1959

RUBY E. DARE LIBRARY
Greenville College
Greenville, Illinois 62246

Virginia L. Hoffman

RUBY E. DARE LIBRARY
Greenville College
Greenville, Illinois 62246

Teaching
for Better Schools

TEACHING
for Better Schools

KIMBALL WILES
College of Education
University of Florida

Second Edition

Illustrated by Mary Purser

1959

PRENTICE-HALL, INC. Englewood Cliffs, N. J.

© 1952, 1959, by
PRENTICE-HALL, INC.
Englewood Cliffs, N. J.

All rights reserved. No part of this book
may be reproduced in any form, by mimeograph
or any other means, without permission in
writing from the publishers.

Library of Congress
Catalog Card No.: 59-12396

PRINTED IN THE UNITED STATES OF AMERICA
89238

Preface

When the first edition of *Teaching for Better Schools* was published, I was convinced by evidence from research in human relations, group development, psychiatry and psychotherapy, counseling, communication, leadership, and the learning process that the role of the teacher is to assist in the creation of the environment in which learning occurs and to relate to the learner in such a way that he will use the help the teacher can give. I am still convinced! Evidence to support this point of view continues to emerge. However, this edition of *Teaching for Better Schools* is a major revision. No chapter parallels a previous chapter! Not even a page remains unchanged! New chapters and sections have been added. Any person familiar with the first edition may wonder why.

Since 1952, I have watched many students use *Teaching for Better Schools*. I have talked with hundreds of teachers who have read it. One point impressed me time and time again: The book frustrated many people. Few have expressed disagreement with the interpretation of the evidence and the description of desirable teaching. However, many have said: "This book is excellent theory, but it isn't practical because there isn't time to do all these things." Few people felt able to fulfill all phases of the teaching role described; reading the book increased feelings of inadequacy.

As I pondered this unexpected and undesirable result, I began to think about the best teachers I know. *Not one is excellent in all phases of the teaching role.* Each one is recognized as a great teacher by colleagues, parents, and pupils because of his unique contribution in one or several phases of teaching. He may be extremely skillful in helping pupils accept themselves and others. He may work in a manner that stimulates a high proportion of his students to creative expression.

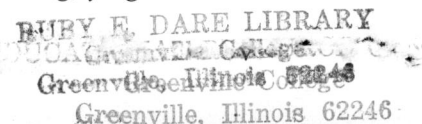

This realization was startling! Throughout the profession we are trying to determine what quality teaching is and to develop ways of measuring or recognizing it. In the forms that we have developed for evaluating teaching, judgments are made about a teacher in several phases of his work, and an average is obtained as the index of the level of quality. Apparently we have been assuming, first, that we could average completely different types of competencies and, second, that quality teaching consisted of being able to do a number of things fairly well. My thinking has led me to the conclusion that these assumptions are wrong.

This edition of *Teaching for Better Schools* has been organized on the assumption that quality teaching is an unusual contribution, by a unique personality, to pupil growth or to the development of the school program. He may not teach like anyone else. He has qualities and abilities different from anyone else. He has studied himself and the learning situation and has decided how he can be most useful; he is giving himself fully and successfully in the implementation of his decision.

It is my hope that this book will assist anyone who reads it to analyze himself and his role, to achieve at least a minimum acceptable level of teaching in the phases described, and to develop special competency in the areas in which he can make a quality contribution.

In conclusion, let me say I hold no brief for categorizing types of quality teaching. However, they are logical in terms of my interpretation of the teacher's role. It is my hope that these categories and the suggested ways of working in each will stimulate you to make an analysis of yourself and your role, and to plan your own steps for increasing the quality of your teaching.

KIMBALL WILES

Contents

Preface v

I—The Nature of Quality Teaching

1. *The Search for Better Teaching* 3
   Certain Teachers. The Minimum Acceptable Level.

2. *Factors Affecting the Role of the Teacher* 14
   The Nature of Teaching. The Learning Process. The Learning Process and Teaching. The Nature of Society. The Basis of Method.

3. *Quality Teaching* 33
   Definition of Quality Teaching. Some Quality Teachers. Approach Necessary to Obtain Quality Teaching. Preview.

II—Types of Quality Teaching

IMPROVING HUMAN RELATIONS

4. *Teacher Acceptance of Self and Others* 49
   The Importance of a Teacher's Feelings About Himself. The Teacher's Feelings About Pupils.

5. *Pupil Acceptance of Self and Others* 61
   The Effect of the Community. The Teacher's Role in Helping a Pupil to Accept Himself. Decreasing Pupil Fears. Decreasing Feelings of Guilt. Decreasing Insecurity Created by Financial Status. The Teacher's Role in Helping Pupils to Accept Others.

Pupil Acceptance of the Teacher. The Process and the Product. *Self-Evaluation Checklist.*

PROMOTING GROUP DEVELOPMENT

6. *The Development of a Class Group* 91
   The Beginning of a Sense of Unity. The Development of Morale. The Formation of a Group Structure. The Planning Committee. Leadership in a Class. Pupil Responsibility to the Group. The Development of Group Maturity. The Determination of Group Progress. The Role of the Individual. The Leadership Role of the Teacher.

7. *A Way of Working with a Group* 110
   Preliminary Planning Is Necessary. Acceptance by Group Essential. The Beginning of Group Planning. The Selection of a Project. The Plan of Work. The Work Period. Controls in the Group. Evaluation of Group Growth. Pitfalls in Group Work. *Self-Evalution Checklist.*

PROVIDING FOR INDIVIDUAL DIFFERENCES

8. *Provision for Individual Differences* 141
   Certain Individual Differences Are Important. Evidence of Concern for Individuals. Types of Individuals. The Underachieving Pupil. The "Less-Developed" Child. The Uninterested Child. The "Aggressive" Child. The "Withdrawing" Child. The "Gifted" Child. Conclusion.

9. *Instruction for the Individual* 164
   Procedures for Learning to Know Pupils. Promotion of Pupil Self-Understanding. The Pupil's Decision. The Pupil's Plan of Work. Pupil Organization of Learning. Conclusion. *Self-Evaluation Checklist.*

STIMULATING INTELLECTUAL GROWTH

10. *The Creation of a Stimulating Intellectual Climate* 183
    Fostering Creativity Essential. Barriers to Teaching for Creativeness. Actions Which Promote Pupil Creativity. Contact with

Scholarship Essential. Contributions of the Scholars. *Self-Evaluation Checklist.*

DEVELOPING SELF-DIRECTION

11. *Guidance in the Formulation of Goals* _____ 201

    All Pupils Have Purposes. The Clarification of Values.

12. *Promotion of the Ability to Make Intelligent Decisions* _____ 221

    The Definition of Goals. The Collection of Data. Records Kept by Pupils. Records Kept by the Teacher. The Pupil's Judgments. Inclusion of the Parent in the Judgment-Making. The Product Sought. *Self-Evaluation Checklist.*

EXERTING LEADERSHIP IN SCHOOL AND COMMUNITY

13. *Exerting Leadership in the Faculty* _____ 249

    Becomes Acquainted with the School. Takes Action in the Faculty. Experiments and Supports Experimentation. Works Through Students.

14. *Exerting Leadership in the Community* _____ 263

    Learns About the Community. Works with Parents. Participates in Community Activities. Students Participate in Community Projects. Reports to the Community. *Self-Evaluation Checklist.*

III—THE SOURCE OF QUALITY TEACHING

15. *The Process of Becoming a Quality Teacher* _____ 283

    Increase in Maturity. Decides on Major Contribution. Evaluates Present Procedures. Human Relations. Group Development. Individual Differences. Intellectual Stimulation. Self-Direction. Faculty and Community Leadership. Seeks New Ideas. Experiments with His Method.

IV—Significant Research

Significant Research _____ 305
Acceptance. Anxiety and Social Pressure. Emotional Needs. Evaluation. Group Interaction. Group-Centered Procedures. Learning. Motivation. Self-Knowledge and Self-Direction. Teacher-Pupil Relationships.

Index _____ 329

I · *The Nature of Quality Teaching*

1 · *The Search for Better Teaching*

The key to better schools is better teaching. New buildings, more transportation, a greater number of special services, a wider range of instructional materials will not result in better schools unless teaching is improved. What the individual teacher does as he works with children is the crucial question.

Teachers are not all equal in ability. Some are effective in their work with students, and others are not. Even among teachers who are able, variation in performance exists.

Although difference in the quality of teaching is recognized, agreement upon the various levels of excellence has not been reached. Attempts to make distinctions among the levels of teaching have become muddled by being attached to the problems of merit rating and salary scales. Instead of examining the teacher and the teaching process, the concern of those seeking to identify quality teaching has been centered in large measure upon the persons who will make judgments about teachers, the fallibility of rating, and the effect upon teacher morale of any effort to categorize teaching performance.

If teaching is to become more effective, however, teachers, supervisors, administrators, and persons in teacher education must seek more agreement concerning the nature of unsatisfactory, satisfactory, and quality teaching. How should the following teachers be ranked? Which are unsatisfactory? Which are quality teachers?

Certain Teachers

Miss Mary Rivers is over sixty. Head of the English department for thirty years, she has established a reputation in the community for being a cultured woman who is well acquainted with our literary heritage.

Miss Rivers will not tolerate loafing in her classes. She gives assignments and insists that all students have them prepared before they return to class. If a student is inadequately prepared or makes mistakes, she chastises him with biting satire before the whole class. And she continues her tirade until he cringes and promises to do better in the future. She fails 10 to 25 per cent of each class in order to keep her scholastic standards high.

Her primary concern is that students learn the material in the course of study. She is willing to help any youngster who will come to her room after school to do additional work. She provides remedial work for youngsters who have fallen behind as a result of illness or absence. She believes it is the teacher's function to help pupils acquire the information that is in the textbook, and she gives unstintingly of her time to fulfill this function.

Miss Rivers is critical of other teachers who do not measure up to the high standards that she sets for herself. She insists that they work for the same objectives and that they do it as efficiently as she does. She accepts warmly the teachers who are striving to meet the requirements she establishes and ignores those she feels are shirking their responsibilities.

Miss Rivers is constantly seeking better ways of teaching her courses. She experiments with new techniques of teaching reading and diligently studies current research to determine if better methods have been devised for teaching grammar.

Jack McDonald, highly intelligent, in his early thirties, is a strong, forceful man who gets along well with other adults. In his college days he was a well-known basketball player and served as an officer in the Navy during the war.

He firmly believes that it is the teacher's job to teach youngsters discipline. He insists that he is in the classroom to tell students what to do and that it is their job to obey. When a student rebels, Jack brings him into line by means of the disciplinary tactics that he knows so well how to employ. He is sure that this approach to teaching pays off in building character because a number of students have come to him after they have left his classes telling him how much they appreciate his having made them do what they were supposed to do.

There is much of the drill sergeant in the way Jack conducts his classes. Students file into the room and stand at attention until they are told that they may be seated. Whenever a student wishes to speak, he raises his hand to secure permission and then stands at attention by the side of his seat while he makes his contribution. Students watch Jack carefully to see when it is permissible to laugh or to determine when it is safe to engage in an activity apart from the customary routine. No time is wasted. Each class period is devoted to hard work on the assignment at hand.

Jack is not exceptionally popular with students, but they respect him. No one makes belittling remarks about him, and students greet him carefully in the halls and on the streets after school. Jack wonders from time to time why students do not talk with him about their problems as they do with some of the other teachers, but he feels that allowing students to become too close to him will be harmful to his teaching effectiveness. He states openly in faculty meetings that "familiarity breeds contempt" and that it is the teacher's responsibility to maintain sufficient distance between himself and the student to insure respect.

Greta Green teaches a primary group. She loves children, but she tries not to show it because she does not want to spoil them. In her opinion, one of her major tasks is to teach children manners. She insists that each child say "Good morning" to her when he arrives at school and shake hands and bid her goodbye as he leaves. She believes she knows the kind of games children should play and enforces her decision at play periods, even though the children, especially the boys, want to play more adult games. Class work is carefully organized and the daily schedule is followed as strictly as possible.

Each pupil knows what is to be done. He is told his responsibilities and Greta repeats them as frequently as necessary.

Pupils may participate in planning. When there are two activities which Greta thinks are equally good, she allows the children to choose the one they prefer.

Jean Allen's life has always been orderly. She is the only child of a mother who stressed neatness and punctuality. Jean has come to value these virtues highly. In her teacher training, she responded immediately to instructors who mentioned the desirability of keeping the window shades even, arranging the seats in straight rows, having all the pupils follow the course of study at the same rate of speed, giving weekly tests to determine what each pupil is doing, and grading on a normal curve. The thought of attempting any variation from a uniform pattern to take care of individual differences frightened her.

Jean teaches all her classes according to the same pattern. The first five minutes are for motivation, the next fifteen for discussion or a predetermined activity, five minutes for an assignment, and the remainder of the period for supervised study. Pupils know what will happen and that it is useless to suggest any change. Pupils also know what the assignment will be (the next ten pages in the textbook) and what kind of test to expect (true or false). They know too that no excuses will be accepted for their failure to do the assigned work.

Jean is against change in content or method. Even the adoption of a new textbook alarms her. The facts will be presented in new ways, and it will be impossible to predict the questions pupils will ask. Everything will be very confusing, and no one will know what is going to happen next.

The administration can always depend upon Jean: reports will be finished on time; the course of study will be followed; pupils will be ready for the system-wide achievement tests; no other teacher will complain about noise or disorder in Jean's classroom; and the children will lead a well-ordered, controlled life.

Jerry Fawcett's clothes are well tailored but slightly extreme. His hair is long and combed straight back. He knows that all the girls think he is handsome, and he tries to maintain his reputation as the faculty fashion plate.

Jerry's classes are dramatic. Whenever possible, he stages an entrance, flinging the door wide, entering with a long stride, quoting some passage from the day's lesson or from an appropriate poem.

Jerry believes teaching is acting. If you want to teach effectively you must put on a good show. He doesn't worry about assignments or whether or not pupils do any work outside the class period. He knows they will learn from watching him and if he is effective enough they will begin to read on their own.

In his opinion, class routine is for the ribbon-clerk type of teacher. Jerry can't be bothered with keeping attendance or any other records. He doesn't believe it is necessary to learn anything about the pupils, even their names. After all, they are in the class to listen to his interpretations. They can do that whether he knows their names or not. And their success can be determined by how well they do on the final examination. If they have merit, they will have absorbed what he has attempted to impart and will make a high score and a good mark. If they do poorly, they just don't have the ability and shouldn't be in a class which requires a cultured mind.

Jerry is in constant demand for out-of-school appearances, especially at clubs devoted to the arts. With the exception of the coach, he is known by more adults than is any other member of the staff. He is considered a public relations asset by the administration and the outstanding teacher in the system by many parents.

Oscar Byrnes wants all the pupils to like science. He has collected many colorful demonstrations which he uses to make every class period a series of exciting incidents. He attends summer schools and conventions to discover new tricks. He is in the height of his glory when he has all his students on the edge of their seats trying to guess what will happen next.

Most students come out of his class thinking that science is amusing and mysterious but without discovering that it has much relation to their home, community, or the way they live. It has little effect on the way they go about solving their problems or on the attitudes they develop.

Oscar is sloppy in his dress, his hair is seldom combed, and his shirt collar is almost always soiled. He rushes in and out of his lab without noticing the pupils in the hall or in his class except for the three or four unkempt boys much like himself who hang around after school to try to learn how he staged the demonstration and tell him of the chemistry set explosion they produced the night before.

Oscar avoids becoming involved in any curriculum discussions—they are so futile and unrealistic. Any improvement in the curriculum will come through efforts of individual teachers to learn better ways of arousing pupil interest. And he has the most interested pupils in school.

Eight-year-olds love Grace Jenkins. She is pretty and gay and wears bright blouses and skirts. She hums and smiles as she works. She loves music and art; consequently, a large part of the day is devoted to singing and art activities. The walls of the classroom are hung with many pictures that the children have painted.

Grace puts high value on creativity and self-expression. The day's program emerges. One thing leads to another. Moods and interests are to be followed. Some days the group does not get around to reading or writing or number work, but that is all right because pupils will learn it faster if it comes spontaneously as a part of some project the class wants to do.

Crises are things to be avoided. Whenever possible, a new idea or a new song is forthcoming when some difficulty arises.

Life is fun in Miss Jenkins' room and the children do not want to leave at the end of the day or the year. Each fall, the nine-year-olds rush back to see Miss Jenkins.

The teacher of the nine-year-olds complains bitterly to the principal that the pupils who have been in Miss Jenkins' room the preceding year are not well disciplined and don't know their arithmetic.

Frank Whittaker is noted for his humor. He is short, with curly hair and blue eyes that dance with merriment. Life is a lot of fun. He can't be bothered with a lot of educational theory, and faculty meetings are a dreadful bore. His students don't do very well on examinations, but his classes are always crowded. He is a punster, with a joke for every occasion. Class periods are poorly organized, and sometimes it is difficult to decide what was accomplished, but they are never dull. Frank insists that if people are happy, they will learn.

Lloyd Lang spends all his summers taking further work in the field of education. He has developed a great facility in using educational terminology and is always abreast of the latest innovations. He writes easily, and the papers that he prepares for his professional courses are always commended highly because they show such professional spirit and insight into modern methods.

In his classes, Lloyd is very concerned about stimulating creativeness, about building his curriculum around "persistent life situations," and about creating the kind of environment in which the "human interactions are easily assimilable."

Because of his great concern for conducting his class in the most up-to-date manner, Lloyd is afraid to do many of the things that he would like to do. He overlooks the aggressive action of students toward one another and toward himself. He does not interfere when he sees students sitting quietly daydreaming or retreating from group activity. He doesn't try to organize the class, because he is afraid that if he structures the situation too firmly pupil creativeness will be hindered. When the class doesn't seem to be making very much progress, Lloyd is happy in the knowledge that he is creating a situation for good group therapy. If students are unhappy about the lack of organization or because they do not feel they are achieving as they should, Lloyd knows that this is simply a manifestation of the tension that must always occur before insight is achieved. Although the room is always cluttered and students wonder what is going to happen, Lloyd is very quick to tell supervisors and parents that these conditions are part of a permissive atmosphere. Lloyd talks so fast and uses the terminology so well that the supervisors and parents usually become embarrassed and retreat before the barrage of pedagoguese.

Ted Davis thinks of himself as a counselor. He spends a large portion of his time getting to know pupils well, visiting their homes, talking with them about their problems. His manner is easy and relaxed, and students have found they can trust him. He doesn't try to tell them what they should do, but they seem to decide for themselves as he talks with them.

Much of the work in Ted's room is individual. As individual students set up goals and projects for themselves, Ted finds many occasions for counseling. Many boys and girls who have had difficulty working with other teachers like Ted's procedure and progress rapidly. Other students who have always been rated superior in other classes say they like Mr. Davis but they don't know how they are doing. They can't tell whether they are doing better work than the other pupils.

June Wilson believes that boys and girls learn most from association with their peers. She attempts to create a classroom situation where there are many opportunities to play and work together. She is attractive, but stays in the background as much as possible. She attempts to help the pupils get to know one another, to plan what they need to do, to organize for action, to carry through their plans, and to evaluate their efforts. Her desk is shoved back in the corner and a visitor to her classroom may find her sitting on the floor with a group making puppets. A story is told about the time the superintendent came to visit her class and found her under a work table helping a girl cut out a pattern. The organization of the furniture and the decoration of the room are the outgrowth of pupil work and planning—sometimes to the great concern of the custodian.

Each individual described believes he is effective. Upon what basis should judgments be made about the quality of teaching in each case?

Unsatisfactory teaching is easy to describe. *The unsatisfactory teacher cannot keep order, does not know his subject matter, has no plan or goals, does what seems expedient at the moment.* He is not respected by students, parents, fellow teachers, or the administration. He is unhappy in his job, and he, the profession, and the community would profit if he left teaching.

The Minimum Acceptable Level

But what are the characteristics of an acceptable teacher? What is the dividing line between unsatisfactory and passable teaching?

Jean graduated from college twenty years ago. She has always taught in marginal schools. She secures the assigned text and copies of the examinations used throughout the system. She announces at the beginning of the year that there will be a weekly test every Friday, a term test every sixth Friday, and a semester examination. Marks will be based on an average of the weekly tests (60% of the mark) and the term test (40% of the mark). The pages for the next day's assignment are written on the board at the end of each class period. All pupils are expected to do the same amount of work. Class periods are devoted to questions and answers concerning the pages assigned. Questions that call for application of the content to topics not mentioned in the text are never asked. If a visitor entered Jean's classroom, it would be difficult to guess the subject matter taught if the class were not in session.

Little change has been made in Jean's teaching procedure or testing methods since the first year of her teaching.

To the writer, Jean represents the minimum level of satisfactory teaching. She helps to meet the teacher shortage, but she does not add luster to the profession; she fills a classroom and draws her paychecks, but she provides only a minimum education. She is not poor enough to be dismissed, but she provides little leadership for pupils, parents, or fellow teachers.

What is the teacher like who meets minimum requirements?

He keeps order. Chaos in a classroom cannot be tolerated. Unless the teacher is able to provide some structure to the teaching-learning situation, pupils might as well roam the streets or play in informal groups. At the lowest level the teacher may obtain order through fear. Physical punishment, threats, sarcasm, and coercion can be used to control. The minimum level teacher may use them. If the teacher has greater skill, he helps pupils move to more self-control. Exercise of coercive pressure is decreased as codes of behavior and purposeful activities are developed, but ability to control and direct the classwork by some technique is essential if the teacher is to fulfill the function of teaching.

He has a plan of work. It is assumed that a teacher will help the class make progress toward some goals that contribute to acceptable education of pupils. At a low level, the teacher follows some course of study. His role, as he sees it, is taking the class through the textbook or course of study. If the textbook is his guide, he may divide the number of pages in the text by the number of days in the school year and assign each day the number of pages necessary to cover the text during the school year. Such a procedure does not reveal much insight into the teaching process or assign relative importance to the aspects of the subject, but it is an organized plan of work which gives some logic to the operation of the class. Without some basis for organization of activities, the teacher and class are overwhelmed by the array of facts or the momentary whims of the teacher or the pupils.

He seeks to determine how much progress his pupils make. Without some effort to collect information about pupil progress, the teacher has no basis for making judgments about his teaching procedures. Some teachers give daily, weekly, and semester tests. Great differences exist in the validity and reliability of the measures used. Some instruments inadequately sample the material covered, and others are only indications of pupil ability to cope with the testing techniques; but any teacher who meets the minimum level attempts to discover whether or not his pupils have learned what he has attempted to teach.

He gives definite assignments. Pupils must know what they are responsible for doing. Leaving pupils confused and without direction is unsatisfactory teaching. At any time pupils must be clear as to what is expected of them and what level of performance is necessary in order to be successful. At a low level, the assignment may be to read the next ten pages of the textbook and be prepared to take a test on the content, but the expectations are stated.

He prepares the reports required by the administration. No school can operate successfully without records. The teacher must prepare some of these, such as attendance records and reports to parents concerning the progress of individual children. Unless a teacher accepts and fulfills these tasks, he is not acceptable at the minimum level.

To judge whether a teacher meets the minimum level of satisfactory teaching, the following questions should be asked:

Can he control the class?
Does he have a plan of work?
Does he test to determine pupil progress?
Does he give clear, definite assignments?
Does he prepare the reports required of him by the administration?

Neither the public nor the profession can be satisfied with minimum performance. Neither are content with maintaining a low level educational system; rather, they want to secure and retain better teachers as the primary means of improving the schools. Within and without the profession, organized efforts are under way to secure a higher quality teacher. But what is better teaching? How can it be recognized?

2 · Factors Affecting the Role of the Teacher

Each teacher has a picture in his mind of the role he should perform. It may have been derived from his admiration for one of his teachers, or it may be the product of careful study of the learning process, the nature of the learner, the school as a social institution, the society, and the social goals. Whatever the source, the role concept a person holds influences his decisions and his behavior.

The Nature of Teaching

All teachers want to be good teachers. All wish to work with boys and girls in the most effective way. Based on their role concept and their beliefs about their ability to achieve it, they make some decisions about the nature of teaching. They answer for themselves the following questions:

Is effective teaching directing and telling? Does the teacher start with the assumption that there is a predetermined body of subject matter which he must organize and present, hoping that each youngster will understand the organization and find it helpful? Does he believe that teaching skill consists primarily of organizing knowledge into some pattern, of presenting the facts and generalizations in a clear, easily understood, interesting fashion, of testing to determine the amount of information acquired, and of marking the pupil's attainment?

Many teachers accept this definition of teaching. They feel that any change from this pattern is a softening of the educative process, a departure from the fundamentals. They are concerned with better ways of telling, explaining, drilling, testing, and marking.

Is effective teaching helping pupils to do what they want? Does the teacher start with pupil interests and follow them wherever they may lead? Is it his function to discover what pupils like to do, to collect materials for them to use, to help them decide upon more effective ways of doing what they want to do, to encourage growth, and to accept the achievement that results? Does he start with the assumption that it does not matter what a pupil studies as long as it seems interesting and desirable to him? Does he feel that pupils should be free to change from one project to another as they choose? Does he accept all types of pupil behavior?

Some teachers believe that they make their contribution by assisting the child to execute his ideas. They do not want to crush his initiative, stifle his creativeness, or cause emotional frustrations. They believe the child will develop satisfactorily if he has the opportunity to do the things that seem important to him with the understanding and support of an adult to whom he can turn if he needs help or counseling. These teachers are concerned with better ways of studying the child, of encouraging him, of recording his growth, and of counseling with his parents.

Is effective teaching working with boys and girls as a member of the classroom group? Does the teacher start with the assumption that the most important outcome of formal education in a democracy is the

ability to be self-directing, which involves having a set of values and the social skills necessary to implement them? Does he believe he should live with pupils in such a way that they experience democratic procedures and come to value them? Does he see himself as having the authority to plan and direct the work of pupils, yet sharing with them the decisions they are willing to accept? Does he believe he should insist that every member of the group abide by the agreements reached?

The teachers who take this position place their major emphasis on working with boys and girls in such a way that increasing responsibility for self-direction rests with the pupils. They constantly stress the why, the what, and the how. Why are we proposing this? What are the values we seek? How shall we do it? What will be the consequences for ourselves and others? How can we improve? They stress group work because they believe that values, skills, and security emerge from interaction with others. These teachers are concerned with helping pupils understand and accept themselves and others; with aiding them to plan, work, and evaluate together and to use the scientific method; with assisting them to analyze their values, experiences, and procedures; and with working with parents and lay public.

Is the teacher an expert to give youngsters the answers to the questions, or is he in a classroom to help students find answers for themselves? Is he primarily concerned with supplying students with information, or is he concerned with helping them develop work skills? Is it his job to establish the tasks for boys and girls and then to see to it that they carry out the tasks, or is it his job to serve as a resource person who is there to help boys and girls examine an area that is important in our society? Is it his job to listen and help boys and girls hear each other and help them interpret the society around them, or is it his job to interpret society and to transmit culture from past generations to future?

The person who is making a professional approach to teaching does not answer questions concerning the teacher's role on the basis of hunch, or sentiment, or personal allegiance. He searches for evidence; he discovers as much as he can about the learning process and how one individual can affect the learning of another; he studies social conditions and goals which determine the role of the school and the types of growth that are socially desirable.

He uses the best data he can discover to decide what his way of working with a class will be.

The Learning Process

How learning occurs has long intrigued man. Philosophers have advanced theories of learning. Psychologists have conducted experiments to test the hypotheses of philosophers and their own. Scientists in fields ranging from physics and biology to psychiatry have contributed knowledge which increased understanding of the learning process. But the answers are not exact yet. Conclusions must be drawn from insufficient evidence and constitute theory which must continue to be subjected to testing and exploration. Unsatisfactory as present answers may be, they give the best basis available for deciding upon the teacher's role.

On the basis of existing evidence, the following conclusions about the learning process seem most acceptable.

Factors Affecting the Role of the Teacher

Learning is occurring all the time a person is alive. A person lives, and through the process of living he learns. As he lives, he selects from his environment the things with which he will interact. Some of the things will be words of other people; some will be the behavior of other people; some will be physical features of the environment. As he interacts with the features of the environment which he selects, he changes. *The process of change in a person through interaction is learning.* He interacts with factors in his environment, rather than reacts to them. *He senses, interprets, and projects future actions and discovers that both the environmental factor and he are changed in the process.* Any object with which he has an experience is changed for him. For example, he narrowly escapes death in an automobile accident. Not only the car in which he was riding but all other cars are different for him. He sees any car as a possible death weapon as well as a means of speedy transportation.

Learning is a process of perceiving and integrating. Perception involves selection and interpretation. A person selects the factors in the environment with which he will interact in terms of his previous experience and present purposes. As he enters a room, he seeks a place to sit. He knows that facing the light has given him a headache in the past. He notes the window and the arrangement of the furniture and seeks a chair where he does not face the light. After determining the general location he desires, he examines the chairs more closely to see which will be most comfortable. He interprets in terms of his past experience with various shapes and textures of chairs. As he moves toward the chair which he believes will be best, he notes a picture hanging on the wall. It is a Van Gogh, in whose works he has a keen interest. To observe the picture from the chair he has selected as most comfortable will be difficult, and he revises his plans and changes his action to secure a chair where he can see the Van Gogh better. Another

person entering the same room, desiring to sit by his friend, would have selected different factors in the room with which to interact.

A person interprets a factor in the environment—an object, sound, color, taste, odor—in terms of his previous experience with it or something like it. If the object with which he is interacting is the telephone, he may notice it is black, especially if he has seen some telephones with red or white plastic covers. He may see it is a cradle phone if he is old enough to remember the box type that hung on the wall. He may observe that it has a dial if other telephones he uses do not have them. He may see the worn cord if he is an electrician. He may note the design if he is an art student. What he perceives as his gaze falls on the telephone is determined in part by his previous experience.

He interprets in terms of what he wants to do. If he is clearing the desk to get more work space, the telephone is an object to move. If he wants to find the railway fare to a nearby city, the telephone is a quick way of contacting the railway station. If he is expecting a call from a friend, he listens for the ringing of the bell in the telephone and may begin to plan what he is going to say.

If he has had a series of unsatisfactory experiences in attempting to share his ideas via the telephone, his concept of the telephone may change. Instead of viewing the black instrument as a convenient way of talking with his associates, he may begin to perceive it as an object to be avoided and used only when other possibilities have been exhausted.

Learning occurs through a person's interaction with the features of the environment which he selects and interprets in terms of his past experiences and present purposes. Through the interaction he is changed. His knowledge of himself, his interpretation of his surroundings, and his purposes are revised by his experience. He sees new relationships among the knowledges, values, and skills he has and between him and the factors of his environment.

Seeing a relationship changes him and his world. A nine-year-old on the way home from a movie in which one of the characters had become a habitual drunkard asked himself and his family, "Could that happen to me?" For the first time in his life he understood that the things he did now would affect him in the distant future. Out of that insight came a concept of himself which changed every fact he knew about himself and a basic belief which will condition each new experience he encounters, helping to determine what he will select or ignore, use or reject.

A five-year-old visited an Indian pueblo with his father. As they climbed from the car a crowd of Indian boys and girls rushed out to greet them, saying, "Take my picture?" As soon as the father had taken the picture, the Indian youngsters rushed the pair, shouting "Gimme a nickel, gimme a nickel. You took our pictures, gimme a nickel." The onrush was so great that the five-year-old beat a hasty retreat to the car, deciding that perhaps Indians weren't very desirable playmates.

But that conclusion was a revision of his previous learning. He had already known about Indians. He had talked about them. He had seen Indians in the movies and on television shows. He had loved Indian stories and wanted to live with Indians. But this new experience supplied him with additional data and caused him to revise his previous beliefs. And future experiences will undoubtedly lead him to further revisions. That's how the process goes. New facts and new experiences lead to a readjustment of previously held opinions and attitudes. And that revision constitutes learning.

The learning of a complex skill illustrates integration too. A person starts with very simple types of coordination and then moves on to more complex types. A boy doesn't learn how to dribble a basketball without previous experience. He has already learned how to walk, how to run, how to move his arm back and forth at the elbow, how to control the pressure exerted by his finger tips. The process of learning to dribble is the reorganization of these skills into a new skill.

Learning involves going out on the frontier. It means breaking through the shell of the present world into a new world. As a person acquires a new idea that gives him a new concept of himself or of his place in the society around him or of the organization of society, he finds himself in a new orientation to everything. He faces a world that for the moment is somewhat chaotic. Things and ideas are not in their accustomed places. He is faced with the proposition of reorganizing his world of knowledge and belief as a result of the new knowledge that has come to him. Thus, disorganization is a stage in learning. It is the entrance to a new organization of knowledge. As a new idea becomes meaningful to him, it is necessary for him to rearrange the ideas and beliefs that he holds to include this new idea.

Learning is done by the individual; it can't be done for him. Other people may share with a person the results of their experience, and he may incorporate some of this knowledge into his own experience through his interpretations of what they have said; but no one can make him accept or be sure he understands what they have said to him.

Learning is unique. The learner does his own learning. He selects from his environment the things with which he will interact and interprets in terms of his past experiences, his needs, and his purposes. In research projects at Dartmouth and at Princeton, displays have been set up which are designed to create the wrong impression by restricting the cues which the observer receives. Viewers are asked to identify an object and then are shown what it really is. People do not see the object accurately. They perceive in terms of their past experiences and interpret in terms of those past experiences. At Chicago, McClellan and others have done some research with perception which indicates that need affects perception. A picture of light and shadows was cast upon a screen. Persons who had been given a test that they could not possibly pass, a test that would make them feel inadequate, were brought in to see the "picture" and asked to tell what they saw. Most of the subjects saw a picture of people having success experiences. Another group was kept from having food for eighteen hours. When they were brought in to see the "picture," they saw a picture of people eating. People perceive in terms of their needs. If a child wants to learn to play baseball and his parents or his teacher try to stop him, the child learns certain things in that process. His proposed learning may be halted momentarily, but he is acquiring new, unplanned understanding. In this case he may be learning to hate authority or that adults don't understand people his age, but learning of some type is occurring. Learning can't be stopped.

Learnings are multiple. A person doesn't learn one thing at a time. He may be in a room where he is attempting to learn American history, but he may learn that certain types of seats are uncomfortable, that small print makes his eyes ache, that Susie Smith likes Johnny Jones better than she does him.

Learning is affected by the learner's purposes. Other people may tell a person what he is supposed to learn, and may try to create a situation in which he will learn what they want him to learn; but he selects from any environment and from any situation the things that are important to him. He selects in terms of what his past experiences have enabled him to understand and what he wants to do or what he desires to become. A boy enthusiastic about hunting may look at a film of a battle of the American Revolution and may learn about the types of guns the soldiers carried. A girl looking at the same picture may, because of her concern about clothing, learn how colonial women dressed. Each pupil selects from the experiences provided by the school the learning that is in line with his purposes.

He also learns much that he didn't plan to learn. As he attempts to execute one of his purposes, he has to select from the resources available to him those facts and those knowledges which will enable him to do what he wants to do. In the process, however, his actions bring him into contact with other facts and with other emotions which color and add to the facts that he wants to acquire. He learns through these additional interactions whether he wishes to do so or not.

The emotional qualities of the learning situation are learned too, and continue to be associated with facts, skills, and other learnings which emerge from an experience.

Emotions condition the learning. A person minimizes certain facts and emphasizes others out of proportion because of his emotional orientation. The acquisition of facts in an unpleasant emotional environment develops an aversion to further contact with similar experiences. Pleasant emotions lead to the desire for more experiences of a similar nature. *Emotions in the situation in which the learning occurs*

affect the use made of the knowledge, understanding, and skills that result from the experience. Further, persistent emotional problems of the individual narrow the range of information that he considers significant.

Learning is affected by the physical condition of the learner. A person who is tired does not learn as quickly or as well as one who is refreshed. Lack of physical maturity may decrease the efficiency of the learning. As the physical structure develops, the human organism is able to interact with its environment in new ways, and new learnings emerge. In some cases, the learnings can be made to occur before the individual is sufficiently mature physically, but the learning process is less efficient because physical inadequacy prevents the human organism from interacting fully. In forced learning of this type, the physical structure may be injured. For example, insisting that a six-year-old begin to read before his eyes are sufficiently mature may impair his eyesight.

The operational intelligence of the individual affects the rate of learning. Some individuals learn more and faster than others. They have more skill in perceiving and in integrating what they perceive. Through their previous experiences they have become more able to see and more able to understand what they are seeing. The extent to which this skill of perceiving has been developed determines how much a person can get from the new experience he is having. Equally important is the skill of integrating the new experience with learnings from previous experience. As mentioned earlier, this process of integration is something the individual learner has to do for himself, and the youngster who sees relationships more easily and more quickly learns more from his experience.

An individual can increase his learning through a procedure called thinking—a process by which he ascertains and tests relationships by mental manipulation of abstract symbols, such as words or concepts. Learning does occur without thinking, but thinking is the key to interacting with factors not in the immediate physical environment.

The Learning Process and Teaching

From the summary of information about the learning process presented, one thing is evident. Every pupil in a class is learning. There are no nonlearners. That term is a name that a teacher gives to a person who does not acquire from the class experiences the types of knowledge, skills, and attitudes that the teacher hopes he will. *Teaching is not a process of causing learning—learning is occurring all the time.*

Teaching is helping boys and girls decide what are the important things to learn and planning with them the experiences through which it is hoped the learnings will occur. The emphasis is on helping pupils establish worth-while purposes rather than on forcing pupils to work on unpleasant tasks. If a teacher attempts to force a pupil to learn, the results are likely to be different from those anticipated. He learns how to avoid, how to deceive, how to resist. And—perhaps—he learns a little of the knowledge it was hoped he would acquire. But it may be in an emotional matrix which will lead him to use it in an undesirable way.

From the above summary of information about the learning process, it is evident that *telling may not be teaching.* The learner selects from his environment the factors with which he will interact. Although a teacher may compel a pupil to sit quietly and listen, he cannot make him learn. The pupil may be interacting with the bird singing outside, the color of the girl's hair in the seat in front of him, or the picture on the bulletin board, and not hear a word the teacher says. If the pupil chooses to interact with the words, the teacher may be able to explain the idea. Lecturing is only one phase of teaching—explaining—and it is effective only if the pupil is seeking to learn what the teacher is trying to tell him.

When boys and girls want to learn the things the teacher hopes they will learn, the situation is easy. The skills of explaining and illustrating are rather simple. *The difficult task in teaching comes in helping boys and girls who don't know what they want to learn, to establish clear purposes, and in helping pupils who have undesirable social purposes to re-examine those purposes and begin to want to learn the things that will make them effective citizens in our society.*

If learning is going on all the time, if it is unique and each pupil learns at his own rate in terms of his perceptions and what he considers significant, it is evident that teaching is not telling and directing and judging. Instead, teaching is a process of relating to youngsters in such a way as to facilitate their learning. Teaching consists of creating the kind of emotional climate in which pupils will feel secure enough to venture and the type of intellectual climate that provides a range of stimuli sufficiently wide to seem significant to youngsters with different backgrounds, needs, and purposes.

A teacher makes every effort to create a pleasant emotional climate in his classroom if he hopes for an efficient learning situation in which pupils have purposes that coincide with his. If he creates a situation in which pupils are under emotional tension, their attention will be

focused on resolving the tension rather than on the ends he hopes they will have in mind. For example, in many situations in which a strong emphasis is placed on marks, pupils are more concerned with obtaining a high score than upon developing skill and competency in the field.

Since all pupils do not interact with the same stimuli, it is necessary for the teacher to attempt to create an environment with many stimuli, if he expects all pupils to learn. He cannot add only one or two new features to the classroom and expect to motivate thirty pupils with different purposes and backgrounds. As he comes to know his pupils well enough to understand their motivations, however, he can be more effective with fewer stimuli because he can use those with which he knows the students are likely to interact.

The knowledge that learning is an individual matter, that different pupils interact with different stimuli, that the facts that are important to one person may not seem so to another, makes individual planning and evaluation a necessity. If a teacher wants to teach efficiently, he studies each pupil, helps him plan his work, and judges his achievement in terms of his purposes.

The teacher helps the individual analyze himself not only in terms of his planning but also on the basis of the outcomes of his experiences. Each person integrates new learnings with previous ones. To further this process, the teacher *provides opportunities for the students to examine the experiences they have had and to evaluate the results.* When a person makes an analysis of an experience that he has had, the process increases the possibility of his generalizing from the experience in such a way that he can use the results to be more effective in new situations.

> A high-school sophomore came to his father complaining that his teacher was not doing a good job. Nothing was being accomplished in the class. The father asked the boy what *he* had done to improve the situation, what responsibility he had assumed. The sixteen-year-old said, "None. I can't tell Mr. Brown what to do. The rest of the class wouldn't like it."

The teacher, in the case cited, was not making progress in the direction of purposes accepted by the students. When a teacher realizes that pupils learn in terms of their purposes, *he attempts to get pupils to assist in the formulation of the purposes for the class.* Unless he brings pupils into the establishment of purposes, the learning situation may be inefficient or even futile because pupils may have different, perhaps even conflicting, purposes.

Since learning is an active process, *the teacher needs to organize his classes so that pupils can do things.* Doing can be making something with the hands, surveying the eating habits in the cafeteria, solving a problem, or writing a poem. The essential feature is that the pupil is doing something for himself, something that he considers important enough to keep on doing.

Failure to understand that learning occurs through action is illustrated by the comment of a teacher who visited a class where pupils were at work.

> In one corner a committee was listening critically to devotions being prepared for an assembly. Another group was practicing a skit to be put on over the PA system. A radio drama showing our war orphan

project was being written by the radio committee. Using reference books and the make-up kit, the art of changing a child into an elderly person was being learned and practiced by the "stage crew." Another group was darting in and out with evaluation blanks. "I think," our visitor commented, "this is all very fine, but when do you get time to teach?"

Since a teacher can't make boys and girls learn what he wants them to learn, he can only create the type of environment in which learning of the kind that he seeks is possible. It is his job to set the scene, to create the situations out of which boys and girls can have the experience through which they can develop the desirable characteristics that society seeks.

The Nature of Society

The nature of the society affects the role a teacher plays. In an authoritarian society the teacher's function is to insure that boys and girls accept the values held by the dominant group and acquire the skills necessary to implement them. If the society has only one set of values and mores, the teacher works to get pupils to understand and accept. But if a society is complex and has competing values, the teacher's task is to help pupils discover, discriminate, and choose the values he will accept. If the society is democratic in nature, the teacher is concerned with helping pupils develop the ability to make wise decisions and the skills to implement the choices made. If a school exists in a society which is making little change, the teacher's task is to explain and promote acceptance. If the society is changing rapidly, the teacher performs his function by helping pupils acquire the skills which enable them to participate effectively in the process of change.

American schools exist in a society composed of people from many cultures who hold many different values. Some values are held in common. Some values conflict with others, and the group subscribing to each compete for domination. Many patterns of behavior exist. The society is in a state of rapid change. To live effectively in the society, pupils must view change as a natural condition, accept responsibility for self-direction, formulate a set of values to guide their choices, and develop the skills which enable them to make and implement intelligent choices. If the schools are to meet the needs of the society, some teachers must conceive of their roles as promoting these types of growth.

If the teachers want to aid pupils to develop democratic values and skills, they are faced with the task of clarifying for themselves the meaning of democracy and identifying the values and skills they will seek to promote—even though they recognize that through their living with pupils their insights will deepen and they will revise their statements of desired values and competencies.

What is a democratic society and what are the values and skills that enable a person to be an effective member of it?

Democracy is a social goal, a symbol of perfection toward which we are striving. Underlying it are two basic concepts:

> That man is intelligent enough, or capable of becoming intelligent enough through education, to make decisions that will promote his own welfare;

> *and*

> That personality is the center of value, and that all social organizations derive their significance from their promise to enhance the individual, to guarantee the sacredness of his person, to safeguard his rights, and to extend his opportunities.

What type of social organization permits these concepts to be translated into reality? Although there is disagreement on specific political, social, and economic structure, most students of democracy agree that the following are essential:

1. It must provide for the uncoerced participation of all members in the formation of policy that will affect them.
2. It must provide for the free flow of information among the members.
3. It must accommodate points of view that diverge from that of the majority.
4. It must be sufficiently flexible to permit any change deemed desirable by the members, except change that would prevent further change.

Within this framework the specific social goals will change. Teachers in a democracy have the responsibility of helping pupils develop a commitment to these basic values and skill in intelligently solving the problems that arise.

The value that democratic society places on the individual demands one task of every teacher—leading each pupil to a deeper appreciation of the worth of each person in the class, the school, the nation, and the world. The way of living in the class furthers democracy as it increases the extent to which pupils accept each other, become concerned about each other, and value the unique contribution that each can make.

The essence of democracy is that values are acquired—not imposed. To force acceptance of values is to contradict and refute the end sought. To help pupils develop an allegiance to democratic values requires that the teacher live them himself and thus promote an atmosphere in which democracy is experienced. But experiencing is not enough. The teacher's responsibility for developing democratic values extends to analyzing with pupils the way they live together and assisting them to verbalize the qualities of the experience which they value. Recognizing and stating are steps in clarifying and developing allegiance to values. Having an opportunity to extend these values in the living together in the classroom increases the allegiance still further.

Self-directing citizens are essential if democracy is to continue to flourish. Democratic forms and procedures require that men and women reach their own decisions and assume the responsibilities inherent in their choices. If the citizens do not exercise their right to participate in policy formation, freedom is lost by default. Unless a high percentage of the population cherishes and utilizes the privileges and responsibility of self-direction, a few members will make the choices and will impose their authority. *Teaching promotes democracy as it aids students to become more self-directing through careful analysis of beliefs held, through participation in class planning and evaluation, and through taking action which implements the decisions made.*

Blind obedience is characteristic of citizens in a dictatorship. In a democracy, where everyone is expected to participate in making decisions concerning public welfare, each person must be conscious of the purpose for which the group is striving and must be capable of making individual and group decisions that will promote that purpose.

Living in a democracy is group living, and effective participation involves group skills. Groups are also faced with solving problems, and the individual assists or hinders the group in solving common problems. Teachers have the responsibility of helping the individual learn such skills of group participation as communication, stating a problem, forming and operating groups to collect and analyze data, sharing information, helping the group reach a decision and organize to execute it. Committee work, group planning, group action, and group evaluation are basic democratic skills.

Closely allied with self-direction is self-control. In a democracy, control that comes from within is sought. Imposition from without is avoided where possible. No attempt is made to proctor the activities of each individual. Instead, effort is made to have each individual develop a commitment to democratic ideals strong enough to guide his behavior. To promote self-control, teachers in a democratic school are faced with the necessity of developing an allegiance to democratic values and the skills essential to solving the problems involved in realizing them in our society.

Self-direction and self-control are not attained by carrying out the directions and plans of others. They are cultivated by giving pupils the opportunity to solve, with the teacher's assistance, the decisions that are necessary in the operation of the class.

All decisions are not equally intelligent. Teachers help the individual further the development of his own potential and that of the society as they help him increase his ability to make wise choices. Throughout the years, scientists have evolved a problem-solving procedure called the scientific method. It involves careful definition of the problem, collection of all the facts available, making judgments based on the facts, and testing the conclusions. Teachers contribute to more effective democratic living as they aid pupils to isolate the issue, to withhold judgment until the evidence is collected from all sides, and to base decisions on facts rather than on whim or prejudice.

The immediate community influences the teacher in the selection of the types of growth he will seek to promote and the way he will conceive and perform his role.

The emotional and intellectual climate of the community plays an important part in determining the teacher's role. Children are educated by the community, of which the school is but a part. They acquire the social, political, economic, and moral attitudes and values of the community through all the experiences they have with its various social institutions, agencies, and groups. The school, and any classroom, is a part of the total environment, and a teacher's role is conditioned by the community.

The attitude of the community toward freedom of inquiry affects the choice of the way of working with boys and girls. If the community, or an influential portion of its citizens, seeks to restrict the areas of study and the sources of information, careful examination of issues and beliefs will be hampered. If the community is proud of its tradition of intellectual integrity and open-mindedness, the teacher will be challenged to exercise all his resources in helping pupils study the culture and its complex or conflicting values, and in developing allegiance to those values held in common.

The level of communication in the community is also a part of the intellectual climate. If the oral communication skills are not highly developed, pupils will be less articulate and more at home working with their hands. In certain rural areas, much of the work of alert English teachers is in oral English. Since the children have been told that they should be seen and not heard, it takes the teachers months of effort to encourage them enough to get them to make a talk before the class. However, English teachers in nearby communities, where children talk, discuss, and sing as a part of their home and community environment, can put much less emphasis on this type of communication. Method, as well as subject matter, is formulated in terms of the skills and needs of the community.

The relationships between adults and young people in the community is significant too. If the children are accustomed to strict, authoritarian control at home, too great a deviation in the classroom may not be understood. If children are allowed an unusual amount of freedom in their homes and other community institutions, a highly restrictive classroom control will be resented and may cause rebellion.

The ability and willingness of the community to support the schools affect teachings. If the average class size is twenty-five, the teacher is in a much better position to individualize instruction than if it is forty-five. When classrooms are small and crowded, or when teaching supplies are limited to a textbook, our possible choices of procedures are restricted.

The way the community believes teaching should be done will affect the choice of method. If predecessors and colleagues have spent a major portion of their class time in having pupils drill and memorize, a teacher may face serious questions if he does not do the same. If no teachers have taken field trips or studied the community, first attempts may be misunderstood. If the community believes good discipline means keeping the class quiet, an effort to move toward pupil self-discipline may be interpreted as lack of skill in controlling pupils. If teachers have been assigning the same homework to all pupils and homework in a class consists of individual projects, parents may protest. A teacher cannot move too far beyond community expectations concerning teaching methods unless he invites the parents to think with him about the ways he can be most helpful to their children.

If certain groups in the community are seeking to control the school, the method of teaching will be subjected to close scrutiny. Any marked deviation from standard practice or procedures will provide the basis for criticism. Under such conditions, thoroughness in planning with pupils and parents, and also in record-keeping, is necessary. Support for the method used in a class is built upon parent and pupil understanding, which comes only through joint planning and the evidence of growth exhibited in the teacher's records.

The reputation of the school in the community will affect the teacher's method of operation. If the community has a high regard for the school and its teachers, few questions will arise concerning teaching procedures. But if the community has lost confidence in the school personnel, any change will be subject to suspicion and quick criticism. Any teacher will be much freer to experiment and more able to teach by the best procedure that he knows if the school has won the support and trust of the community. If the teachers have shown themselves to be conscientious, worthwhile, mature citizens, and if the parents and lay personnel of the community accept them as such, they will not have to hesitate about making needed innovations. But if the community, rightly or wrongly, is suspicious of teachers and resentful of the school program, teachers must be careful to insure that pupils and parents thoroughly understand and approve all the changes recommended. Much more time must be spent in building rapport with pupils and in planning with parents.

A community may be more or less advanced in its conception of teaching than the teacher is. Parents in the community may be more concerned about pupils' emotional development than the teacher. Members of the community may have greater insight into the ways in which boys and girls can be brought into active community participation than the school staff. The reverse may be true also. A community may help a teacher grow in skill or retard his development.

The Basis of Method

Teaching method consists of judging each teaching situation—and there may be a thousand or more a day—and choosing at the moment the procedure deemed most likely to be successful. To be able to make the decisions intelligently and with assurance, a teacher must have thought through his philosophy of teaching and have decided upon the functions he should perform.

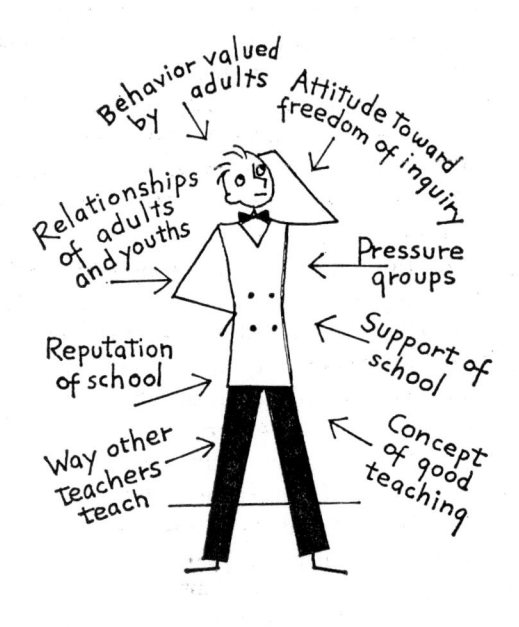

Behavior valued by adults
Attitude toward freedom of inquiry
Relationships of adults and youths
Pressure groups
Reputation of school
Support of school
Way other teachers teach
Concept of good teaching

3 · Quality Teaching

Even a brief comparison of the description of minimum acceptable teaching with the psychological and sociological factors which bear upon the function of the teacher makes it evident that minimum teaching will not enable the school to fulfill its social responsibility. Securing better teaching is essential. To make the contribution indicated by the review of factors presented in the preceding chapter, a teacher would need to operate a class in which:

1. each pupil feels accepted, at ease, successful, and responsible for helping others;
2. pupil leadership and self-control is developed;
3. individuals and groups increase their skill in collecting and recording evidence of growth, making judgments, and revising plans;
4. each individual grows in understanding of himself and more adequately selects from the environment the experiences and resources which he may use to further his purposes.
5. each individual's creative potential is fostered;
6. each individual lives in a stimulating intellectual environment;
7. differences in achievement among individuals is constantly increased;
8. each individual explores the values found in our society, learns to discriminate among them, and develops commitment to those he finds good.

Definition of Quality Teaching

Although all teachers should provide these conditions in their classes, not all can hope to accomplish it. Merely considering the possibility of attempting it discourages some, and they call such a statement of functions idealistic and impractical. Others try and find themselves overwhelmed and retreat to the minimum acceptable pattern.

The time has come to rethink the meaning of quality teaching and how it may be attained for more pupils. It is no longer acceptable to consider continuing to staff schools with mediocre teachers.

Many teachers are quality teachers. They stand out so that pupils, parents, and even their colleagues recognize them. They give the teaching profession its lustre and are the persons the public has in mind when it indicates its willingness to pay higher salaries.

Difficulty has occurred in attempts to identify quality teaching because of the assumption that excellence in a teacher is determined by averaging the scores assigned to him on a variety of qualities. This approach is doomed to failure. An individual is unique, and he makes a particular type of contribution. He is recognized for his ability in some phase of teaching. *Quality teaching is not an average of many qualities; it is an exceptional contribution in some important phase of teaching.*

Analysis of work in other fields leads to support of this conclusion. Leadership research has arrived at the point where it is possible to recognize that people may contribute to leadership in many different ways. In sports, only a few super stars are proficient in many fields. A quality musician is not expected to be competent on all instruments. In industry and the armed services, special types of excellence are valued and few are expected to do all things well.

Once this concept is accepted, the task of identifying quality teachers becomes easier. Let's meet some teachers who make a contribution far beyond the minimum call of duty.

Some Quality Teachers

Jack teaches science. He is looked upon by his students as more of a scientist than a teacher. He seldom shows an interest in pupil problems or sports or school activities unless they relate to science. But all pupils know Jack will take as much time as they wish to explore a scientifiic idea. His office is a hangout for pupils who want to talk about scientific development.

Students in Jack's class have freedom to move into special projects as soon as they have demonstrated a real interest in science. In one class one committee may be working on the preparation of a rocket, or a boy working alone may be investigating the effect of radiation of seeds on subsequent plant history.

Jack treats the students interested in science as contemporaries and fellow scientists. He has no patience for those who question the importance of investigation of the field of science.

Jack is a scholar in his own right. The text is merely an aid. He knows what he wants pupils to learn in the field of science and organizes a variety of types of experiences and information from many sources to achieve the results he desires.

This teacher enriches the program for his pupils. He is not content to follow a text. He knows his field well enough to deal with topics and questions not specifically answered in the text. His classroom contains displays, specimens, books, and pamphlets which attract the attention of pupils. He brings resource people into the class and takes pupils out on field trips. From time to time he shares his knowledge which supplements that of the text. He is a scholar in his field and shares his enthusiasm with his students.

Mary, who teaches kindergarten, is one of the best teachers in her system in producing a desirable emotional climate in the classroom. All pupils love her. One pupil, when his mother told him if he were not good no one would like him, replied, "Oh yes. No matter what I do, two people will like me. God and Miss Mary." She makes each child feel wanted and worthy. She greets each one and reacts to him many times each day. She is always alert to emotions and moves in to give support as needed. Frequently a pupil goes to her, tugs at her skirt and says "lap." She sits down, pulls the youngster into her lap and holds him until he is ready to get down and face the world again. As she works she looks for the good things about each pupil, the types of strength she can encourage. Never does she accentuate or reprimand weakness. She provides, in a soft voice, constructive suggestions as to ways to solve the problem when she sees a child in difficulty or misbehaving.

She learns about each pupil. She talks with his parents and listens to his observations. She encourages him to bring his pets and toys to school and to share his sorrows and joys.

She helps a pupil feel adequate and worthy. No matter how immature the child, she notes with him the progress he is making in solving his problems. It may be decreasing the number of times he cries each day or increasing his help in the distribution of the milk. Verbal note is always made of progress, not lack of it.

Miss Mary promotes pupil acceptance of each other. She never makes belittling remarks about a child, and the habit is contagious. She constantly plans with pupils about what we are going to do, talks about what we have done and how we feel. She encourages them to share their experiences and to listen to the things others say. She steps in quietly to divert attention to other pursuits when conflict begins.

Parents plead to get their children in Miss Mary's room. Pupils are happy there and remember it with such pleasure that some children continue to return for visits for two or three years after they leave. During the first grade a number of pupils bring their personal problems back to Miss Mary.

Although Miss Mary does what other kindergarten teachers do about pre-reading, pre-arithmetic, art and music experiences, it is in the contribution to mental health that she is a quality teacher.

This teacher excels in her ability to meet the emotional needs of pupils. She accepts pupils, helps pupils accept themselves, and promotes pupil acceptance of each other. Her concern for pupil emotions arises from her knowledge that the emotional climate affects the amount and type of learning pupils do. She recognizes, since one out of ten persons spend some time in hospitals for treatment of emotional or mental disturbance, that promoting good mental health is basic citizenship education.

Betty cares for individual differences through her organization of her fifth-grade class, the type of assignments given, her evaluation procedures, and the establishment of different sets of standards for youngsters within her room.

The school day in Betty's classroom is divided into two parts. During one portion of the day the entire class works on a single project and the remainder of the day each youngster works on his own tasks to develop his individual skills. When students work on the total class project, committees within the group assume responsibility for a portion of the project. Students choose the phase of the project which is important to them. The members of a committee plan with Betty what each will do. Assignments differ from student to student in terms of the type of commitments each makes as he plans with the committee how it will accomplish its purposes. The more able students exert more leadership and assume responsibility for a greater amount of work. The less able students make the type of contribution that they can. No one compares the amount of work of one student with another. Each student is working for goals he established for himself as a member of a working committee.

During the portion of the day that the students work on the development of individual skills, each student has a different assignment. He has his work materials in arithmetic, language, and spelling. He moves ahead at his own rate as fast as he can. For example, Jack, a student in Betty's fifth-grade class, is able to do arithmetic at only the third-grade level, as measured by standardized tests, but can read at the eighth-grade level. When Jack is working on individual skills he is working on typical third-grade arithmetic tasks, just a little ahead of of his present achievement. During some of the time he is reading, his selections are from eighth- and ninth-grade books, even though he is only a fifth-grader.

Betty helps each youngster establish standards for himself. Her ambitions for this class do not consist of having all youngsters work at the fifth-grade level. For many youngsters working at the fifth-grade level would be a very low standard. To have Jack read at the fifth-grade level would merely convince him that school was not challenging. For a teacher to maintain high standards, as Betty sees it, she must know where each child is and insist that he work at a level just beyond his present achievement.

Evaluation is on an individual basis. At the beginning of the year, Betty provides each student with a manilla folder and asks each one to put in the folder samples of his work of which he is proud. Betty realizes that no teacher can record all of the evidence concerning a pupil's growth. To secure a more adequate record, she brings students in on the record keeping. It should be noted that Betty does not ask any student to keep a record against himself. Instead he is asked to collect evidence of his best achievement.

The evidence is then used as the basis for judgment making concerning next steps. For example, in January Betty asks each student to go through his folder and make a list of the ten most important things for him to work on in the second semester. Each student does this. By this process Betty helps each youngster to assume responsibility for the direction of his work. She helps youngsters set up individual goals in terms of their present achievement. She encourages each student to plan his own work in terms of his needs. She participates in the process by going through the list with students and with their parents and adding other goals that she thinks should be considered.

This teacher makes an unusual contribution through her skill in providing for individual differences. Most teachers give verbal allegiance to meeting individual differences, but some consider that they care for individual differences by the fact that youngsters get different amounts of information from the same assignment. Such an approach does not call for teaching ingenuity. The differences within the pupils determine what happens to them. The classroom is not organized to provide for individual differences. If a teacher really attempts to provide for individual differences, he plans his assignments, evaluations, and organization of class activity to make possible individual programs for students. He seeks constantly to increase the difference in achievement among pupils. Instead of striving to provide the same content for all, he devotes his efforts to organizing a different program for each.

Jim, a clean-cut, athletic young man with a crew-cut, teaches in the ninth grade. He wants students to learn the subject matter he teaches, but he also wants them to understand themselves and to be able to plan their own work.

To increase their self-understanding he is willing to talk with students about their concerns and their purposes. Between classes and after the school day, students hold conferences with him to discuss their problems. During the regular class period he spends much of his time in conferences with individuals while the other students work in small groups. He encourages each youngster to be honest with himself and has established a reputation for maintaining confidences and being a helpful listener.

Jim could plan the work for the class and announce the assignments. Instead of that, he decides upon a large area of work to be covered in his science course. He tells students that there are many phases of the topic that they might investigate and then brings the class in on deciding the specific questions that they will study. He helps them to make this decision by talking through with them what they already know about the topic and securing from them a list of questions to which they would like to know the answers. He supplies some of his own questions, questions that are real for him, not ones that could be answered by reading certain pages of the textbook.

After the class has formulated the questions they wish to investigate, Jim does not proceed to tell them how to study the area. Instead he asks them for suggestions. He may contribute several possibilities himself, but one of his primary concerns is to help them decide on ways of attacking problems. He feels this is an important skill, one that they will need to use throughout the rest of their lives. In his opinion, developing this skill will be as useful as any concept learned in his science class. He sees two major purposes to his teaching: (1) to develop a knowledge of the field of science and (2) to develop skills in the use of the scientific method.

As the class works through the plans they have made, they pause from time to time, under Jim's direction, to make some judgments about the progress. Jim recognizes that evaluation applies to purposes, procedures, progress, and production. He is attempting to help his class see this. He wants them to look at the plans they have made and to decide upon their effectiveness in terms of efficiency and achievement. He helps them look at the evidence and make judgments about it. He could make the judgments himself. He could tell the class how well it is doing. If he did, however, he would feel that he was depriving them of one of their major learnings. He judges his teaching by whether or not the students become better able to make accurate judgments about their individual and group progress and to revise their plans in light of the judgments.

In the beginning some of Jim's students feel that the planning and the evaluation are wastes of time. They cannot see how it is helping them to become better science students. They would prefer to have Jim direct and judge. As they work together during the year, many students begin to see that the way they become more efficient is to use the judgments of all the people involved. Some of the students never do see this, but they tolerate the joint planning and evaluation because they respect Jim as a person and as a scientist.

This teacher makes his special contribution through skill in joint planning and evaluation. He is very helpful in helping students become self-directed; he brings youngsters in on the planning and the evaluation processes; he promotes self-direction; he helps each student to know himself, to establish his goals, to make plans and to carry them out and to make judgments about the effectiveness of present procedures and devise better ones. If the function of formal education is to help people develop a skill for continuing their own education after they leave school, a teacher who performs the role of increasing self-direction makes a major contribution.

Bill promotes creativity. Whenever a class has completed an activity, he asks each student to interpret it in his own way. Bill believes that he is able to do his best guidance and counseling by discussing with pupils the interpretations that they make of events. He believes that no teacher can really know how to react to a student's behavior or comments unless the student is free to interpret his behavior and comments to the teacher. Bill views listening as a major facet of teaching. He deems it necessary in order to know how to relate to pupils' present knowledge.

When students prepare book reports in Bill's tenth grade English class, he does not ask that they all use the same form of 500 words in length on pages with exact margins. Instead, he makes possible utilization of different ways of sharing ideas about books. Sometimes the class goes to the library for a free reading period, and the next day those students who have read books of the same type sit together in a small group and tell each other about the books they have read. Sometimes Bill will tell the class to use color and materials as well as written comments to express their feelings about a book. Sometimes he suggests that students pantomime an interpretation of a book. His primary concern is not the book report but rather to help students feel that their interpretations have validity and want to share their feelings.

Bill wants students to do things with facts rather than to acquire a set of facts. If they have analyzed an author's statements about a short story, they may test them by writing a short story in which they attempt to use the ideas. If they have been examining student life in the school, they may compose a code of beliefs or propose a revision of the school government. Preparation of their proposals constitutes a method of increasing skill in communication. If they have been studying their community, they may prepare a pageant depicting the history of the community. In any kind of situation Bill hunts ways of encouraging students to do things with facts rather than memorizing them. He emphasizes helping people draw generalizations and making application of them.

This teacher makes an extra contribution by promoting creativity in youngsters. He is not content to have students learn information that is in a textbook or to have students acquire the knowledge and concepts that he has. He believes that each person is a unique individual with a special contribution to make. He teaches for creativity rather than for conformity. He wants each pupil to feel that he has a special contribution to make and to search for effective ways of sharing it. He recognizes that no two children learn the same things from an experience they supposedly have in common. He accepts the fact that each child perceives in terms of his background of experiences, his purposes, and his needs. He believes that to insist that all children learn the same thing from a common experience is to compel students to lose their integrity. He wants each child to interpret his own experiences and to share this interpretation with others. He encourages each person to interpret in the way that seems best to him. He recognizes that some youngsters express themselves best through one medium while others are more effective through a different one. He is concerned that people use facts and ideas to formulate their own organization of knowledge.

> As he works with students, Bill helps them examine values. If they are reading *The Merchant of Venice,* the class may stop reading about Shylock and begin discussing how stereotypes of people are formed and what stereotypes they hold. Bill believes that being able to recognize the teachable moment when people are examining their values is one of the most important competencies of a teacher. He feels that any contribution he can make at the teachable moment to a student's formulation of values that will guide his behavior is more important than any skill or concept he might have taught during those minutes.

This teacher also believes that a major part of his role is helping pupils find something by which to live. He wants them to know values people hold, to be able to understand and accept difference, to discover which values are significant for them, and to develop a commitment which will give purpose and meaning to life. He does not believe he could or should give others his values, but he sees his role as helping pupils examine and evaluate the values inherent in problems and crises they encounter.

> Alice is a leader on the faculty. She is in her mid-thirties, has her Master's degree, and each summer selects an experience that will, in her opinion, contribute to improvement of her teaching. One year she went to Europe, another year she attended a workshop in Human Growth and Development. A third summer was spent in a creative-writing clinic. A fourth vacation period she worked as a member of a

state committee in the preparation of a language arts guide. Alice makes no outward show of her leadership, but she demonstrates daily by her teaching her ability to apply what she believes. Parents of the children in her room tell other members of the community how happy they are with the work she is doing.

In faculty meetings Alice is not an ardent advocate of any particular point of view. Whenever an issue arises she shares her opinion and any evidence she has that bears on the issue. As she talks she makes clear the values that she holds and why she takes the position she does in terms of these values.

She encourages the faculty to undertake new projects and to try out new ideas. She helps those who hesitate by suggesting that any good proposal be tried out on an experimental basis and that it be revised if it does not achieve the expectations the faculty had.

She proposes that plans be made for evaluating the action that is being tried out on an experimental basis. She never argues about who is right. Instead, she encourages the faculty to investigate and make judgments in terms of the evidence.

Alice has tenure and the security of knowing what she believes. She does not hesitate to question or disagree with the principal. She feels as free to be a professional person of integrity with him as with any other member of the faculty. She is not aggressive, but she insists that all points of view be tested in terms of the effect that the implementation of the ideas will have upon children.

During the years that Alice has been in the school she has won the respect of the administration, the other faculty members, and the community. If anyone were to ask about Alice as a teacher, she would be labeled as a highly professional person and one who seeks constantly to improve the school in which she teaches. She is recognized by all persons as a teacher who is constantly seeking better methods, who is willing to experiment and engage in active research to test the new ideas she has. She can be counted on by the rest of the faculty to help them formulate plans for action research or to participate in action research projects related to her field.

This teacher makes her special contribution by exerting leadership in a faculty. Any faculty has certain teachers to whom it turns for leadership. They may exert influence for the advancement of the program or for maintaining the status quo. The quality teacher in the area of faculty leadership is a person who has good insight as a result of additional experiences or study and works in a way that leads to the sharing of this insight and the acceptance of higher standards by the rest of the faculty.

> Jinny is in her late forties. She has been teaching in the community for fifteen years and is a leader in church, civic, and welfare activities. She is the educational director of her church Sunday School;

she is chairman of the membership committee of the League of Women Voters; she devotes one evening a week to a committee working for better housing. At times she wonders whether these community activities do not take too much of her energy and if she would not be a better teacher if she spent more hours away from school in her own recreational activities.

But the principal and the members of the classroom teachers association urge her to continue. They know that community members trust Jinny and ask for her comments when questions are raised about school practices or proposals. And Jinny actually prefers her community work to sports or women's clubs.

This teacher makes an unusual contribution in working with the community. She is an average teacher in her work with students, but she adds to classwork great skill in bringing the school and community closer together. She participates in community activities, church work, recreational programs, and even fund-raising campaigns. She encourages members of the community to visit the school and to learn more about the school program; she uses her activities in the community as a method for increasing the respect of the community for the school and the teachers; she spends much of her time interpreting the school program and the methods used by modern teachers. She recognizes that education for children is provided by the total community and that the school performs one portion of it. She believes that the best education will be secured if the school and the community personnel plan and work cooperatively.

All of the teachers presented here make a special contribution. Each is unique, and each is a quality teacher in his area.

Approach Necessary to Obtain Quality Teaching

Not one of the teachers presented could make all of the contributions described. Mary, the kindergarten teacher, would laugh at anyone who suspected her of depth of scholarship, yet she is recognized throughout her section of the United States for her quality teaching; Jack, the science teacher, would resent the implication that he can or should care for emotional needs, yet he is valued highly by his pupils and their parents.

If quality teaching is to be secured for large numbers of children, teachers must be encouraged to develop their uniqueness and seek the place in the school where their contribution can be of most worth. School staffs must be selected to secure and make available to pupils a variety of contributions. Pupil placement must be made to provide the kind of teacher contribution and relationship that will be of most value to the student involved.

Preview

Throughout the remainder of this book, the types of quality teaching which the author considers most significant will be described with illustrations and suggestions for those who wish to improve their contribution in an area. At the close of each section is a self-evaluation checklist which summarizes the specific suggestions made and a bibliography of references which presents the viewpoints and research of other writers dealing with that aspect of teaching.

Bibliography

Beatty, W. H., "When Does Knowledge Change Behavior?" *Progressive Education,* 33 (May, 1956), pp. 85–90.

Cantor, Nathaniel, *The Dynamics of Learning.* Buffalo, New York: Foster and Stewart Publishing Corporation, 1946.

Davis, Allison, *Social Class Influences Upon Learning.* Cambridge, Massachusetts: Harvard University Press, 1948.

Hart, Joseph K., *Education in the Humane Community.* New York: Harper & Brothers, 1951.

Kelley, Earl C., *Education For What Is Real.* New York: Harper & Brothers, 1951.

Lewin, Kurt, *Resolving Social Conflicts.* New York: Harper & Brothers, 1948.

Murphy, Gardner, *Personality: A Biosocial Approach to Origins and Structure.* New York: Harper & Brothers, 1947.

National Society for the Study of Education, *Learning and Instruction.* Chicago: University of Chicago Press, 1950.

Prescott, Daniel A., *Emotion and the Educative Process.* Washington, D.C.: American Council on Education, 1938.

Rasey, Marie, *This Is Teaching.* New York: Harper & Brothers, 1950.

II · *Types of Quality Teaching*

- Improving Human Relations
- Promoting Group Development
- Providing for Individual Differences
- Stimulating Intellectual Growth
- Developing Self-Direction
- Exerting Leadership in School and Community

· · · Improving Human
Relations

The emotional climate of a learning situation determines how efficiently the pupil will learn the facts and skills desired. Unless the emotional content of the situation is right, the desired subject-matter learnings will not occur. In any situation, boys and girls are striving to feel right about themselves, to feel that they have worth, to feel that they are accepted. Other learnings are secondary and will not receive the full attention of students until these first learnings receive satisfaction.

The type of human relations that exist within the school teaches the youngster how to feel toward others and what to believe about others. To varying degrees he learns: to accept all people, or to reject certain people who do not measure up to standards imposed by the group or by the teacher; to encourage people and have faith in them, or to suspect the other person and expect only failure to live up to responsibilities; that it is good to work together, or that he must work alone, without help; that adults are people who are helpful and can be trusted, or that he must cover up his true emotional beliefs and feelings when he is talking to them; that most situations offer many choices, or that most situations are either "all good" or "all bad."

The emotional climate determines the significance with which a learner endows an idea and the use to which he will put it; the potency of the idea is determined by the emotional matrix in which it is embedded.

UNSATISFACTORY TEACHER

By his actions he teaches hate, prejudice, violence, and lack of respect for the worth of the individual. Such a teacher uses his classroom to vent his hate, frustration, and feelings of inadequacy. Pupils who come into contact with him are blighted and warped by the experience.

MINIMUM SATISFACTORY TEACHER

He does not make a positive contribution to pupil growth in the area of human relations. He acts more as a restrictive force to poor human relations. He prevents chaos. He has his class under control. He fights injustice. He protects the weak from the aggressive and strong. He stops fights and attempts to prevent name-calling and labeling. Pupils do not increase in understanding, in sensitivity, in empathy, or in skill in living more effectively with others as a result of their interaction with him; they are merely protected.

4 · *Teacher Acceptance of Self and Others*

The teacher plays a major role in determining the quality of human relations that exist in the classroom. Through the status and authority of his role, the teacher can do much to force pupils to accept the way of living together that he deems desirable. He has the authority to establish a social structure and processes and to determine the method and rate of change. How he uses his position to influence the human relations will be determined by his values, his feelings about himself, and his feelings about his pupils. The quality teacher in the area of human relations will attempt to treat pupils in a way that helps each to feel more worthy, wanted, and adequate.

The Importance of a Teacher's Feelings About Himself

Park's study and others indicates that a person is more able to accept others if he can accept himself. An important asset or liability to the establishment of a good emotional climate in a classroom is how the teacher feels about himself.

If he feels inadequate, superior, or rebellious, he doesn't help pupils create a wholesome emotional climate in which all feel that they belong, accept others, and help each other.

If he is not confident of his ability to work successfully in situations that arise, he is always on guard. He seeks ways of covering up his incompetence, of proving his superiority, of gaining personal security, even though the techniques he uses mean infringing on the rights of others. He must always win. He develops any technique that he can for making people aware of his superiority. One way is to hold up exceedingly high standards in the area in which he is highly competent, and to reject boys and girls who cannot achieve these competencies. He keeps pupils from ever getting close enough to know him in order to prevent their discovering his weaknesses.

To the extent that he feels superior, he decreases his potential for promoting good human relations. When he feels and demonstrates feelings of superiority, he alienates the other person. When he feels superior, he makes it impossible for him to really appreciate others and to understand the contribution that they can make to group living and to him! When he can't appreciate or understand or really know the others, he can't expect to have good relationships with them or to help them have good relationships with other people.

On the surface, feelings of superiority may seem to come out of an ability to do more complicated mathematical operations or to handle verbs with more skill. Or a teacher may feel superior because he knows certain facts that other people don't know or because he has a different color or religion or nationality, or even because he has more money. All these feelings of superiority, however, are based on a feeling of insecurity that makes it necessary for a person to be superior to other peole in order to be safe and secure within himself.

Some feelings of superiority are very subtle. Some teachers feel that pupils grow only as they become more and more like them. This is a hard stereotype to avoid. Their experiences have led them to certain conclusions and have given them certain skills. They have been employed by boards of education to help boys and girls grow. By the very process of employing them, the board of education may seem to them to have put the stamp of approval on the type of growth that they have made. Some have moved from that assumption to the belief that it is their job to help boys and girls to be like them. No doubt they are quite sincere. They really believe that they have the answer to the world's problems, that they are the type of person who succeeds best in the world. Because of these beliefs, they attempt to have boys and girls become like them.

But when a teacher attempts to get others to be like him, he rejects the multiplicity of values that are within the culture. He fails to recognize the many contributions that people can make that are different from his own contributions. He fails to recognize that in a plural culture there are many skills, understandings, and values that contribute to the welfare and development of the total social group.

When a teacher feels that others must attain his status, he sometimes provides the type of teaching and guidance that leads people to move in the direction of goals that may be blind alleys for them. For example, a study conducted in the late thirties showed that 95 per cent of the boys and girls in American high schools were seeking white-collar jobs. This same study shows that only 5 per cent of the jobs in America at that time were white-collar jobs. Approximately 90 per cent of the population in American secondary schools were moving toward jobs that they could never occupy. Teachers who believe that youngsters should be molded in their pattern must accept a share of the responsibility for such false guidance.

If a person feels that teaching is unworthy of his best efforts and is rebellious against an unkind fate that has forced him into teaching, he has feelings that interfere with his creating good human relations in the classroom. If he feels that teaching is just a job and that he must put up with the "brats" to draw his salary, it is easy to guess that his classroom will be one in which he will be on one side and the pupils will be lined up against him. Pupils sense how the teacher feels toward them and formulate their own relationships in terms of the attitude that the teacher takes first toward them. Pupils respond to the type of treatment that they get, and any attitude of superiority or resentment on the teacher's part will alienate them and prevent them from considering him as a person to be trusted or accepted.

If a teacher feels superior, inadequate, or resentful, he cannot be satisfied with his present status and expect to provide quality instruction. He can change by recognizing that all persons have these feelings in varying degrees, and understanding that they decrease as his attention is focused more sharply on how he can help others. If he wants to promote good human relations, he begins his teaching by examining himself and identifying and working to eliminate those qualities within himself which hinder him. He seeks to increase his sense of personal adequacy.

A major portion of a person's feelings of inadequacy comes from pretending that he has no weaknesses, from creating a false picture of himself. All persons have weaknesses, teachers as well as pupils. Unless an individual recognizes and accepts this condition, he has to resort to tactics that make it impossible for him to work on a friendly, cooperative basis with children. A teacher needs to be able to say, "I don't know," simply, humbly, without shame, confusion, or hesitation. Knowing that all have weaknesses makes possible all contributing from their strengths. A teacher can recognize with children the weaknesses that each person has, but at the same time he can bring to the fore the special contributions that each can make. This stress on the positive is something that applies to the teacher's contributions as much as it does to the contribution of pupils. If he makes this approach, it puts him in a position in which there is no need for proving his ability to others. He accepts himself as he is, and he knows his own competencies. He contributes what he has and expects others to do the same. He works to eradicate his weaknesses so he can be of more help to others.

He needs to feel sufficiently confident and mature, so that he can consider pupil behavior objectively. If he is, he examines constantly the type of treatment that he gives boys and girls to see whether or not it is an attempt to get even for something that they have done to him. As a teacher, he cannot wear his feelings on his sleeve. A mature person can accept the action of a less mature person, can analyze that action, and can take the steps necessary for the less mature person to grow more mature. To the extent that he fights back at youngsters to get even with them, he is reflecting his own immaturity and is revealing his inadequacy to help create an environment in which boys and girls can become more mature. He must have enough security within himself to be able to put the welfare of the pupil first. Only then can he recognize that there are times when it is better for him to lose than to win, when it is more important for an insecure boy or girl to have the experience of winning in an issue with the teacher. An expression of hostility may be a symptom of disturbance rather than a token of personal dislike or antagonism.

To be effective in the area of human relations, a teacher must understand himself, recognize his strengths and his weaknesses, and see his role as a helping, sharing, rather than as a controlling one.

The Teacher's Feelings About Pupils

A college professor was conducting an inservice program for nurses. During one session she asked the nurses to write down the words that came to their mind when the professor mentioned "boys." The three words found most frequently on the papers were "noisy," "dirty," "brats."

Obviously these nurses did not hold positive feelings toward boys.

To contribute to desirable human relations in the classroom the teacher must accept his students. *Accepting pupils means that the teacher looks for the strengths in them rather than concentrating attention on the things he dislikes about them or the weaknesses he feels that they have.*

A beginning teacher in Kentucky found an eighteen-year-old boy, homely and weighing over 200 pounds, in her sophomore English class. His appearance and reputation as a trouble-maker and poor student made the teacher wish that he had been assigned to the class of a more experienced colleague. For two months the teacher endured him, dreading the period when he appeared in her room—and he made no progress. One night, in a moment of soul-searching, the young woman suddenly realized that she hated the boy, that she was wishing him failure rather than success. Conscience-stricken, she asked herself if there wasn't at least one good quality in the youth and resolved to search for one the very next day. By her own testimony, the teacher was amazed by the change that came over the boy in the next few weeks! Actually, the basic change was in the teacher. She began to see strong qualities in the boy which she had been overlooking.

An individual finds what he expects to find in other people, and persons tend to live up to what is expected of them.

If a teacher is to be effective, he wants each person in his class to succeed. He is not with the class to sort and classify and label. He is not there to help some to succeed and cause others to fail. His job is to hope and to work for the growth of all. It is his function to help each pupil develop his strengths and overcome his weaknesses.

If a teacher is going to help the total class, he has faith in each pupil. He believes that each has potential leadership and the ability to make a contribution to the group and to society. Even though his talents are hidden beneath a surface of indifference, hostility, filth, or social ineptness, he believes that each child can be better than he is, and the teacher's success is judged by the extent to which each realizes his potential. Like the Kentucky teacher, he starts looking for the good points.

All students, like teachers, have weaknesses. None will have all the answers or all the necessary skills. These weaknesses are opportunities for the teacher to be of assistance, not stigmas for which he condemns a child. A machine-scored test can locate a lack of knowledge or skill, but a teacher by faith and by providing the experiences that will promote the needed growth can help a child to improve.

If a teacher is to provide leadership for all, he is willing for pupils to be different. He will find that strengths vary from pupil to pupil. Elementary teachers, who work with pupils in many different types of activities, have a better opportunity than secondary teachers, who work with children in a limited field, to see the range of abilities possessed by the individual and the group. Because of this greater breadth of experience with the child, many elementary teachers have gone further in accepting and encouraging different kinds of contribution and leadership. All teachers can go still further in accepting and utilizing different patterns of development. Singing, art, humor, human relations, and sensitivity are as important as abstract mental manipulations.

Moreover, the teacher will be willing for pupils to have purposes that are different from his own. If he recognizes that motivation comes from the vision developed through past experience, he knows it is useless to expect pupils from different backgrounds to have the same purposes and ambitions that he has. He recognizes the difference, and lets the pupils know he understands it, but he does not proclaim their goals less worthy than his.

In short, the teacher wants to know pupils, to understand them, to recognize their strengths, weaknesses, and purposes, and to have faith in their potential and his ability to help them realize it.

At the very lowest level, acceptance means that a teacher seeks to know his pupils. He learns their names, where they are from, what their parents are like, their background, their likes, their interests, their dislikes, their prejudices, their ambitions. Also, the teacher must be careful not to hold their previous behavior against them as he learns more about them. He does not say, at the first sign of behavior of which he disapproves, "Oh well, that's all you can expect from a youngster with such a record." He avoids analyzing the records simply as a means of spotting trouble-makers and choosing allies.

Parenthetically, using the records to determine which students should be guarded against is highly unprofessional. The only valid reason for a teacher to see a pupil's record is to gain information about his strengths or weaknesses that will make possible providing the kind of help needed.

Because a teacher recognizes that each pupil perceives in terms of his own background and his purposes, it is necessary for the teacher to understand that background to interpret pupil behavior accurately and to relate to the pupil in a way that promotes desirable growth.

> In a California junior high school a fourteen-year-old girl was wearing a skirt that was so tight that the boys began to whistle at her and to make remarks that the teachers considered improper. Some of the teachers on the staff drew the conclusion that this girl needed some advice on relationships with boys. The dean of girls called her into the office and began to talk with her about proper behavior for adolescent girls. The girl began to cry and ran out of the office and went home. The dean of girls followed her and discovered that the girl's father and mother had been divorced two years before. The girl had loved her father and wanted to go with him, but the court had assigned her to her mother. The only thing she had left that her father had given her was the skirt.

It is so easy to misinterpret behavior unless the teacher knows the background and the needs of the students with whom he works. Taking the steps to learn and know about pupils not only helps a teacher to understand and relate to pupils but also is an indication to pupils that he values them.

Accepting a youngster also means refusing to take advantage of him. Because a teacher has had more experience and has had an opportunity to study the techniques of winning situations in the classroom, he knows how to win. But if he uses his advantage unfairly, he will destroy whatever progress he has made in winning the confidence of the youngsters. Any action of an adult which decreases their faith in his sincerity and willingness to help them lessens his opportunity to be of real assistance to them. One break destroys the fabric. If children find that a teacher has passed along to another teacher something that they have told him in confidence, they will classify him as unreliable if they are charitable, or a dishonest fraud if they have a long-standing distrust of teachers.

A teacher shows his acceptance of boys and girls by really wanting them to be themselves. When he asks a youngster to be like him or like certain children of whom he approves, he is keeping the pupil from being himself. He is saying to him, "You aren't as good as I am. The only way you can be acceptable is to be like me." If pupils happen to have come from a different social background, it is impossible for them to behave just as the teacher does. It is impossible for them to have the same beliefs, social graces, prejudices, and values.

The following questions help a teacher to examine his acceptance of people:

Am I agreeable to boys and girls having different purposes, values, and social skills? Do I lead my pupils to feel that I am thinking with them and that all of us together, through the process of interaction, are gaining new insight into what constitutes good human relations? Or do I assume that I alone know what constitutes good human relations? Am I willing to think with all the members of the class about ways in which everyone working together can help one another to grow? Do I believe that I can learn from each of my pupils?

Accepting pupils means that a teacher wants them to have the opportunity to improve, that he tries sincerely to find out what they are like and what they believe; that he supports them in their belief that they have value and the ability to improve; that he has faith that they will become more worthwhile.

Accepting dirty youngsters, for example, does not mean that a teacher likes their filth. It does not mean that he allows them to stay dirty in his class. It means that he does not establish prejudices against them because they are not clean but that he makes provisions for them to take baths at school, that he encourages their parents to provide clean clothes for them and to help them stay clean, that he continues to believe they will improve even though they fail numerous times, that he does not isolate them or encourage the other pupils to shame them. He wants them to learn to value cleanliness, but he is willing to keep working with them, even when they do not respond as readily as he had hoped.

> In one of the New York City junior high schools, special emphasis was placed on the acceptance of pupils who were having difficulty in the school. A teacher was placed in charge of an ungraded group. Children who were not getting along in other classes were allowed to join the group, and others were assigned to it. No child was forced to do anything during the time he was there. Facilities for work and play were provided, but the pupils could simply sit if they wanted to. They could say or do anything they pleased as long as they did not harm other pupils. As each child behaved in the way he chose, the teacher studied him and talked with him in order to help him determine the causes of his difficulties and what he really wanted to do. When a pupil felt like working, he did so. When he felt that he was ready to return to the group from which he had come, he was permitted to. The emphasis was on encouraging the child to help himself rather than on trying to change him in accordance with a teacher's pattern. But the teacher's acceptance of a child did not entitle him to engage in behavior harmful to the other children.

The remedial treatment applied in helping these pupils re-establish themselves as worthy members of the school was simply the teacher's acceptance. If all teachers in the school had accepted pupils more fully, the remedial group would not have been necessary. In this school this procedure succeeded where disciplinary action had failed. If a teacher accepts pupils, he gives them support when they need it.

A major aspect of acceptance is empathy, the ability to put one's self in the other person's role and feel as he does. When a teacher can do this he understands pupils' behavior more fully. He sees aggression or withdrawal in a different light and has a greater recognition that *his role is helping rather than controlling*. Understanding the causes of behavior is a part of acceptance.

Accepting a pupil also means that a teacher listens patiently to him. His stories about himself and his family may be uninteresting and repetitive. The stories may be similar to those heard many times before from other pupils. But to accept a pupil means that the teacher is listening wholeheartedly to his problems and his concerns. If the teacher is really interested, the stories will always be new, even though the general pattern of his difficulties is familiar.

A teacher can contribute to a student's feeling of acceptance in many ways:

1. *Calling by name.* Every person likes the recognition that comes from having his name used. Calling youngsters by other than their first names creates a situation in which no one is very close to anyone else. The choice of names is symbolic and revealing.
2. *Responding to ideas.* Listening is not enough. Since learning occurs through the interaction of ideas, teaching will be made most effective through thoughtful response to pupil ideas.
3. *Taking questions seriously.* Although some questions seem very naive, they are important to the pupil who asks them. Any question seems simple to a person who has already worked out the answer. Respecting the other person and working with him in a way that helps him grow requires accepting his questions as being worthy of consideration.
4. *Avoiding ridicule and sarcasm.* Respect for human personality is taught by example. If a teacher ridicules individual students, he makes clear to all that he does not respect the personalities of children. But by showing proper respect for each child, he increases the chance that the boys and girls with whom he works will respect each other.
5. *Avoiding action that embarrasses.* Embarrassing a pupil splits the group into two camps. All the members feel that they must take sides. They are forced either to defend the injured person or to declare their allegiance to the teacher. Such issues can be avoided if the teacher takes the misbehaving youngster aside and talks over with him the effect of his behavior on the group.
6. *Encouraging friendliness.* By complimenting pupils on their acts of friendliness, friendliness in the group is increased.
7. *Welcoming children.* Welcoming new children into the group makes it clear that friendliness and belonging are essential qualities of that group. As a teacher plans with the members of his class how they can make new members feel at home, he shows

that all people belong and are wanted. He assures the newcomers that they are welcome, and at the same time he increases the security and acceptance of the other children.
8. *Letting absentees know that they are missed.* When absentees know that they have been missed, they feel that they are making a contribution to the group. But when they return unnoticed, they gain the impression that no one cares whether they are part of the group or not.
9. *Permitting students to choose their own seats.* If the teacher assigns seats arbitrarily, he makes it clear that the room is really his room and that the students are simply doing his bidding. But if he allows students to sit with their friends, he shows that he is working with them in a situation in which friendship is valued and respected. By separating friends, he makes clear that friendship is not a quality that he values in the classroom.

The problem of what to do about cliques can be effectively handled after the children have come to recognize friendship as a positive value. Then the problem can be attacked by all the members of the group working together. The solution worked out by this method will be far more satisfactory than when the teacher sets out to destroy the cliques by seating youngsters away from the people with whom they would prefer to sit.
10. *Having the class work in committees.* As pupils have an opportunity to work closely together in small committees, friendships and sense of belonging increase.
11. *Stressing common qualities.* By emphasizing common interests, a teacher decreases the importance of differences. Group unity is built around common purposes, interests, and beliefs. If differences are stressed, they loom so large that unity is never achieved.
12. *Refraining from sending youngsters from the room.* When a teacher sends a youngster from the room, he decreases his self-respect and isolates him from the group. The effects of such isolation are particularly harmful to children who are already having difficulty getting along with others.

The behavior of the adult leader in the group determines to a great degree the pattern of living in the class. If a teacher accepts all pupils, he helps create the conditions in which pupils will accept themselves and each other.

Acceptance of children is shown in courtesy to them. A teacher teaches courtesy as he creates an environment in which people are naturally courteous toward each other, and the major factor in developing such an atmosphere is his attitude and bearing. He teaches more by action than by statements.

If he hopes to teach boys and girls to be courteous to each other, he is courteous to them. Courtesy includes such things as remembering and calling them by name, speaking to them as they come into the room, acknowledging requests, saying "please" to them just as he expects them to say "please" to him, asking permission of individuals and the group in just the same type of situation in which he expects them to ask permission. He is as much bound by the code of behavior as the pupils are, and any deviation from it on his part requires as much of an apology or explanation as any deviation on the part of a pupil. If he sets himself above the code of behavior that is accepted by the group, he signifies that codes are binding only on those who are not in a position of authority. He teaches respect for manners and mores and ways of behaving by the way he accepts his role within the group as a member of the group and lives by standards that have been established by the classroom society.

If a teacher expects boys and girls to call him by the title that he prefers, he has the same responsibility to them. If a child wants to be called "Lucky" rather than Nathaniel, the teacher should abide by the choice. If a high-school pupil wishes to be called "Bill" rather than Mr. Smith, that too should be a decision of his that the teacher respects.

Working with children in a courteous manner requires that the teacher treat them as adults. When he talks down to children, he belittles them. When he treats them as inferiors and as persons of lesser ability, he is making clear to them that he behaves toward people in accordance with their power and position rather than in accordance with their individual worth.

The teacher's acceptance of himself and his pupils is the foundation for creating a healthy emotional climate. If the teacher does not believe in himself or the people with whom he works, he is too concerned with these dissatisfactions to take the necessary leadership in creating a quality teaching-learning situation.

5 · *Pupil Acceptance of Self and Others*

Unless each student can believe that he has worth and is able to contribute to the group, his potential for aggression or withdrawal is strong and his attention will not be focused on the learning task at hand.

If optimum learning conditions prevail in the class, each pupil feels that:

He belongs—is accepted, will be missed if he is not present, will be welcomed back after each absence, and has equal opportunity in the group;

He is at ease with the group—recognizes that he will make mistakes but knows that they will be accepted as learning experiences;

He is successful—is accomplishing, knows where he is going, is putting forth his best effort to reach his goals, and feels confident;

He has a responsibility to the group—can help others, and can make a positive contribution to the success of the group.

The Effect of the Community

When a class meets for the first time, it brings with it to the classroom the groupings, attitudes, desires, and ways of working in the community from which its members come. The background of community living serves as a springboard from which class activities grow.

Each class member has a picture of his family's position in the community. He knows how other people look upon his family; he knows it from the expressions on their faces when his family's name is mentioned; he knows it from the attitudes that other people have displayed in their actions toward the members of his family; he has seen how other members of the community treat his father; he has seen how other women talk down or play up to his mother; he has seen his sister accepted or rejected by other girls; he has seen his brother a part of a team or excluded from it.

Each youngster not only has a picture of his own family and its place in the community but he has a knowledge of the position of every other family that he knows. He knows which families have power, which families can exert influence in the church or with the local city government, which families belong to the controlling group of the community, which families are accepted by the community, and which families are rejected by the community.

These impressions may not be accurate, but they influence his behavior. They give him confidence or lack of confidence. They move him to aggression, withdrawal, or active participation. Youngsters who are members of privileged groups, formed by parental contacts or by youth organizations, formal or informal, within the community, bring their acceptance to the class as foundation stones for *total* group acceptance of each other. They also bring their feelings of superiority and lack of consideration for the feelings of non-members as barriers to *total* group unity. Parenthetically, such handicaps are multiplied when the school has social fraternities and sororities within its organization.

Members of the same gang, children who attend the same church, pupils who come from the same rural elementary school to the consolidated high school, members of a minority racial or nationality element of the community may all constitute social groups within a classroom. The pattern varies from community to community.

Youths who have been excluded bring their desire to belong as a positive inclination, and their resentment and overt aggression toward the more privileged as liabilities, to the building of satisfying group relations.

But a class differs from a community. It has the advantage of being a frontier where people can meet together in a new environment and develop the type of social organization they find good. As a new social group, it has an opportunity to look at its surroundings and to make judgments concerning the types of relationships that bring satisfactions and those that are not as satisfying, and then in terms of those judgments begin to devise ways of working together that will increase satisfactions for all. If the teacher is willing to provide the leadership, this can be accomplished.

The Teacher's Role in Helping a Pupil to Accept Himself

The emotionally healthy person believes in himself. He knows he is worthy, wanted, and adequate. He is confident of his ability to meet the problems that will arise.

A teacher helps a pupil accept himself by doing the things which enable the pupil to recognize his achievement, to decrease his fears, to reduce his feelings of guilt and to lessen his financial insecurity.

Recognizing Achievement

Many classroom problems center around the teacher's concept of leadership. If he believes that a leader is a person who is superior to the other students, his attitude will color all the relationships within the class. Emphasis will be placed on being better than other people. Honor rolls will be posted on the bulletin board, and contests will be held to see which students can make the highest scores. Pupils will be strictly ranked from top to bottom of the class, and each one will know where he stands in the rank order. Emphasis will be placed on becoming a leader by beating someone else. Obviously, such an atmosphere restricts leadership to a very few pupils.

On the other hand, if he conceives of leadership as being any contribution that a boy or girl makes toward establishing and carrying out group purposes, everyone has the chance to be a leader. Whenever a student shares a worthwhile idea with the group or contributes a skill to the completion of a class project, he will manifest leadership. Everyone is encouraged to lead. Leadership will not be limited to two or three of the more gifted members of the class. All the children will take pride in the things they have done together rather than in the achievement of the superior members of the class. In fact, when leadership is restricted to only a few, the other class members frequently come to resent the activities of the teacher-appointed "elite" rather than take pride in their abilities.

If he uses any system of determining achievement that labels some people as leaders and others as inadequate, a teacher leads many youngsters to feel that they have no contribution to make. They rebel against a situation and system that makes it impossible for them to have a sense of achievement.

> In a junior high school in Ohio there was a seventh-grade boy who was three years older and much bigger than the other members of his class. Still, he had a hard time keeping up with his classmates in academic activities. Moreover, his family was not well accepted in the community. Because of his size, he was able to excel at athletics and was capable of winning his way in any physical combat that occurred in the school. To compensate for the rejection of his family and his inability to attain the scholastic achievement of other members of his class, he was constantly making fun of the youngsters who were more studious than himself. He belittled all types of academic and social achievement. He took pride in the fact that he did not wear a necktie or a white shirt or a coat. He took great joy in hitting and shoving other youngsters who were superior in academic achievement and who did not accept him socially. Refusing the role of an inferior, he began a struggle to achieve a different type of social order in which his particular talents and abilities could function. Since his school and his teacher were inflexible, dropping out of school as soon as he reached the legal age to obtain working papers was the only course open through which he saw an opportunity to maintain his self-respect. His teacher and the school lost the opportunity to contribute to his development as a citizen as soon as he was sixteen.

How much of adult insecurity and mental disturbance is due to a method of measuring achievement under which only a few can feel successful?

Achievement under the broader concept of leadership is an individual affair. To achieve a pupil does not have to excel others. He is concerned with making better contributions than he has made in the past. The teacher's task is to take the steps that will enable him to determine and evaluate his contribution. He does this by:

1. *Helping each pupil and the group as a whole to determine the progress they are making.* Procedures for helping pupils to collect evidence of progress will be discussed fully in the section on evaluation. At this point it is noted that it is the teacher's function to help each pupil determine his present status, the kind of growth he seeks, and ways of collecting evidence of growth to be used as a basis of judgment concerning the amount and quality of achievement. Evidence of growth is proof of achievement.
2. *Giving encouragement at times of failure.* All persons fail at times. Despite their best efforts they do not always measure up to the goals that they set for themselves. A teacher can perform a valuable service to youngsters if he lets them know by a word of encouragement that he recognizes that the going is tough and that the achievement has not been as great as they had hoped.
3. *Making possible many kinds of achievement and recognition.* By encouraging the class to recognize various kinds of contribution, a teacher can assure that the efforts of each pupil will be noticed and valued.
4. *Praising youngsters for their accomplishment.* No one receives enough praise. Frequently he is criticized for the things that he does not do, with little recognition of his contributions. The teacher can help youngsters to gain a sense of achievement by praising them for the things that they have done well.

5. *Varying standards for different individuals.* Children's inclinations and abilities vary greatly. A single set of achievement standards will not serve for all members of a class. Some students will never experience a sense of achievement simply because they will be able to achieve the standards with almost no effort. Others, no matter how hard they try, will never be able to measure up to them. When a youngster has no hope of attaining the standards of achievement that have been established for the group, he begins to despair and to lose interest in his work.

A sense of achievement and a feeling of personal worth are closely intertwined. If it is hoped that all pupils will develop self-respect, a teacher works for the kind of class organization where many different contributions are used and acknowledged, where each pupil maintains a record of his own progress, and where judgments are made by pupils, parents, and teacher in terms of standards appropriate to the status and ability of the individual student. If marks, which are only a way of reporting to parents, jeopardize the possibility that all can feel worthy, new ways of sharing with pupils and parents the evaluation of pupil work should be developed. The chapters on self-direction will suggest techniques for helping pupils and parents determine pupil achievement.

Decreasing Pupil Fears

Fear eats away a person's sense of personal worth. It decreases his self-confidence and his trust in others. It forces him into a defensive position and makes constructive forward steps difficult. If the fear is great enough, it brings regression.

The present world is one in which many adults are afraid—afraid of death, ghosts, atomic bombs, hunger, snakes, high places. The list is endless. How much more children face! They encounter these fears in adults and are affected by them. In addition, they face the special fears associated with their period of development—fear about physical changes occurring in themselves, fear of not being normal, fear of being left out, fear of failure.

> An anecdote reported in the *Reader's Digest* tells of a girl who was sitting on a high school stage in Washington, D.C., about to give a valedictory address. She was shaking, very much embarrassed and

afraid. The man sitting next to her noticed her fright and leaned over and whispered, "I'm scared too." He was the principal speaker of the evening, Franklin D. Roosevelt.

He put the girl at ease by letting her know that he was tense too, but that both of them could go ahead and face the situation that confronted them.

A teacher can help pupils by letting them know that he too has concerns, that he understands how they feel, that he is willing to talk over their disturbances with them. Children are less fearful when they know they can turn to grown-ups for help. Of course, they don't want help unless they ask for it, but they like to have the assurance that help is there when they need it.

The instructor helps, moreover, by assisting the pupils to concentrate on solving the problems of the immediate present rather than anticipating the dreadful things that may occur. As he enables them to meet current difficulties successfully, they form the strength, courage, and skill to face new problems as they arise. In some cases preparation for future possibilities, such as fires or atomic explosions, must be undertaken in schools. But even these grim exercises can be used to build up security and assurance if they are conducted coolly and without expressions of fear.

Protection of youngsters from physical violence is essential to decreasing fear. When smaller pupils are beaten by large ones or threatened with bodily harm by a pupil gang, a school staff member is forced to take action. He may bring the situation to the group for decision if it is within the class. Or the student government may be the agency to which the problem is referred if the pupils involved are from different groups. As he works with pupils in reaching a solution, his function is to increase the concern of all for their fellows and to encourage older youngsters to assume responsibility for smaller ones. But in the process a teacher does what he must to protect the weak from aggression.

Unless a teacher is sensitive, his own behavior may increase pupil fearfulness and insecurity. Does he utilize their fears as an easy means of motivation? Does he threaten them with failure or with punishment? Such phrases as, "I don't want to mention any names, but some of you will repeat this grade next year unless you show improvement," are destructive threats to the peace of mind of a large proportion of the class. Constant scrutiny of the way assignments are made, counsel is given, or disorder discussed is essential if threats and fear-inciting words are to be eliminated.

Being willing to listen and share their concerns, helping solve immediate problems, facing realistically and unemotionally the necessity for preparing for crises, protecting from physical violence, and avoiding the use of fear as motivation—these are all steps the teacher can take to decrease pupil fears.

Decreasing Feelings of Guilt

A person with guilt feelings is unable to believe in his own worth and thus is less secure in his relations with others. If a teacher takes action that increases a child's sense of guilt, he hinders the development of good human relations in the class.

Guilt is appropriate only when the person who performs an act is aware of the other ways in which he might have behaved. Youngsters are often unaware of these other possibilities and react in the only way they know to a given situation. Some teachers, who do know of alternate ways of behavior, are horrified and seek to instill in the children a feeling of guilt so that they will not behave in such a manner again. Such action is detrimental to the child's mental health. Making a youngster feel ashamed is appropriate only when he has had an opportunity to consider possible ways of behaving in the situation, has decided that some ways are more satisfactory than others, and yet has acted contrary to his decisions.

Throughout the consideration of behavior that a teacher thinks is unsatisfactory, he can be constructive if he stresses the desirability of examining several courses of action and deciding which is the most intelligent choice. If he helps pupils to see several possible procedures and allows the choice to remain theirs, he provides the opportunity for them to change their behavior and still maintain their self-respect.

PUPIL ACCEPTANCE OF SELF AND OTHERS 69

Guilt feelings are decreased as a teacher emphasizes pupils' socially acceptable behavior. He makes a positive contribution to their well-being as he helps them see within themselves the qualities that respected people have. When the emphasis is placed on the qualities they have that are different and unacceptable, they begin to lose hope that they can become like the respected members of the community and begin to adopt other ways of behaving to get attention. It should be noted that the persons respected vary from community to community and from age-group to age-group. A part of a teacher's task is finding the kinds of persons all can agree are respected.

If a teacher is shocked by pupils' activities, language, or dress, he avoids letting them know it.

> A psychologist and a teacher were walking through an Alabama school. As they passed, a seven-year-old youngster held out a picture that he had drawn, a picture that he considered obscene. The psychologist took it, looked at it, made a passing comment, and handed it back to the youngster. He had not displayed any disgust, any horror, or any indication that the picture was out of the ordinary. He had not added to the youngster's guilt-feelings, nor had he given him the satisfaction of knowing that he had been successful in shocking adults.

A pupil's behavior is objective evidence that a teacher uses in deciding how to proceed. The teacher's job is not to judge or to punish, but to study each child and to work with him in such a way that he can grow in self-respect and wisdom. When in doubt about how to proceed in a situation, the question to ask is: "What course of action will give me the best opportunity to work with this child again?" If a teacher's behavior causes pupils to lose faith in him, to resent him, to fear him, or to feel rejected by him, that teacher has little chance of helping in the future. When someone wants help or counsel, he goes to a person who accepts him and who has faith in his potentialities. Pupils are people!

A teacher increases guilt feelings if he sets standards so high that few children attain them. Boys and girls who want to do what is right and socially desirable find themselves unable to do so through no fault of their own. If a teacher wants to make it possible for all children to feel worthy, he formulates with them standards suitable to their ability and purposes.

The positive teacher can stress pride in one's family, nationality, and cultural group. When he finds that some members of his class feel less worthy because they belong to a minority group of the particular community in which they live, he can take the lead in demonstrating respect for the group and gratitude for the contribution it has made. He can let students know that he opposes name-calling and labeling of groups and recommend that they include a prohibition of such action in their code of behavior.

Decreasing Insecurity Created by Financial Status

To the extent that the school emphasizes economic differences among pupils, it increases the insecurity of children whose families do not have economic stability. Studies have shown, in high schools particularly, that many hidden costs tend to cause youngsters from lower economic levels to drop out of school sooner than others. Even those who remain find themselves handicapped unless teachers exercise leadership in reducing the number of situations in which inadequate finances cause a pupil to feel different or embarrassed.

A school staff can provide economic assistance without advertising it. When free lunches or free glasses, or other types of aid are provided, students who receive such aid should not be made known to the other students. Lack of ability to pay is no fault of the youngster, and he should not be penalized by his peers because he does not have the financial backing to purchase all the equipment that is needed in the school. In one school in Ohio, free lunch cards were supplied to youngsters who could not afford to pay for their lunches. But the free lunch cards were yellow, while those that were paid for were green. Each time they went through the lunch line, the youngsters who could not afford lunch were forced to advertise the fact that they were different, that they were recipients of charity. The emphasis was on pointing out the differences rather than on decreasing them. It is not surprising that a large number of the pupils unable to afford lunch cards chose to stay in the study hall without lunch rather than carry the yellow card through the cafeteria line. Other schools have handled this problem by giving free lunch cards that are exactly like the lunch cards that are purchased.

Teachers can encourage youngsters to dress sensibly and inexpensively. When the youngsters in a class dress in a manner that all can afford, those who come from homes in which money is not plentiful have an opportunity to be working members of the group without feeling the insecurity that comes from having clothing that is not like that of other boys and girls.

Any teacher can eliminate special Christmas gifts for the teacher. If he teaches in a school in which giving presents is the custom, he can insist on being a member of the group and having his name drawn by lot with the same price limit on his present as on the others.

A teacher can work for decreasing extra fees. Requiring extra money for papers, laboratory fees, and activity fees emphasizes economic differences.

He can assure pupils that economic handicaps can be overcome. By bringing to the class stories and illustrations of youngsters who have succeeded, he increases the belief of each class member that he can achieve success in our American society with or without financial backing. This type of assurance is important for the mental health of some boys and girls.

Any teacher can work with students in such a way that those with superior socio-economic status do not dominate the group. By encouraging all members of the group, no matter what their background is, to use and develop their leadership talents, he builds up acceptance of a way of life in which leadership is the reward of ability rather than the prerogative of status. The children will gradually learn that true leadership depends on an individual's contribution to the group, not on his official or social position.

Ultimately, the individual accepts or does not accept himself. The teacher can only do the things which create an environment in which it is possible for more individuals to accept themselves.

The Teacher's Role in Helping Pupils to Accept Others

A person's acceptance of self is determined in large part by the extent to which he is accepted by others. He increases his belief in himself as he sees that others value him.

Many times it is difficult to get persons to accept each other. If the youngsters come from a community that has sharp cleavages between nationalities, races, and religions, community attitudes of intolerance and distrust are brought into the classroom and affect relations among members of the class.

Some teachers have tried to promote acceptance by having the class study the cultural and national backgrounds of various groups within the class. They have assumed that knowledge and acceptance are synonymous! Often, however, this procedure has resulted in an overdevelopment of national pride and a heightened antagonism, rather than in a greater understanding among the groups, as the teacher had intended.

Acceptance is more than gaining knowledge about someone. It develops through recognizing common goals and sharing attempts to reach them.

A teacher can't tell students what to think of one another. If he tries they may decide to act in just the opposite way.

> A new pupil entered a New York City junior high school from a private school in Chicago. On his way home from school the first day, he was attacked by the boys in class because he had come from Chicago. On the second day, he was beaten by the same group because he had come from a private school. They did not feel that he was a typical American boy and wanted to prove to him that he would have to earn his spurs before he would be accepted in this particular neighborhood of New York City. A few days later, the class began to discuss how wool was produced. The new boy, having been in the midwest where sheep were raised, knew much about the subject. In the class discussion, when he had the opportunity, he described the shearing process. After he had finished, the teacher called him to the front of the room in an obvious attempt to help him gain acceptance in the group. She put her arm around his shoulders and commended him highly for having contributed so much to the class from his study and experience. On the way home that afternoon the boy was once again slugged by his fellow classmates because of the teacher's demonstration of approval.

By such an obvious attempt to direct the attitudes of the class, the teacher succeeded only in increasing the new boy's isolation.

However, by proceeding carefully and sensitively, a teacher can often arouse the concern of the class for a child who is having difficulty in finding his place in the group.

> A new youngster from out-of-state joined a first-grade class in a Florida elementary school. It was a large school, over a thousand children, and the boy was insecure in the new situation. He found a type of teaching that was strange to him. He was permitted less freedom and was expected to remain more quiet than had been customary in the kindergarten that he had attended. He rebelled. He began to play hookey. He was absent three days in a row. Finally, the teacher decided that she would try to improve the situation for this one boy. *She approached the problem by inviting the class to help work out the solution.* While the new boy was still absent, she asked the other children to think about what they could do to help him feel at home in the class. They responded to her appeal. In their attempts to help, they succeeded in developing better human relations among all members of the group. The new boy was made to feel welcome and accepted, and at the same time the children's new awareness of the feelings of other people led to a classroom situation that was more satisfying for them all.

Strong emphasis during the early stages of class activity on the effective functioning of the group will help students to become concerned about the welfare of others.

One way of helping pupils understand how the other person feels is to have them play out the incidents of conflict within their group.

> Two third-grade boys started an argument over a cowboy lasso. Soon other youngsters gathered around and began to encourage each of the protagonists to stand up for his rights. Both boys, beginning to feel that their honor and the honor of those yelling for them were at stake, crowded closer together until one accidentally touched the other. The fight was on.
> The teacher came around the corner of the building, saw the struggle, walked over, took each boy by the shoulder, and asked them to tell her what was happening. Through their tears, for both had become angry and hurt, each told his story. Other pupils added bits of information. The teacher asked the boys if they would try an experiment. When they agreed, perhaps as a way of avoiding punishment, the class was requested to sit down in a circle and then the teacher asked the fighters to go back to the beginning of the disagreement. She had them trace the development of the argument up to the point when the first blow had been struck. She had each boy tell how he

> felt at each stage of the argument and also asked the bystanders to describe their feelings.
> Then the teacher asked each boy to play the role of his opponent while they went through the scene again. Once more the boys were asked to tell how they felt, but this time each was finding out how his opponent had felt. The entire group joined in the discussion and sought to suggest how a fight could have been avoided in a way that would have satisfied both disputants.

The technique described is a simple form of a psycho-drama. The participants in the real-life situation act out their roles in the play situation and interpret their feelings. After each has played his own part, the roles are reversed and each person plays the part of his opponent.

The role-playing can be carried a step further by having two other pupils play the same roles. Each pupil is asked to explain his feelings and his emotional reactions as the situation develops. Seeing the dispute acted out in this way, the original participants become aware of factors in the situation that they had not recognized before. They gain a greater understanding of how the other person felt. They have a chance to see themselves as others see them. When all the members of the group have shared in one another's emotional reactions, they are ready to suggest more effective ways of dealing with similar problems. Then these suggestions of better ways of behaving can be acted out, and the whole class will have had an opportunity to become involved in meeting a human relations problem.

> At the high-school level a social studies class, studying labor management relations, staged the following socio-drama.
> The son of a manufacturer was cast in the role of a labor leader and the son of a union member played the role of an industrial leader in a negotiation situation. Both pupils, as well as the rest of the class, gained insight through their roles into the values and techniques of groups toward which they might not formerly have been sympathetic.

Understanding is increased through opportunities to experience as fully as possible the reactions of others in given social situations. The alert teacher seeks constantly to devise ways of helping his students to feel and to respond to social situations in roles other than those to which they are accustomed. He gives students an opportunity to put themselves in the place of the persons with whom they usually disagree, and social sensitivity is increased through a widening of experience.

From these first steps in becoming concerned about others, members of the class can gradually move on to a real understanding of one another. They will develop this understanding through sharing experiences, through bringing hobbies and personal projects to class, through taking part in social activities, and through talking out together individual and group problems. As they share their interests, they will begin to accept and to want to help one another. *When people share, they care,* not only about the outcome of a particular project but also about the people who have been involved in making the project successful.

There are many cues which indicate the type of pupil-to-pupil relationships that exist in the class. One of them is the kind of remark pupils make about the total group.

> In one school, in which the pupils were grouped homogeneously on the basis of their I.Q. scores, a class that was at the bottom of the list was making very little progress in school and displayed a lackadaisical attitude toward school work. When their teacher attempted to help, through an evaluation session in which the class was asked how their effectiveness as a group could be improved, one of the pupils remarked, "We are the dumb-bells of the school. None of us ever do anything worth while and we are waiting until we are old enough to quit school."

Even though this school attempted to fool boys and girls by revising the names given to the low and high sections each year, the students were not misled. They knew their classmates, and they knew the students who were in other sections. They sensed the frustration their classmates felt, and they had been able to detect the attitude that teachers held toward them. As a defense measure, they had adopted the attitude that not much could be expected of them. As the conversation continued, the student added, "We don't have a chance. Not one of us has ever won anything." The class had lost its pride and its sense of ability to achieve. They felt that the cards were stacked against them and that no one from their group could exert real leadership in the school. When any group of people has been taught to feel about itself as this class did, two things have been destroyed: self-respect, which is the basis of good mental hygiene, and initiative, which makes possible continued growth.

> One teacher, working with a similar group, put her major emphasis during the first few months that the group was together on building confidence in the group. When the school undertook a paper drive, the teacher put more time and effort into helping the class win the drive than she did in teaching basic skills. She was more concerned that this group of boys and girls should feel the confidence that came from winning recognition from the total school than she was about moving ahead on scheduled class work. She knew that until this group came to respect itself most of her efforts in teaching skills and facts would be futile. And they won.
>
> After the group had regained some of its self-confidence through this achievement, she was ready to move on to other activities in which the group had constantly failed. An interesting side light on this particular class was that most of the members came from homes of the lower economic level. In previous contests held in the school, such as raising money for the Red Cross or selling student activity tickets, they had never been able to compete successfully because their parents had not been able to contribute as much as those from a more favored economic status.

When schools allow their competition between class groups to give the privileged economic groups an advantage, they tend further to decrease the self-respect of youngsters who are already faced with many difficulties.

On the other hand, some groups never question their status or their rights. Such comments as "We always win," "We have the best students in the school in our class," "We have so much we will give our old toys to the poor boys and girls," all indicate feelings of superiority. These groups need to work on the concept of sharing on an equal basis rather than of giving out of their riches to those who are of inferior status.

Another indication of the way class members feel about themselves is their attitude toward the classroom itself. When students take pride in the appearance of their room and continually want to improve it, teachers have an indication of high morale in the group. When they begin to think about decorating their room for special holidays or their own enjoyment and begin to analyze the special contributions each can make, a sense of groupness is developing. When they bring their friends and parents to see the classroom and the activities that take place there, evidence is mounting that the relationships in the room are moving in the right direction. When they want to come back after school and work on projects or plans, the atmosphere is good.

The social relationships of a class group are shown by whether or not the students want to be together. Does the class want to have class parties, or do certain members hold back and say that they are too busy? Persons make choices in terms of the things they value most. When a percentage of the class group indicates that they value other relationships more than associating with members of the group, they are making clear that the human relationships within the classroom have not moved to a high plane.

By observing the class members at dances and football games, it is possible to tell whether or not they have developed enough liking for each other to enjoy being together.

Another index is the kind of remark that pupils make about each other. When one pupil makes a remark that belittles another member of the group, he is belittling the entire group. He is saying that the class has not become a group as far as he is concerned. It doesn't include the person he is belittling. On the other hand, when members begin to show concern in off-the-record conversation about the ways they can help other class members to grow, class relations are moving in the right direction. When one student says, "Don talks too much and is too dogmatic in what he says—what can we do to help him?" it is evidence of growing concern for each other. If three months later ten children out of the thirty are raising questions about how they can help others, group feeling within the class is growing.

One of the technical devices for finding out how students feel toward each other is the sociogram, in which students are asked to indicate the persons with whom they would like to work. Although it is an effective device for revealing grouping and isolation within a class, it has certain disadvantages. Care is necessary to insure that its use does not start boys and girls thinking about people they like and dislike, thus increasing differences rather than developing common concerns. It can be an instrument for building exclusiveness rather than cooperation.

Why use a sociogram at all, then? Isn't it better simply to be with the students and observe them closely? Hasn't the sociogram technique been validated by comparing its results with the results obtained through the insight of teachers who study children in other ways? What if the evidence from the sociogram contradicts the evidence from observation? Which is more valid?

The sociogram is a short-cut technique to help a teacher collect data about a group when time for individual child study is limited. It helps a teacher identify quickly the pupils who need the most help in improving their human-relations skills. But the evidence it provides is not superior to other evidence that a teacher collects through continued association with the children. After rapport has been established in a group, the use of the sociogram may be planned with pupils as one way of collecting additional data to be used in planning how to work together.

As a quality teacher works with a group, he strives to assist the children to discover things they enjoy doing together and to diminish the procedures that separate and cause dissension. He seeks to live with them in a manner that encourages them to accept each other, to develop concern for each other, and to have pride in the achievements of all members of the group. He wants them to know each other's strengths and weaknesses and to assume responsibility for helping each other to grow.

If the teacher wants pupils to help each other, he provides many opportunities for them to work, play, and think together. He uses class committees. He suggests that pupils undertake projects together. He recommends that less skilled pupils ask the more skilled to help them.

> In a Michigan high school an English worshop has been established. Student volunteers from the study hall come to the workshop and serve as coaches and counselors for other students desiring help with their English work. Students are encouraged to help each other—not penalized or punished for doing so.

This practice can be utilized in any classroom. The more advanced pupils can be of service to the other students if the teacher encourages them to help. And the roles will change constantly. One student will be superior in one area while another will lead in a different phase of the work.

A teacher also promotes in pupils a sense of responsibility for each other by encouraging children to share. When he invites them to share trips, books, the movies, television shows, problems, joys, successes, and sorrows, they increase their concern for each other. Time spent in "show and tell" or other types of sharing periods serves a real purpose in developing pupil interest in each other as well as opening up areas for more intensive study.

Using class time for the sharing of problems when they desire it is a way of increasing pupils' willingness to help each other. At first, pupils may hesitate to bring their concerns to the group—particularly if they are older boys and girls. The teacher makes it easier for them to seek the help of the group if he lets them know that he doesn't have all the answers either, that he is still seeking for answers to problems in his own life, some that recur and some that are new. When pupils understand that an adult is still facing and attempting to solve problems, they are freer to share their concerns.

When a teacher opens the class period for pupils to use in seeking solutions to their problems and does the things that free them from fear of ridicule, he is taking positive steps to create the type of situation in which the group members begin to seek help from each other.

He further stimulates pupils to help each other if, during the evaluation conferences he holds with individual students, he asks such questions as:

Which students have been most helpful to you? Why?
Which materials have you brought for others to use?
Which students have you helped?
What have you done to help the class?
What additional things could you have done to help others?

Pupil Acceptance of the Teacher

A group of California teachers concerned with good human relations in the classroom stated that they wanted their pupils to believe they were:

1. *Friendly.* We want our students to believe that we want to be friends with each member of the class, that we are approachable,

and that we accept each one as a person of importance and worth.
2. *Trustworthy.* We want our students to believe that we can be trusted, that we can be depended upon to live up to our word, that we will not take advantage of persons less able than ourselves, and that we will play fair with all students at all times.
3. *Helpful.* We want our students to believe that we are with them to help them, that we are resource persons to whom they can turn for assistance in solving their problems, that we believe our job is to work with them and provide guidance as needed or requested, and that we respect their purposes and problems.
4. *Wise and skilled.* We want our students to believe that even though we make mistakes we know our subject matter fields, that we keep informed of developments in our specialization and in world events, that we are versatile and can apply our knowledge and skills to many problems, and that we are still learning with them.
5. *Consistent.* We want our students to believe that we have a set of values that we live by, that we are predictable, that we will exercise the same type of self-control from day to day, and that we will work honestly with the group.

But all boys and girls do not regard all teachers in this light. Children bring to the classroom the stereotypes of teachers which are a part of their social environment. In the past, teachers have been looked upon as outside the typical community pattern. Parents have said that the teacher was supposed to set an example and that actions in which he engaged should be judged by an even higher standard than the action of parents. In some homes the teacher has been looked down upon as a person slightly inferior or, if the teacher was considered to be a person who knew more, certainly an impractical person who went into a less remunerative type of activity. Children acquire the attitudes of their parents and of the community toward teachers.

After the first few months in school, pupils develop attitudes toward teachers that grow out of their experiences with them. By the time a child gets to third, fourth, or fifth grade, he has had many experiences that condition the point of view he takes toward any new teacher whom he meets. Either he is willing to accept that teacher and to give him a fair break or he schemes to put the teacher in an unfortunate, undesirable position. Some pupils believe that teachers are persons who cannot be trusted. Their experiences with teachers have led them to the conclusion that you can't tell teachers anything and have your confidences kept. Other students look upon teachers as persons who punish. They have had sufficient experience with authoritarian teachers to conclude that all teachers are dictators, people who force boys and girls to behave in a set way without any consideration of their feelings, interests, and purposes.

Still other boys and girls come to the classroom with a watchful attitude toward teachers. Their experiences have led them to believe that some teachers are good and that some are bad, and that one tries to determine first of all the type of person the new teacher is. In some classrooms, boys and girls have developed signals by which they communicate to each other their idea of the teacher. During the first few weeks with any teacher, they test him to see if he is fair, if he is understanding, if he can be trusted, if he will keep his word and respect confidences.

The experiences of some students have led them to look upon school as a game. They see the teacher and themselves as opposing teams, each trying to put over on the other as much as they can. They see school work as an activity that teachers try to manipulate them into doing. They conceive of themselves as successful when they are able to outwit the teacher and do the things they wish rather than the things they think the teacher wishes.

Other youngsters come to school with the conviction that the teacher is a helpful person, concerned with helping boys and girls to grow into more useful citizens. The child whose father or mother is a teacher will have a favorable attitude toward the teachers he meets at school, if his home relationships are satisfactory. And pupils who have found their former teachers lovable and helpful will be favorably inclined to a new teacher, at least until he proves himself an unsatisfactory person.

A teacher may expect all these attitudes, and others, in his classes. He may expect to be on trial for the first few weeks with any class. Distrust, antagonism, or hate can be overcome in time if his behavior is satisfactory to pupils. But, by the same token, love and respect for teachers can be dispelled if he is the kind of person who deserves hatred and recrimination. He has an opportunity with each class to build in pupils either a favorable or an unfavorable attitude toward him.

When the group comes together for the first time, he has an opportunity to take positive steps in helping it get organized. In the process, he may or may not win a place in it for himself. If he is joining a class that has worked together before, he moves into a society and a culture that have already been created. He is a new force in the situation, but he can become effective only as he is accepted by the group. As long as he is outside the group, the attitudes, values, and points of view that will really matter will continue to be those of the members themselves. He may be able to force the group by physical power or by other clubs to accede to his wishes, but mere submission will not be effective in improving human relations within the group or the efficiency of the learning situation. If he hopes to be accepted as friendly, trustworthy, helpful, wise, skilled, and consistent, his actions must show that he is worthy of such an evaluation.

The Process and the Product

The human relations in a class are not static. They change with the experiences the children have together. The quality of human relations either improves or deteriorates, and the teacher's responsibility is to demonstrate constantly that he values a way of living together in which each person is accepted, respected, and encouraged to achieve. If he wants boys and girls to feel free to dare to try new things, he develops a situation in which students feel they are among friends, and he strives to be more secure within himself. He tries to become a person to whom pupils will turn for help—a person who does not become jittery in the face of difficult circumstances, a person who does not release his frustration, spites, and emotional difficulties by aggression against pupils; he assists pupils to know and understand one another and become more concerned about helping one another; he creates a situation in which pupils can focus their major attention and effort on self-improvement rather than on how to become accepted by their peers.

In a class with excellent human relations, each pupil feels that he belongs, that the other members of the group want him, that they are trying to help him rather than to hurt or make fun of him. It does not mean that he is never criticized or told that he is wrong, or even occasionally punished by the group. It means that he feels free to come to the group at any time without being afraid of crowding in or being in the way. He also feels that it is safe for him to leave the group when he wants to go. He may be talked about after he is gone, but he knows that the other members will not try to hurt him or deprive him of his rights. He feels "free to come and safe to go."

SELF-EVALUATION CHECKLIST
Improving Human Relations

Do I:

1. Seek to eliminate personal feelings of inferiority, superiority, or aggressions?
2. Learn the name, background, likes, dislikes, interests, and purposes of each pupil?
3. Try to understand why each pupil feels as he does?
4. Try to examine pupil behavior objectively?
5. Listen to a student's stories about himself which he considers important for me to know?
6. Look for the good qualities in each pupil?
7. Stress the socially acceptable phases of each child's behavior?
8. Have faith in the potential of each pupil?
9. Recognize that all persons have weaknesses? Accept each as he is?
10. Encourage each member of the group to contribute his special skills, and work to help him overcome his weaknesses?

11. Believe that all pupils can exert some type of leadership?
12. Display as much courtesy to pupils as I expect them to display to me?
13. Call each student by the name he prefers?
14. Follow any established code of behavior as closely as students are expected to do?
15. Seek to be accepted by the pupils?
16. Respond to pupil ideas?
17. Take pupil questions seriously?
18. Display friendliness and encourage friendliness?
19. Strive to help each pupil gain a sense of achievement?
20. Vary standards to individual abilities?
21. Give encouragement when a pupil experiences failure?
22. Give praise for accoplisment?
23. Attempt to help a pupil solve his present problems instead of worrying about his future?
24. Let each pupil know I am willing to talk through his personal problems?
25. Let children know they were missed when they have been absent?
26. Observe pupil behavior in non-class situations to get clues concerning the quality of human relations in the group?
27. Attempt to help each child feel he belongs, is accepted, is achieving, and is responsible to the group?
28. Have the class make judgments about their satisfaction with existing human relations in the group?
29. State values and purposes held in common in the group?
30. Give pupils an opportunity to choose their seating arrangements as long as they behave in an acceptable manner?
31. Protect younger children from physical violence of older pupils?
32. Eliminate fear, as far as possible, as a motivating technique?
33. Welcome new children to the group?
34. Secure necessary economic assistance for needy pupils without letting other pupils know?
35. Seek to develop in pupils a concern for the feelings and welfare of others?
36. Encourage pupils to put themselves in the place of persons with whom they disagree?
37. Oppose name-calling and labeling of minority groups?

38. Take the lead in recognizing contributions of minority groups in class and nation?
39. Use socio-dramas to help pupils gain greater understanding of the feelings of others?
40. Ask the individual during evaluation sessions how he has helped others grow?
41. Expect some students, as a result of their past experiences, to dislike and distrust teachers?
42. Allow pupils to express their feelings?
43. Avoid ridicule, sarcasm, and other actions that embarrass students?
44. Refuse to allow my feelings to be hurt?
45. Fight against any desires to get even with a child?
46. Lose an issue if it will help an individual or a class?
47. Avoid sending pupils from the room?
48. Take a course of action in a problem situation that makes possible working with the child in the future?
49. Encourage the faculty to become concerned about improving human relations in the community?
50. Give pupils the opportunity to apply the generalizations they have drawn about human relations to the organization and operation of the community?

BIBLIOGRAPHY

Improving Human Relations

Albrecht, M., and L. Gross, "Nondirective Teaching," *Sociology and Sociological Research*, 32 (June, 1948), pp. 874–81.

Allen, Frederick H., *Psychotherapy with Children*. New York: W. W. Norton Company, 1942.

American Council on Education, *Helping Teachers Understand Children*. Washington, D.C.: The Council, 1945.

Arnold, D. L., "Quality of Our Living Together," *Ohio Schools*, 33 (September, 1955), pp. 8–9.

Association for Supervision and Curriculum Development, *Fostering Mental Health in Our Schools*. Washington, D.C.: N.E.A., 1950.

⸺, *Toward Better Teaching*, Washington, D.C.: N.E.A., 1949.

Axline, Virginia Mae, *Play Therapy: The Inner Dynamics of Childhood*. Boston: Houghton Mifflin Company, 1947.

Baxter, Bernice, *Teacher-Pupil Relationships*. New York: The Macmillan Company, 1941.

Berger, Donald W., "Handling Human Relations in Cooperative Learning," *Progressive Education*, 26 (April, 1949), pp. 180–83.

Bernstein, J., "I'll Be Forever Grateful," *National Education Association Journal*, 44 (January, 1955), p. 27.

Bradley, Phillips, "Labor-Management Relations in the Classroom," *The Education Digest*, 16 (January, 1951), pp. 45–47.

Campbell, C. M., "Human Relations Techniques Useful in School Administration," *American School Board Journal*, 130 (June, 1955), pp. 31–32.

Collings, Miller R., "Let My Children Go," *Clearing House*, 25 (October, 1950), pp. 103–06.

Dale, E., "In the Other Fellows' Shoes," *School and Community*, 43 (April, 1957), pp. 32–33.

Dean, Berta, "Of Such Is the Kingdom," *N.E.A. Journal*, 37 (January, 1948), pp. 22–23.

Dent, C. H., "Do You Have Permissiveness in Your Room?" *Instructor*, 67 (November, 1957), p. 6ff.

DuBois, Rachael Davis, "A Tension Area Becomes a Neighborhood," *N.E.A. Journal*, 38 (February, 1949), pp. 114–15.

Dunbar, Helen Flanders, *Mind and Body, Psychosomatic Medicine*. New York: Random House, 1947.

Eiserer, Paul E., "Children's Perceptions of School and Teachers," *Educational Leadership*, 11 (April, 1954), pp. 409–12.

————, "The Implications of Nondirective Counseling for Classroom Teaching," in *Growing Points in Educational Research*, 1949 Official Report. Washington, D.C.: American Educational Research Association, 1949.

Farnsworth, O. L., "Emotions and Learning," *Harvard Educational Review*, 25, No. 2 (1955), pp. 95–104.

Fenton, Norman, *Mental Hygiene in School Practice*. Palo Alto, California: Stanford University Press, 1943.

Franklin, R., "Effective Workshops in Human Relations," *Journal of Educational Sociology*, 28 (May, 1955), pp. 381–88.

Gardiol, Yvonne A., "An Adventure in International Relations," *N.E.A. Journal*, 38 (September, 1949), p. 425.

Hanszen, M. W., and W. G. Hollister, "Teaching Human Relations Through Spontaneous Pupil Play Writing and Play Acting," *Understanding the Child*, 25 (October, 1956), pp. 103–10.

Kay, Lillian W., "Role Playing As a Teaching Aid," *Sociometry*, 9 (May–August, 1946), pp. 263–74.

Keliher, A. V., "You Are a Good Teacher If . . . You Believe in Boys and Girls," *Grade Teacher*, (October, 1954), p. 105.

Kissell, Lucy, and Mayne A. Sweet, "Second Graders Find Security and Acceptance," *Educational Leadership*, 8 (December, 1950), pp. 138–43.

Kurtz, J. J., "Enabling Children to Achieve," *Educational Leadership*, 14 (December, 1956), pp. 147–51.

Lane, Howard, and Mary Beauchamp, *Human Relations in Teaching*. Englewood Cliffs, N.J.: Prentice-Hall, Inc., 1955.

Martin, M. F., "Teach Without Tension," *Parents Magazine*, 22 (September, 1947), p. 17.

Raths, Louis E., *An Application of the Needs Theory to Education*. Bronxville, New York: Louis E. Raths, 1949.

Rogers, Carl R., *Client-Centered Therapy*. Boston: Houghton Mifflin Company, 1951.

Russell, David H., "Reading Disabilities and Mental Health: A Review of Research," *Understanding the Child*, 26 (January, 1947), pp. 24–32.

Sskwor, H. M., "Human Relations Education in St. Louis," *Educational Leadership*, 13 (November, 1955), pp. 102–05.

Stanfield, E., "Yellow Blouse," *National Education Association Journal*, 42 (October, 1953), p. 417.

Taba, Hilda, et al., *Diagnosing Human-Relations Needs*. Washington, D.C.: American Council on Education, 1951.

Wood, Helen C., "Children Who Move with the Crops," *National Education Association Journal*, 47 (March, 1958), pp. 170–73.

Wright, E. G., "Human Relations Discussions in the Classroom," *Progressive Education*, 33 (November, 1956), pp. 171–73.

• • • Promoting Group Development

Out of an increased understanding of human development and the learning process has come a greater recognition of the importance of the nature of the class group. Although it has been demonstrated that group procedures can be used to decrease deviation in thought, it is also true that membership in other types of groups can give the security of being accepted which makes it possible to dare to be different.

The fundamental question is not whether a person will be in a group or not. It is rather what type of group development should be encouraged if the school is to produce individuals who are thoughtful, creative, and self-directing.

When a teacher seeks to develop a group which will release and nurture individual growth, he shares the leadership, the decisions, and the evaluative process.

He invites students to share the planning with him; he seeks to establish common purposes; he develops an organization through which students can participate in the administration of the class; he stimulates the emergence of other leadership; he encourages each member to accept other members and to feel a responsibility for helping them.

UNSATISFACTORY TEACHER

He is not aware of the group as a factor in the learning situation. He sees his relationship with pupils as a person-to-person proposition in which he must control the aggressive and coerce the idolent. He prevents cooperative activities whenever he can and remains as insensitive to group opinion as he can. He stresses the importance of being superior by winning over others. The attainment of personal success is portrayed as the primary goal to be sought. Morale is low in the class. Students do not like to attend and dislike the teacher intensely.

MINIMUM SATISFACTORY TEACHER

He does not oppose the development of group feeling. He finds that teaching is more fun for him when students like to be together. But he believes group activity should be a nonclass enterprise. He supports the formation of intramural teams and the holding of class parties. However, when students begin class work, each must work separately and decisions as to what should be done are the exclusive responsibility and right of the teacher. Of course, he knows that some students help each other with homework, but that can't be avoided. Perhaps some benefit comes from this out-of-class help.

6 · *The Development of a Class Group*

A class may become a group, but a group doesn't exist merely because a school assigns a number of youngsters to work in the same classroom. A group is born; it emerges when a number of individuals form some common goals and some common plans.

The Beginning of a Sense of Unity

One of the functions of a teacher is to help the group develop a sense of unity and a belief that they belong together, that the welfare of each depends on the welfare of the group.

As a class meets for the first time, he will want to take time for students to talk together and get to know each other. Until pupils know the names and personalities of other class members, they have a tendency to be a little bit afraid, to feel a lack of common purposes and interests. But when they can sit down together and discover their common experiences, their sense of belonging together grows. Knowing names is important. If the teacher learns the names of class members quickly, he encourages each student to know the name of every other person. A simple device like knowing one another's names will help immeasurably in leading pupils to feel that they do have things in common and that they are a social group working together.

Social activities in which students get to know each other in out-of-class situations are also helpful. As they have a chance to play and joke and eat together, they begin to understand and to know each other.

A group grows in a sense of unity and belonging as it helps one of its members out of trouble. When the group as a whole accepts the responsibility for helping a pupil who is having difficulty, there emerges from that experience a sense of belonging together and a pride in achievement. Each student comes to feel that if he is in difficulty, he can rely on the group for the assistance he needs.

Undertaking a joint project is another basic way for people to come together. As they plan and work as a group, boys and girls get to know one another and to respect the contribution that each can make. A sense of kinship is developed by common pride in the thing that they have done well together.

The Development of Morale

The morale of a group depends upon the extent to which its ways of living and working together satisfy the basic desires of the members. Boys and girls, like adults, are concerned with having a feeling of belonging, a feeling of security, a feeling of achievement, a belief that they will get fair treatment, a part in deciding what shall be done, a satisfaction of their own wants and comforts, and a chance for advancement.

Class morale is influenced by many things, but mostly by the way in which the teacher operates. By his procedures the teacher can contribute to conditions that will bring about high morale. If boys and girls feel that they will receive fair and just treatment and know that no one will be granted special favors, if they can trust the teacher and know that he will always stand by his word, if the teacher is consistent and can be depended upon to behave in the same way from day to day and to abide by the same values, group morale will be improved.

If the teacher works in such a way that pupils know where they stand and see the progress that they are making, if he helps them know where they began and the achievement they have made, they will be more satisfied with their working environment.

A teacher can contribute much to the morale of the group by looking after the comfort of the pupils. He can see that there is enough light, check on ventilation, keep down distracting noise, arrange furniture properly, choose a pleasing color for room decorating, and generally attempt to make the room a beautiful, satisfying place in which to live. The morale is even higher if he brings pupils into the process of securing more satisfying working conditions.

Pupils contribute to one another's morale by being friendly, by accepting other members of the group, and by showing a willingness to help others to solve their problems. They are contributing to group morale when they share materials and ideas and do not compete with one another for the credit. The teacher can encourage boys and girls to value acceptance, friendship, sharing, willingness to help, willingness to share credit, and all the other qualities that make it possible for everyone to find in the situation the satisfactions that go to make up high morale.

If a teacher gives boys and girls an opportunity to sit down with him and revise unsatisfactory situations, he is creating a procedure through which morale can be strengthened. Factors that destroy good morale are eliminated by this process. He increases students' real belief in the work of the class by bringing them in on decision-making. As boys and girls grow older, they want to move more and more toward independence and self-direction and want to be controlled less and less by the judgment and decisions of the teacher.

The Formation of a Group Structure

The transformation of a roomful of children into a group is a difficult process. Students must decide that group purposes may be more important than their own individual purposes—a decision that never comes easily.

The class seems to bog down for a while and the pupils feel that they are not getting anywhere. They may turn back to the teacher and ask him what he wants them to do. He should recognize this step for what it is, *gear shifting*, one operation in the transfer of control and responsibility from him to the group.

When pupils ask a teacher to tell them what to do, they are using a technique for avoiding the necessity for giving up individual purposes in order to achieve common purposes. As long as he is the person in authority and gives the directions, the individual pupils do not feel the pain of giving up their own purposes—they never expected to have the opportunity to use their purposes in school anyway. But when a teacher is willing to share with pupils the development of group purposes and when they really begin to believe that their purposes can play a part, the strength of the impulse to have their purposes prevail has to be brought against the same strength in others, and in the process people feel the pain of pushing and striving with others for domination. It is hard, at first, for a group to see that greater satisfaction is achieved by agreeing upon common purposes than through each pursuing his individual purposes.

It is a hard transition for the teachers too, but it pays great dividends.

When he shares his authority with pupils and brings them in on planning how to use that authority, he is sharing with them a sense of responsibility. Having a part in making a decision involves them in responsibility for the success of the conclusion reached. Their judgment is at stake, and they exert their best efforts to prove that they were correct. *Shared authority and shared responsibility go hand in hand.* A teacher does not lose power by sharing a decision with the class. He gains it, because pupils will assume with him responsibility for the success of the use of authority that they have made. From this point the full power of the total group is supporting the decision.

In order to avoid confusion, frustration, and disillusionment, the areas of shared authority should be clear in the minds of all. Students should know the regulations within which the teacher operates: regulations established by the legislature, the state department of education, the local board of education, the principal, and the faculty. Items such as attendance, tardiness, courses of study, and the examinations may be a part of the framework created by these regulations. But a teacher misleads youngsters and invites their distrust when he fails to inform them of the limitations that have been set on the authority he shares with them. Or it may be that he will want to reserve certain areas of his authority. He may believe that he should organize content or work out necessary punishment, for instance. If he does, he should make these stipulations clear, along with his reasons for reserving such authority. By being open and straightforward with students, he will avoid the embarrassment of having to veto group decisions or of going back on his proposal to share authority with them.

The amount of authority a teacher shares will depend upon the maturity of the learners. Pupils in the seventh grade can be expected to share in a wider range of decisions than can children in the second grade. But it is unwise to say arbitrarily that certain decisions can be shared with a fifth-grade but not with a fourth-grade pupil. Rather, a teacher should encourage a group to share in decision-making in accordance with its ability to do so. Some sixth-grade groups can deal with problems that some ninth-grade groups cannot.

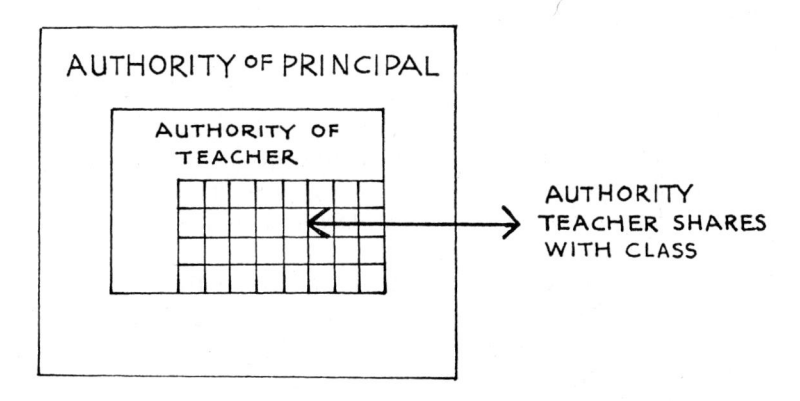

```
┌─────────────────────────────────────┐
│  AUTHORITY OF PRINCIPAL             │
│   ┌─────────────────┐               │        AUTHORITY
│   │ AUTHORITY OF    │               │        TEACHER SHARES
│   │   TEACHER       │  ←────→       │        WITH CLASS
│   │                 │               │
│   └─────────────────┘               │
└─────────────────────────────────────┘
```

At the first-grade level much teacher direction may be necessary. One teacher had the following experience.

> In my class this year I have thirty-seven first-graders with a chronological age range of five and a half to seven and a half. Their readiness range at the first of the year ran from very low to superior.
>
> I have found that "work committees" are one of the best ways to begin group living and group experiences. Each child is given some small duty in the care of the room. Many of the immature children have to work on individual jobs until they progress to the point they would like to have a "friend" to help them. I always let them choose this friend.
>
> The more mature children work in groups of two or three on a job like cleaning tables—if I carefully explain what is to be done, and each person's part of the job. This last point bothered me a great deal because all I had read or heard about group teaching led me to believe that the children should do their own organization work, and I did not seem to be able to get them to do it successfully. I have talked to other teachers and the resource people who were brought in, and now I feel much better about the whole thing, as they too seem to feel that in the beginning it is necessary for the teacher to play a very prominent role, since these young children have to be taught

to organize and share duties in order to bring the project to a successful conclusion.

We change our committees about every two weeks, and each person chooses someone to take his place. In most instances the children have grown and matured enough so that they are now able to work out their own organization without too much help from me.

The superior pupils have progressed to the point where they can carry a group project through to a conclusion. For example, they will set up their tables for painting, paint their pictures with tempera paint, and clean up, putting everything back in place with little supervision.

The quality of teaching is judged by the progress made—not by the status of the class at any given moment.

The teacher's task is to study the group and to extend its range of decision-making as rapidly as possible. *He helps by continually expecting more from pupils than they are able to deliver, rather than by protecting them from making major decisions simply because he believes that they are not yet ready.*

By sharing authority with pupils, he increases their maturity. As pupils gradually assume more and more responsibility, they mature and become increasingly more self-directing.

In the process of moving from teacher domination to shared control, a teacher helps the group to analyze itself and the situation and provides appropriate guidance in formulating and testing various courses of action. Transformation does not occur spontaneously.

As a group organizes to carry out common purposes, there needs to be an opportunity for the members to size one another up to determine one another's capacities and the types of leadership that each person within the group can exert. As students do this, they make several types of growth: they grow in ability to select leaders; they grow in ability to analyze the qualities that provide leadership; they determine who among them will be most effective in doing the things the group needs to have done.

It is wise to suggest to students in the beginning that they keep their organization flexible. Some of the choices they make will be poor, but if their organization is flexible and if officials are not chosen for long periods of time, they will have an opportunity to recover from their mistakes and to make wiser choices.

If the class is organized in such a way that each person can see his place in the total class and know that he is represented on the planning committee that determines how the total group will operate, he will begin to feel that he is a real and important part of that class. And if the various committees are held responsible to the total group rather than to individual pupils or to the teacher, as discussed in the following chapter, there is bound to be an increase in the feeling of unity within the class.

The Planning Committee

A planning committee may be desirable if the class is large. If the group is less than nine, all the members of the group can plan together intelligently. In a large group of twenty or more, a planning committee serves as a short cut to save time for the class. It makes possible the meeting of a small number of people who can exchange ideas easily and quickly to form a plan which they will then submit to the total group.

A good way to form a planning committee is to have each work-group appoint one pupil to work with the teacher and representatives of other groups.

What are the functions of a planning committee? Its primary task is to secure the suggestions that have come from the total group and to prepare a proposed course of action for the submission to the total group. In other words, it does the "spade work" which shapes into a proposed course of action the many ideas that have come out of the total group. *The planning committee does not start with its own ideas; it starts from the basis that has been established from the suggestions of the total group.*

In some classes the planning committee has developed into a steering group that tells the class what to do. This procedure is just as detrimental to developing strength within the total class as teacher domination is. If a steering committee tells the class what to do, the organizational structure gives certain members of the class experience in leadership and a share in the responsibility, but it does not bring the rest of the pupils into these very important positions. All proposals of the planning committee should be submitted to the total class for acceptance or rejection.

The planning committee serves another function. It has a special responsibility for discovering ways in which the group can improve itself. Of course every member of the class has this responsibility. But the members of a planning group have additional responsibility in this area because of the position to which they have been appointed or elected.

Still another function of the planning committee is to make it possible for students who are timid about suggesting ways of improving the class to get their ideas out in the open. When a planning committee is composed of representatives of each small work-group, members of the small work-groups who do not feel secure in presenting ideas to the class can have their ideas come out as group suggestions and not as individual suggestions. In this way their suggestions will receive the consideration of the total group without their status being jeopardized.

The planning committee also may serve as an executive committee to conduct the official operations of the group. Such a plan provides the teacher with an opportunity to share control easily. He no longer has to chair class sessions or appoint someone else to do so. Responsibility for the detailed operations of the class sessions is shared with the students themselves.

A good way of assisting the class to understand the function of the planning committee is to have some of its first meetings held in the classroom, with all the class members as observers. In this manner, all the pupils see how their representation contributes to class plans and how representatives can operate most effectively. It also provides an opportunity for everyone to see how the teacher works with the planning committee. The students are shown that it does not simply give rubber-stamp endorsement to teacher ideas or submit its plans for teacher approval or veto, but rather that it is a true committee in which each person has equal voice and vote.

Whatever the decision regarding a planning committee, it is well to suggest that the class organization be as simple as possible. Not all classes need a president, secretary, and treasurer. Some classes may decide that the only type of organization they need is a chairman and a recorder working in each group. If the organization is simple, and designed by the pupils as they plan their program, it is their organization; and it is their responsibility either to see that it works or to change it. A teacher promotes the pupils' sense of responsibility for the class organization if he avoids recommending an exact organizational pattern.

Leadership in a Class

Every group has leaders.

Sometimes a teacher ignores the leadership that exists within the class or honestly believes that there is no leadership in the group because it is weak for the age he is teaching. He finds it hard to remember that any class that has not had much opportunity to exert its native leadership will want to be dependent upon teacher direction and domination and will feel insecure without them because the pupils do not know how far they can go or under what conditions they can work.

But he cannot be most effective if he discounts the leadership in the group. His function as teacher requires that he start with the basic assumption that every person has the potential for leadership and that it is his responsibility to help this leadership to emerge.

A teacher must step out of the way to let other leadership emerge. As long as his leadership dominates the situation, other, less mature leadership will be overwhelmed. He can discover the leadership within the group by watching the way the group operates before and after school, in the gymnasium, on the playground, or in the club. Students who, because of their past conditioning, are afraid to attempt to exert leadership in the classroom have freedom to exert it in these areas. He can learn much about the kinds of native ability and leadership of the children in the group just by watching.

Unless a teacher understands the need for his standing aside as pupil leadership emerges, he will feel threatened and challenged. To be happy in the process, a teacher must recognize that he succeeds when he can get pupils to assume responsibility for leadership, not when pupils are doing what he wants them to do.

A teacher makes it possible for leadership to emerge as he creates an atmosphere where people feel free to be themselves. As long as he establishes a stereotype of what constitutes satisfactory behavior in the classroom, people are free only to conform unless they want to challenge authority. He makes it possible for many types of leadership to emerge as he creates a permissive atmosphere in which people feel that many types of behavior and leadership are accepted.

The basic step is to allow the group to plan. As long as the teacher does all the planning for students, he cannot know what leadership is there, and he cannot give it a chance to function.

As a teacher plans with boys and girls how to carry on a picnic or to put on a class play, he is utilizing situations in which they can exert leadership without feeling strange and restrained. As they find that they can exert leadership with him in this kind of a situation, they will, if he gives the opportunity, move on to greater freedom and exert leadership in the planning and operation of the class.

If a teacher refers his suggestions to the pupils for their decisions and their examination, he is creating the possibility for other suggestions to be made and for other leadership to take hold.

A teacher provides for the emergence of leadership to the degree to which he accepts class mistakes. As long as he is afraid of a class's making a mistake and always steps in to protect its members from what he considers their mistakes, he is continuing to keep the leadership function within his own hands. *The opportunity for exerting leadership is restricted in great measure to those who have the opportunity to make the mistakes.*

One of the basic techniques by which the teacher can help leadership emerge is by being willing to sit still when he thinks students can't handle the situation.

> At a May Day celebration a kindergarten group pretended they were going to the maypole in a covered wagon. Their prairie schooner consisted of a coaster wagon with a barrel in it. One of the youngsters sat on the barrel and the others pulled and pushed. As the group started to go before the parents who were watching the performance, the wagon upset and youngsters, barrel, and wagon piled up on the ground. The teacher could have run to the situation to rescue the youngsters and help to re-establish the wagon on four wheels—but she didn't. She sat still and the five-year-olds turned the wagon right side up and placed the barrel back up on top. Four took hold of the hands, legs, and arms of the youngster who belonged on top of the wagon and hoisted her up again, and the group moved on to the maypole.

By being willing to sit still through what was apparently a catastrophe, the teacher made it possible for the students to exert the leadership potential that they had within them and to solve the problem before them satisfactorily. If she had rushed into the situation and taken over, the boys and girls would have been denied the chance provided by the situation to develop their leadership qualities.

A high-school teacher describes his first attempt with group work as follows:

> One of the most difficult things I had to learn was to just sit back. Many is the time I wanted to step in and say to one of the groups, "I wouldn't go ahead that way. I know from experience that. . . ." But I let them go ahead and merely answered questions when asked or suggested something here and there. After a time, the group realized that nothing would happen to them if they went contrary to my suggestions. Whenever we arrived at a decision that didn't "pan out" too well, we changed it and tried something else. It has been hard for me to change habits and ideas more or less fixed after twenty-odd years of teaching. Although I have handled clubs and other special activity groups in the past, this is the first time where I tried to sit back and let students decide things for themselves. Too often, teachers are judged by results in an activity. Therefore, we are fearful of students' making the wrong decisions. We find it necessary to interject our wisdom, based on years of experience, into all decisions. Perhaps we are not entirely at fault. Perhaps supervisors and administrators should be more understanding.

This teacher states forcefully one of the strongest pressures a teacher faces while waiting for pupil leadership to emerge.

The development of leadership is encouraged if a teacher allows the class to undergo frustration in thinking through its problems. Whenever he becomes frightened by frustration within a group, he tends to move too fast in giving the pupils the answers that come from his experience. He feels that if they suffer too much frustration, they will become disgusted with the class and with the activity. He fails to recognize that one of the most powerful motivating forces for any one is to be confronted with difficulty and then to have the experience of satisfactorily overcoming that difficulty. The pleasure that comes with the emergence of leadership and successful experience motivates the continuation of the leadership and the willingness to attempt even more difficult things in the future.

Even after a teacher has worked with students for a period of time and has decided that they have taken real steps in developing initiative and leadership, he finds that they have periods when they do not want to assume responsibility. Leadership in the group may seem to grow erratically. One week the students may really want to step out into active leadership and the next week they may want him to resume control of the class. If he is to keep the development constantly moving forward, he must be skillful enough to know when to take over and when to withdraw. He must be alert in recognizing the desire for self-direction and work with it whenever it becomes evident.

Pupil Responsibility to the Group

The concept of leadership that a teacher holds affects the extent to which all pupils develop a sense of responsibility to the group. *If he honestly stresses the idea that everyone can lead, that everyone can contribute, all the pupils will be more inclined to accept responsibility.* But if he reserves leadership for the superior students, the less gifted will be inclined to let them carry the major responsibility. He releases the less gifted from responsibility as he rejects their contributions.

There are a number of ways in which a teacher can encourage boys and girls to lead by contributing rather than by demonstrating superiority over others. A simple way is to praise the contribution rather than the contributor. Another way is to center the attention of the class on group achievements and group projects rather than on individual showmanship. If assemblies and plays are class projects rather than opportunities for exhibitions by individual students, all the students can feel that they have a part. A third way is to stress contributions to improved living in the school. Developing service groups with membership open to all who wish to assist, rather than honor groups open only to students who show special skills, is one way to emphasize a broader type of leadership.

Choice of pronouns helps to set the stage for assuming responsibility for the group. If a teacher stresses "his," "her," "me," and "mine," he encourages differences and feelings of superiority. But if he uses "we," "our," and "us" as often as possible, the group begins to come together.

All pupils begin to feel that ideas and achievements are contributions to the class and each has a responsibility to do his part.

Basic, however, to the assumption of responsibility for the group is its participation in the decisions that affect the group. If the teacher encourages the group to organize in such a way that all members share in making decisions, he helps each child to assume responsibility. This point was analyzed in detail previously.

If the class assumes, by group decision, a responsibility to the total school, individual members will feel more responsibility to the group. Whether it is a beautification-of-grounds project or serving as a hospitality committee for an open house, the knowledge that other members of the student body know that the group has a task to perform will keep the individual from "letting the group down."

The Development of Group Maturity

A group has attained maturity when it has accepted the responsibility for its own actions and has become self-directing. Not all groups attain this status. Since maturity grows out of experience, a teacher can expect that most pupils will make some progress in maturity every day they live. However, he can consciously aid them in this progress by encouraging certain activities and attitudes that are characteristic of mature persons.

There are many ways to foster maturity.

One technique is to praise pupils for facing the problems that arise and for seeking their own answers. He can further this process by not giving answers. When he gives a class his answers, he deprives them of the opportunity of becoming more mature.

One device for avoiding giving answers is to suggest several possibilities and leave the choice to the class. Help is provided, but the responsibility for decision is left with the group.

Still another way in which a teacher helps a class achieve maturity is by letting students discover their own mistakes. When a mistake is made, it is very easy for him to say, "You are making a mistake. We will do it this way." Every time he takes such an action, he checks their growth toward maturity. A mature person lives with his mistakes, accepts the responsibility for them, and grows in the process of finding out the consequences of his behavior. By denying pupils the right to discover the consequences of their behavior, he robs them of the opportunity to grow. He assumes the responsibility and continues their status as dependent, immature persons. Through continuous evaluation, a teacher can help pupils to discover their mistakes quickly and to revise their plans in terms of the evidence rather than in terms of his judgment.

The teacher helps a class become more mature by accepting disagreements as a definition of work to be done. Too many teachers pretend disagreements don't exist. They feel that disagreements within the class are an unhealthy sign, that they should be covered up and ignored in class discussions. If, however, a class has the opportunity to bring harmony out of confusion by struggling with the confusion rather than by holding fast to some demonstratedly inadequate idea or policy, that class grows in the process. Pupils widen their horizons and become more mature when they have a chance to think through conflicting positions and arrive at a new synthesis. Discovering new truths and establishing new policies and codes of conduct constitute processes by which they move from immaturity to maturity. By making it possible for students to face their problems realistically, to work out their own answers, and then to live with the decisions they make, a teacher can help them move forward in their development into responsible, mature citizens.

His basic contribution, however, lies in teaching the steps in problem-solving which enable (1) pupils to meet new situations intelligently and (2) the skills of analysis which make it possible for them to interpret the experiences they have.

The Determination of Group Progress

It is important for every group to feel that it is achieving, that it is growing in maturity. If a group lacks this feeling, if it feels it is making the same mistakes that it made a week, a month, or six weeks before, it begins to lose confidence in itself. But if pupils have some way of checking the progress they are making, they will be able to experience the satisfaction that comes from growth.

The use of a tape recorder makes it possible for pupils to review their progress in discussion and planning techniques over a period of time. Or certain members of the class can be delegated to keep records of class decisions and the reasons why they were made. Then these records can be used by the class as a whole in analyzing its progress. Observers who can discuss and analyze with the class the steps that have been taken during a class meeting serve, in effect, the same purpose.

It may be necessary for the teacher to help pupils interpret the data they collect. Through his greater experience he has insights which he should share with the group. By comparing current behavior of the class with its past behavior, by pointing out areas in which progress has been made, and by indicating failure to improve in the handling of certain problems, he can show the students how the class looks to him. Whether or not they accept his observation as valid depends upon the way he works and the objectivity and fairness they have seen him display. In all these procedures he is helping students to compare previous with present behavior to see if they are satisfied with their progress or lack of progress.

Visiting groups from other classes from time to time can be asked to comment on what they see happening. Or, when another teacher or the principal or the supervisor stops by, he can be asked whether or not he sees evidence of progress. Any device by which the teacher can help pupils sense the changes that are taking place in their ways of working and thinking will lead them to a clearer knowledge of the progress that is being made. The evidence collected by such devices also constitutes the basis for judgments concerning the quality of work being done. This process will be discussed fully in Chapter 7.

But not all evidence is the kind that can be recorded. The way people feel is equally as important in maintaining high group morale. Evaluation sessions in which students discuss their feelings about what they are doing constitute a form of reassurance or an indication of need for revision of procedures. As students hear their fellow students state that they feel this way now as compared to how they felt earlier, they are getting evidence concerning achievements or lack of achievement of the group. Oral evidence of this type is as important to the class as the written evidence of secretary's minutes or tape recordings of earlier work.

Real group responsibility is developing when members of the class begin asking for evaluation sessions.

> A California class had been meeting for four weeks. One member opened a session by saying, "Les, John, and I have been discussing this class. We don't believe people are really working in here. Is that right?" The question was addressed to the group, not to the teacher. This group had grown to the point where its members were assuming responsibility for its success and were exercising leadership in raising it to the level of its potential performance.

In such situations, the teacher must be careful not to destroy the growth that has been made by regarding the students' comments as criticisms of him. If he goes on the defensive and attempts to give the answers to such questions, he is proclaiming that all the responsibility is his and denying students the right to share in it. But if he can sit back and let the class think through its procedures, simply supplying pertinent data, the pupils will have an opportunity to face reality and to grow in maturity.

The Role of the Individual

Every member of the group has responsibility. He cannot ignore it. Simply because he is living and working with other people, he must be considerate of them and of their feelings, and he must work as an effective member of the group.

A class member has a responsibility for participating in the planning, for getting his ideas and his purposes considered, for helping the group arrive at a plan. When he holds his ideas and his suggestions back, he is not contributing the full leadership of which he is capable. He must also question other ideas. Unless he questions decisions that to him seem wrong, he is not exercising his group membership. He is responsible, too, for taking the necessary steps to help the group reach consensus, for suggesting integrations of purposes and activities that no one else has seen. As a group member, he is committed to carry out the plan arrived at by the group. This will involve contributing skills that he already has, seeking to acquire new skills that will enable the group to put its plan into action more effectively, and doing his share of the work.

As the work proceeds, he must help the group evaluate its progress and work out changes that will make its efforts more effective. He serves as the group conscience, calling attention to things that are being overlooked or to departures from the original plan. And, at every turn, he is responsible for helping the other members of the group grow more efficient and effective. It is clear, then, that *the role of the individual class member is similar to that of the teacher.* He has the same responsibilities and the same functions. Although he probably will not be able to contribute as much as the teacher, he will work and participate in the work of the group in much the same way. *When a class is a group, everyone exercises the same functions in varying degrees.* Leadership and followership shift constantly.

The Leadership Role of the Teacher

Effective group development in the classroom depends upon the leadership role played by the teacher. To be successful, he must demonstrate the type of behavior that is frequently used by groups as a part of leadership.

Sharing the leadership function is a vital concept. If the teacher attempts to be "the leader" and to control the class, he will not develop a class group of which he is a part.

Sharing leadership with children may seem to be a dangerous and difficult undertaking. No teacher wants to lose the respect of pupils. He doesn't want the class to run wild, without control. What kind of relationship between teacher and pupils permits shared leadership and shared authority?

It is not one in which the pupils are afraid of the teacher. Or one in which the pupils control the teacher. Or one in which students are in opposition to the teacher.

It is one marked by mutual trust and respect, in which the teacher believes in the worth of the students, and they in turn believe in his good faith and abilities; one in which pupils and teacher help each other, talk out problems together, and depend upon each other.

A major element in developing this type of relationship is faith. Sometimes it's hard for a teacher to have such faith. It's hard to see how a group of boys and girls who have not had previous experience in self-direction, who seem very immature, who do not appear to have any worthwhile purposes or values, can be persons in whom it is possible to place faith. But faith is necessary. If the teacher doesn't believe in them, he can't help them believe in themselves.

The teacher must believe that each student in his class is important and is necessary to help a group develop and has a potential contribution to make. Otherwise, the teacher finds himself shutting the pupil out or ignoring him or doing the things in the class that will cause the other students to leave him out or to ignore his contributions. He searches for each youngster's contribution while guiding and planning with him.

The teacher must believe that each child has worthwhile purposes. Boys and girls are human beings with the drives and the instincts that other human beings have. They have some purposes that are judged good by society, and they have other purposes that are judged bad. The classroom provides an opportunity to help boys and girls to implement their socially acceptable purposes. They will make mistakes along the way, of course. Otherwise, schools would be unnecessary.

The teacher must believe, too, that each child can improve. Unless improvement is believed possible, education becomes a farce. With sufficient teaching skill, it is possible to help the child to improve his values, his ways of working, and his skill in living with others.

The teacher must believe that each pupil wants to belong and will work with others as soon as he feels that he does belong. It is a basic aspect of human nature to want to be a part of the social group. If it is realized that a child is sincere in his attempts to win membership in the group, teaching becomes, in part, a process of helping him discover the most effective techniques. Certainly faith in him is not lost when he first enters the group, for not already having developed skills in working with others.

The teacher must believe that boys and girls can be trusted. People tend to live up to what other people expect of them. Demonstrations of distrust provoke a child to be untrustworthy. Belief in his trustworthiness makes it very difficult for him to deny the faith in him.

A teacher must believe that each student will live up to the best that he knows. No student wants to be inadequate. Often he will do things that appear unsatisfactory simply because he does not know the best means of achieving his goals. A phase of teaching is to help him set higher standards for himself, to help him develop concepts of the good life that will cause him to aim a little higher than when he first came to the class.

The teacher fulfills his leadership role by showing in his actions with the class that he has a commitment to these beliefs about his pupils. As he works, it is *his task to provide enough direction to give the pupils a sense of security, but not enough to discourage initiative.* There will be times when students will hesitate and feel lost, when they do not have a sense of direction as a group. At such times the teacher will need to step in and suggest to the group solutions that will get them over the hurdle. When the class wants to relapse into less responsibility than they have grown to accept, he will need to help them accept that feeling in themselves. He will assume the job of helping the group move ahead during the time they feel this desire for dependence. And then he will retire from directing the group as the initiative once again starts to surge forward among members of the class.

7 · A Way of Working with a Group

Skillful planning with pupils is the very core of teaching for efficient learning. Without pupil-teacher planning, motivation may be superficial and class time may be a waste of the teacher's energy and the pupils' opportunities.

Preliminary Planning Is Necessary

If a teacher is to feel secure and at ease when he faces a class for the first time, he must have done serious preliminary planning.

There are many ways of planning, and they aren't all formal. Before beginning work in a new school, it is helpful to go through the community in which the school is located and to talk with the citizens. In this way, the feel of the community, some understanding of the problems of the youngsters who live there, and familiarity with community attitudes and mores are obtained. Knowledge of the community gives meaning to references students make to local points of interest and sly remarks about problems they face, and suggests the types of material and information that will prove most stimulating to them.

But knowing the community is not enough. It is also desirable to know the different children who will be in the class as well. One way to learn about students is by reviewing their personnel folders, studying their test scores, looking at remarks that other teachers have made about them, noting their strengths, and discovering their problems.

Another step to take is to collect information on problems which seem likely to be important to the group to be encountered. Some general clues exist. Pamphlets on child development, such as *How Children Develop,* published by the Ohio State University School, give a good analysis of the interests, needs, and physical growth of the particular age-group. These characteristics of an age-group constitute valuable guideposts in selecting materials to have on hand when the class comes together. In addition, the study of the individual folders gives information on special interests of the boys and girls in the class.

The syllabi and regulations of the system provide additional direction. The work that has been done by individuals in charge of the curriculum organization in preparing courses of study and curricula for various grade and age levels constitutes the framework within which a class will work. These written materials at least give guidance and illustrate the teaching that has been customary in the school.

Also, thought can be given to the physical appearance of the room before the students arrive. Some teachers deliberately avoid making specific arrangements because they want the boys and girls to develop the environment as a group project. They feel that if the class members set up a room and collect and organize the material and furniture in a way in which they want it, they will feel more responsibility for the room and a greater interest in what goes on. Other teachers take the point of view that it is their job to have on hand as many stimulating materials and exhibits as possible. If there is clay in one corner, a reading table in another, a tape recorder in a third, students will know that these are some of the types of equipment and materials that they may use. They are stimulated at the start by the possibilities of doing things with the materials. The displays of work that previous students have done or listings of questions that previous groups have undertaken to solve are other ways to suggest some activities that may go on in the class.

Plans of several ways of getting acquainted with the students should be made. They may not be used, but they're good to fall back on if nothing else suggests itself at the moment when the class arrives. This is especially important for the beginning teacher who has had little experience in meeting groups.

Acceptance by Group Essential

As a teacher walks into a classroom for the first time, he is "sized up" and evaluated by all the members of the group, especially if he is new in the system and the students have had no reports from their predecessors about what kind of person he is. Of course, if he has taught in the school before, his chances for success are either increased or decreased by the reputation he has made for himself. If previous students have found him to be a satisfactory person to work with, his task of winning the acceptance of a new group will not be hard. But if he has a name for being a nagger, a disagreeable person, a tyrant, or an inefficient worker, his hopes for winning acceptance by the group are greatly reduced.

As he undergoes this first trial, the teacher finds that certain things may hinder his winning acceptance. If he attempts to bluff his way by being very strict and by making an example of the first pupil who steps out of line, he creates an undesirable relationship that he will have to overcome later. If he attempts to be exceedingly friendly, he risks losing the students' respect. Students welcome evidence of the teacher's willingness to be friendly, but they resent synthetic, elaborate displays of friendship. They know that friendship develops as a result of shared experiences that bring about mutual respect.

In beginning to work with students, the teacher should attempt to create the kind of situation in which they will feel free to express their personal reactions. When the students are free to say what they think, their comments will guide the teacher in deciding what steps he should take to win acceptance in the group.

Boys and girls must feel that they have independence. This is particularly true at the high-school age. Whenever a teacher attempts to crowd students into accepting his plans, he forces them either to abandon their self-respect or to rebel. If he draws the battleline so that rebellion is the only respectable course, he can't win acceptance by the group. He may win respect based on fear, but he won't be accepted as a member of the group. If he wants to be a working member of the group, he must begin to work with the class in such a way that he makes clear to them that the class is theirs as well as his, that he wants help in planning how class experiences can be conducted most effectively.

A teacher cannot win acceptance unless he has faith in the youngsters with whom he works. *Acceptance means mutual faith,* and faith on the part of students does not come until the teacher has shown them that he has the faith in them described previously. This faith can be shown in numerous ways. It is demonstrated by expecting the best from students as he begins work with them, by refraining from making comments about unsatisfactory past performance, by looking for the good things they do rather than for things to stop them from doing, by encouraging them to work together rather than attempting to isolate them from each other, by allowing them to sit and work with the people they like to work with. Faith is the most powerful tool a teacher has in winning acceptance and in working with boys and girls at all levels.

> A Florida teacher met a class for the first time. He noticed that there was a great deal of confusion and disorder, but he made no point of it. Finally, he raised a question with the class, and one of the students said, "Don't you know that we're the most unruly class in the school? Hasn't anyone told you that we've had that reputation ever since we were in the fifth grade?" The teacher sat quietly for a moment and then said, "Is this a challenge?" The students looked back and laughed. Then one of them said, "No, we just want to tell you so you won't be too discouraged."

The situation illustrates the way a class tests a new teacher. They were finding out whether he was for them or against them, whether he was going to attack, become frightened, or try to be friendly.

Students need to be able to look to the teacher for the kind of friendly help they would get from their parents. Parents do not condemn their children because they do not measure up to some artificial standard; they accept their children as the best possible children and then work with them in moving in the direction that both parents and children feel is important.

If a teacher wants to be accepted as a working member of the team, he must make it possible for students to work with him without having their personalities violated. Students must find in working with him the kind of experience that allows them to be themselves, to think their own thoughts, to maintain their own integrity, and to develop in terms of the things they think are important.

A teacher loses any chance of working successfully *with* a class when he allows himself to be drawn into a struggle for domination with the more aggressive pupils. It should never become evident to a class that he is taking issue with a given student. If it does, he creates a situation in which one or the other must win. When a student creates a problem by challenging the teacher, as some students are certain to do, it becomes a problem for group solution rather than one for him to solve by himself.

If a teacher assumes that he alone should give the answer, then it becomes a question of whether or not he can enforce it, whether or not the other students will accept it as better than that of the aggressive student who has challenged him. He cannot engage in a person-to-person quarrel with a student and expect to retain group acceptance; the student group as a whole will automatically be on the side of their age-peer.

A teacher moves toward acceptance by the group by sharing with members of the group decisions on appropriate action. If he raises the question with students as to what is the most important thing to do and what is the best way to do it, the issue of who will decide what is to be done will never arise. He moves toward acceptance by making the issue *what* is right rather than *who* is right.

He moves toward acceptance more quickly by learning the names of students. If he is careless or slow in learning them, he is saying brutally to the students that it doesn't matter to him who they are, that they aren't even important enough for him to learn their names.

By familiarizing himself with the interests, purposes, desires, and experiences of pupils, the teacher manifests to them that they are important to him. *As they become important to him, he becomes important to them.*

A teacher wins acceptance more easily by avoiding such statements as, "This is what *I* want you to do," "*I* have decided that we are going to begin this way." Rather, he should proceed by asking pupils, "What is the best way to work together?" "What are the next steps for us to take?" As pupils share decisions with him, they come to accept him. Through the process of sharing decisions, the teacher wins group acceptance.

Whether or not a teacher continues to enjoy the acceptance of the group depends upon whether or not he lives up to his responsibilities to the group. If he ignores the decisions that he has shared with the group, if he doesn't play fair in carrying out the plans and policies that have been made together, he loses the ground that he has gained. Acceptance by the group on one occasion does not guarantee life membership. Acceptance is a dynamic condition; it grows either stronger or weaker. Day-to-day behavior either helps to develop whatever acceptance has been won or it decreases that acceptance.

The Beginning of Group Planning

One of the questions a teacher has to face is whether or not to bring pupils in on planning the program. If a teacher believes that it is a major function of a teacher to develop democratic values and skills, there seems to be only one answer to this question.

The only way to learn to plan is through planning, and if a teacher wants to develop this democratic skill, he brings students in on the planning. But the manner in which he proceeds, and the types of decisions that he shares may vary. He will be guided here by a number of factors, including the pupils' maturity and background, and the attitudes of the community and of other staff members.

Teacher-pupil planning can be foolishly misinterpreted.

> A wrestling coach in a midwestern high school had been asked to teach a section of tenth-grade English. In the third month of the school year, while he was talking with the principal, he commented, "There has been so much talk about pupil-teacher planning in our faculty meetings that I have begun it in my English class. The students are helping me plan our spelling work. Last week we decided that if we did not miss more than three letters in a word we would count it right."

Here was a teacher who accepted the idea without any understanding of the reason for it or its purpose. Joint planning is not intended to decide whether or not facts are correct. Pupils are brought into the planning to increase agreement on purposes to help them to develop more effective methods of problem-solving.

Even limited student participation helps. Here is what the teacher of a tenth-grade Spanish class in Connecticut has to say:

> In using "La Linterna," a little paper printed entirely in Spanish which is published twice a month, I had noticed a marked drop in student interest. To arouse more interest I made the following changes in procedure.
>
> Previously, I had read the paper first myself before distributing it to the students, and then made assignments sometimes to the class as a whole or to individual students. I tried to assign articles that I thought might have special interest for them. Evidently I must have failed—at least in some of this.
>
> I changed this procedure to distributing the papers to the students and suggesting that we plan together what we should read either as a class or individuals. The class was slow at first to accept this suggestion but later did very well. I made a few short summaries of the articles—just enough to give them a slight idea of the subject matter. After a few weeks I decided to allow the class to do all the planning, of course with the help and suggestions that they asked me to give. They usually were given the paper to look over by themselves for two or three days to become acquainted with the various articles and subject matter in general. Then they reported to class ready to volunteer for the reading assignments. I was amazed and more than pleased with the very thorough way they handled this.
>
> The result is that they now show more interest in the paper and have even done some reference and research work on some of the articles. This was done and planned entirely by the students. Although every pupil does not read the entire paper, they all get the information; the pupils, by making their own assignments and assuming responsibility for their share of the work, give what amounts to a report of the entire paper. Each one reads or translates or tells in his own words what he has read or prepared.
>
> Immediate results are better prepared work, better group spirit, more interest, and finally no more "lost" or "mislaid" papers.

Ordinarily, pupils will not express a desire to take part in the planning. They don't expect to.

Only through a period of encouragement can a teacher get boys and girls who have been conditioned to teacher domination to move to the place where they are willing to say, "This is what seems important to me in terms of my purposes and in terms of what I hope to become."

Many students are suspicious when a teacher begins to plan with them, especially those who have had unsatisfactory experiences in the past with teachers who have said that they were going to share the planning. They wonder what is going to happen. They suspect that it is just another technique for getting them to do what the teacher wants them to do.

Of course, a teacher cannot force pupils to plan with him; he can only extend to them the invitation to participate when they are ready. All he can do is say, "Here is a decision that I can make. I would like you to help me make it if you will. We'll abide by the decision that we reach as a group if you undertake to join me in this decision. Otherwise, I will have to make it for us." This attitude clearly shows that it is up to the students to decide whether or not they will enter into the planning. In the beginning, they may wisely choose not to accept the invitation. They may know how much they are willing to undertake, but they may not yet know how much faith and trust they can have in the teacher. He may have to extend this offer for a month or more before the students will undertake any joint planning with him.

An easy way of getting started with students in planning is the teacher's proposing some method of work. Then, if they do not want to make any revision in it at the time, he can simply start to work by that method. As soon as the class has had a chance to experience the method and to find out what it considers its strengths or weaknesses, he can take time out to say, "Are we doing what we should? Is the method we are following helpful to you? Or are there changes we should make to improve it so that all of us will be happier with it and make more progress together?" Such questions bring students into an evaluation session and give them an opportunity to participate in revising the procedure. It is true pupil-teacher planning.

Another way to bring pupils into the planning is to propose several plans of work and then let them choose the one they like best. After they have tried their wings in carrying out some plan they themselves have chosen, they will probably be ready to help in developing the next plan.

Whatever plan the class decides upon should be put into operation and later the members of the group given an opportunity to evaluate and revise it in terms of how effective they feel it to be.

A class difficulty sometimes leads to the first real acceptance of pupil-teacher planning. Here's what happened in a seventh-grade physical education class:

> On one volley ball court the arguing grew louder and louder until the umpire threw up her hands and began screaming to be heard. It sounded like a department store full of ladies on bargain day.
> It was early in the year, and some new seventh-graders were trying hard to assume their role of junior-high girls, but occasionally it proved too much.
> Across the way two other teams played, with squeals of delight and cooperation.
> Feeling the complete contrast of the situation, a hunch told me this might be one of their teachable moments.
> I called Betty, the class leader, and we watched the two games. "Looks a little like war and peace," she told me. She thought they would really laugh if they could see the contrast. We walked over to the peaceful teams, and asked them to come over and observe the other game. Then we told them to play the way they had seen the game played.
> After the observation, the peaceful team staged a sham ruckus. Betty ran over to the quarreling teams and asked them to watch the others play. We then called both groups together and talked about what they had seen. Each team contributed facts, and we discussed which way of playing was the most fun.

The steps in planning are very simple. They consist of deciding what needs to be done, choosing the things that should be undertaken immediately, and figuring out a plan of attack.

A teacher makes a mistake if he tells pupils that they can do anything they please during the class. Students are smart enough to see that this philosophy carried to its logical conclusion would mean that they could go fishing during class time if they so desired. Instead of telling pupils that they can do as they please, *it is the teacher's function to stress the idea that the class is a place where students can engage in activities within the field of work that are of most value to them.*

When students consider a particular way of attacking a problem, it helps to ask such questions as: "Will it accomplish what we want? Can we do it in the time that we have? Is it better than the other solutions we are considering?" These criteria will help any group from elementary classes through high school to determine whether or not the proposed plan of study should be the one undertaken.

Many teachers have felt that the time spent in setting up criteria by which to judge problems is wasted. They have felt that it would be easier and more helpful if they suggested to the class the criteria by which problems should be judged. Actually, the establishing of criteria to apply in selecting problems or courses of action is a form of planning, with long-range implications. The effects of even two class periods at the beginning of a year given over to establishing criteria will carry through the whole year. They are probably the most important planning periods that the group will have. Naturally, it will be necessary during the year to revise the criteria as the youngsters learn more about self-direction, but this beginning statement of criteria is the level from which the group starts and the foundation on which it builds.

Many teachers find it helpful during early planning sessions with the group to talk about the interests of various members of the class. This gives the boys and girls a chance to learn about one another and to discover which classmates share their interests. It also gives the class direction in selecting the projects that will be valuable to the total group.

Others talk with the pupils about the best way to work. Pupils are given an opportunity to say what they would like from the teacher, and the teacher says, "This is how I like to work with a class and these are the relationships I like to have with students." The points of view expressed may not be identical, but out of the discussion may come criteria which the class will establish as rules of behavior.

The Selection of a Project

In deciding what problems to study, it is helpful to take a problem census. Each student may say, "These are the problems that I would like to work on. These are the things that are important for me to learn. These are the skills that I hope to develop." *Since the teacher, too, is a member of the group, he should feel free at all times to suggest problems that he believes are important.*

Students are encouraged to make their own decisions by such questions as, "Are you sure this is what we need to do? Is this the most valuable thing we can do?" When a student answers these questions, he is in effect justifying, to anyone concerned, the activity being undertaken.

As a technique for reaching group agreement, taking straw votes proves to be very helpful. Opinions are expressed through informal votes which do not commit the individual or group. For example, the class may have suggested seven topics: South America, How To Win Friends, Farm Animals, Ships, Gold Mining, Getting Along with Parents, and Japan. Through discussion, it has been found that all seven meet the criteria for study units that the class has established. A choice has to be made among them. A straw vote in which each student may express his preference is suggested. The class accepts, with the understanding that the straw vote is for the purpose of helping to reach a decision. The vote is: South America 2, How To Win Friends 10, Farm Animals 2, Ships 3, Gold Mining 12, Getting Along with Parents 3, and Japan 3. After the straw vote, the persons wishing to study South America, Farm Animals, Ships, Getting Along with Parents, and Japan are given an opportunity to present additional arguments for their preference, with the understanding that if they do not convince anyone, the choice will become a decision between studying How To Win Friends and Gold Mining. After the choice has been narrowed down, either a big majority will shift their votes to one side or the other, or else efforts will be made to reach a compromise agreement. Official votes are avoided as much as possible.

Through the use of a straw vote, it is possible for the group to gain an understanding of the general feeling about the various projects that have been suggested without making a commitment to follow any one course of action. If, after more discussion, the group comes to an agreement on what is to be done, the problem is solved. But if no consensus is reached as a result of the straw vote, more planning will be needed. The straw vote, then, is a technique for revealing the opinions of various members of the group, for determining which people should have further opportunity to explain the proposals they have made, and for moving toward consensus on the ultimate course of action.

The Plan of Work

Every group should agree on an agenda or a plan of work. The agenda may simply list the problems that the group wants to study during the year, or it may outline a more detailed schedule. Most classes find it helpful to agree on only one project at the first few sessions. Then the pupils concentrate on that problem for a while until they get to know each other and develop a deeper understanding of the field being investigated. Later on, when they feel ready, they may decide to establish a long-range schedule for the remaining portion of their time together. But some classes never move beyond scheduling the problem to be studied next. They feel that it is better not to establish a long-term agenda because the work on the present problem may lead to greater insight into the things that need to be done next.

In any case, whether only one problem is agreed upon or the agenda for the total year or semester is established, the class needs to have a definite plan of work, with agreement on actual dates for the completion of various tasks. Such a plan gives students security. They know what is expected of them and they know where they are going.

Pupils are expected to honor this contract until they work out an agreement for change. Adjustment and changes in the plan must be cleared with the class. The teacher serves as executive and coordinator.

The Work Period

After a class has developed a plan, freedom of movement is necessary to carry it out. During the planning stage, the teacher works with the total group, but as soon as a plan is agreed upon that includes individual projects or committee activities, students need to be free to engage in the activities they have planned.

During the work period the class is in effect a workshop where the teacher works with individuals or with groups that need help. He serves as a resource person, moving from group to group and giving help whenever the students request it or he sees it is needed. He does not hesitate to move voluntarily into any situation in which the students seem to have lost their sense of direction. That is a part of his guidance function—spotting difficulties and helping students surmount them without being deflected from their course. He does it by asking questions that contrast what students are doing with the plans they have made or questions that suggest other possibilities.

As he works with students, he stresses that information is to be *used*, that it is not to be memorized as an end in itself. To help pupils use facts to solve problems and form generalizations is the teacher's goal. Research experiments report that within two years 70 per cent of unused facts are forgotten.

The class schedule should provide for work to be done by both large and small groups, and also by individual students. It is a mistake to assume that all the work can be done by the total class.

The teacher makes a major contribution as the class begins small-group work by counseling individual groups and by using one group to demonstrate small-group work to the total class. If all pupils watch one work-group and offer suggestions for improvement of its operation, all groups will profit by the suggestions given to the demonstrating group.

In the early elementary school, pupils may work best in pairs or trios, with larger groups used occasionally.

In secondary schools small work-groups formed within the class are more effective when their membership ranges from five to nine. In committees of less than five members, the stimulation decreases and students tend to become less interested. They see less real opportunity to coordinate and pull their work together. On the other hand, in work-groups that include nine or more members, individual students find that they are getting in one another's way, that duplication occurs, and that lack of time prevents adequate communication.

Unless the members are experienced in group work, most small work-groups will require help in deciding the kind of organization they need, in defining the functions of such persons as the chairman and recorder, and in formulating work plans.

A teacher should be careful to have the small work committees within the larger group recognize their responsibility to the total group in which they are functioning. If each individual committee is permitted to go its own way without any responsibility to the total group, the class will soon disintegrate into a number of small, independent groups. The feeling of belonging together will be weakened. Individual students will begin to identify with their smaller work-groups and thus lose their feeling of belonging to the total class. In planning sessions the class should develop a total plan, and then within this total plan individual committees should set up procedures by which they can delve into the special phases of the plan that seem important to them. The responsibility of the pupils in a small group should not be to themselves alone, but to the total group for whom they are undertaking research.

Frequent progress reports made by each small group to the total group increase the sense of responsibility to the total group. Such reports help stimulate ideas in other groups, and develop cooperation among small groups with common problems.

Arrangements should be made that will encourage the small committees to share with the larger group. Unless the original planning includes provisions for sharing, the small committees will feel less responsibility to the larger group. They may know that they are going to share their experiences eventually, but unless some time in the original planning is spent in deciding how this sharing will take place, its importance does not really make itself felt.

Individuals want time to work by themselves to explore individual problems, to work on individual skills, and to follow their own reading tastes. The class may reject the teacher's suggestion that time be provided for these individual pursuits. And he should accept their rejection at that point. But during subsequent evaluation sessions he will again want to raise the question, even though it is voted down. *The teacher's role is to suggest the best he knows and to help the group decide whether or not his suggestion and others will improve their living and working.*

The operation of a class group was illustrated by a sophomore biology class in a southern high school.

> A class was discussing diseases. They found that 50 per cent of the class had had malaria. Shocked, they decided to undertake a study of the disease, its causes, and possible preventive measures.
>
> At first, the teacher assumed leadership in defining the problem and in suggesting various methods of attack. After talking the project through, the members of the class decided that they would begin interviewing various citizens in the town in order to get the facts on the extent of malaria in their town—the health department did not have the information. One student, who was skilled in the communication arts, volunteered to help train the interviewers in the most effective techniques of drawing forth information. When the interviewers had returned with their findings, the best mathematician in the class assumed leadership of a committee responsible for organizing the data into a meaningful pattern. Another student, interested in politics, suggested that they should make their findings known and recommended submitting them to the city council. After discussing the desirability of such a step, the class decided that it was a good idea. But first, they felt the material would have to be prepared for effective presentation. At this point, other students, with experience in drawing and lettering, offered to work out graphs and illustrations of the group's conclusions and proposals. Then the students selected their most eloquent speaker to make the actual presentation to the council. After the council had listened but taken no action, the teacher raised the questions that caused the group to evaluate the results of their efforts.

All during this project, one student after another had assumed leadership as successive group needs became evident. The teacher stood ready to offer assistance, but his greatest contribution had been in helping the group to uncover and develop its own potentials for leadership.

Controls in the Group

Policy formed by the group, definite plans for work, and high morale serve as controls in a class in which the teacher makes a group.

Participation in forming the policy that will govern behavior is the basic control. A code of behavior established by the class itself guides its actions most effectively. It gives the youngsters security because they know the kinds of behavior that are approved and the kinds that are not. It also puts the pressure of group opinion against undesirable behavior. The control is even stronger if pupils are helped to realize as they plan that policy-making is not play; that they are substituting group control for teacher control; that they are agreeing to live by the rules and regulations they formulate.

After a code has been formulated, there will be times when certain members of the group will want to question it. They can. Even such commonly accepted values as truth, honesty, acceptance of other people, and respect for the individual, if they are established as values by the class, will become issues at various times in the daily living. Out of questioning comes new insight for the individual, and perhaps for the entire class. The rethinking of class procedures necessitated by a class member's challenging the existing practice is a real learning situation. But the fact that the code can be questioned, re-examined, and revised gives it more power as a control. The possibility of change gives any group policy greater influence because each student knows that it is accepted by all—otherwise, it would be changed. Because it is respected by all, he feels a greater responsibility to live by it.

Agenda and deadlines decided on by the group serve as controls too. They make it clear to each pupil just what the group expects him to do and how much time he has to do it. If the agenda and schedule are tight enough, there will be no time for lackadaisical effort or for sidepath activities. The members of the group will be controlled by the plan of action that they themselves have set.

Once policies and plans have been established, the teacher is in the position of serving as the group conscience. It is his function to call to the attention of the group any deviations from the policy or plan that has been formulated. It is not necessary for him to say to the group, "Let's get back to the work." He can say, "We have departed from the plan. Is this the course of action that is most important for us to take?" or "The thing that we are doing now is not within the scope of the policy that we established. Do we want to re-examine the policy?" By encouraging students to make decisions concerning their own behavior when they begin to depart from agreed upon policy or plans, he creates a situation in which they have to think through their answers and reach their own decisions and accept their own responsibilities.

If individuals or small groups within the large group depart from the total group plan, it is the teacher's responsibility to have them explain to the total group why they are doing so. It may be that they can convince the total group that the plan should be revised. But it is the responsibility of every group to get clearance from the total group before it undertakes a departure from the established course.

High morale developed by the way the group has lived together serves as a control. An individual who is proud of his group will not take action that will discredit it.

Participation in policy formation and planning does not mean that the classroom can be as noisy as any student chooses to make it. No teacher can allow the classroom to become chaotic. Some order must prevail. Order may be imposed by the teacher, or it may be developed by the students within the class. If some class members will not abide by the regulations imposed by the group, it is the teacher's responsibility to enforce these regulations.

Group punishment is not an answer to any problem and should never be used. Certainly all the youngsters in the class haven't departed from the values to which they are committed. Mass punishment decreases chances of working effectively with pupils who have failed least in self-discipline. Whenever it seems that the class as a whole has departed from its code of behavior, a class session for group evaluation is in order. As a member of the group, the teacher has the right and responsibility to call for an evaluation of the group's code of behavior whenever the members of the group seem to be departing from the course that they have set. So does any other member of the group.

When punishment of an individual seems to be the only course left in a certain situation, the first step is to seek agreement on what has occurred. The first question should be, "As you saw it, what happened?" Once it has been decided just what happened, the next step is to determine the causes for the pupil's behavior. A helpful question is "Can you add any information that will help us understand your action better?"

If the pupil, as a result of analyzing with the teacher what he has done and why he did it, recognizes that he has made a mistake and shows that he is willing to correct it, there is no need for punishment. If he can say, "This is what I did and this is what I am going to do to correct it," the situation has gone as far as it needs to go. *Punishment is only one way of affecting behavior, and it is one of the least effective.* It is used only when other procedures have failed, and it will probably fail too.

When punishment is necessary, the third question to ask is, "What do you think should be done?" It should be kept clearly in mind that punishment is not getting even with a pupil but helping him face the reality of the situation. If the situation has advanced to the stage where something must be done, the student is in as good a position as the teacher to make recommendations concerning the way to help him gain an understanding of the full significance of his behavior. If he does not propose an acceptable solution, the teacher is forced to make the decision himself.

Any movement into this third step with any pupil must be an effort to help a youngster see the full implications of his behavior and not an attempt to salvage the teacher's dignity.

Certainly the teacher must do all in his power to keep punishment from becoming a personal issue between himself and the student. To insure that he is not taking revenge or satisfying his ego, it is well never to administer or recommend punishment while angry or hurt.

Punishment should not be a routine thing. One of the major difficulties in high schools is that time spent in detention halls is looked upon as a way of paying a debt to society. The student who has done something that is unsatisfactory pays his debt, and that is all there is to it. Instead of being a routine payment in terms of time or privileges, punishment should be a corrective measure. Once a student sees that he has made a mistake, the teacher should work out with him what he can do to remedy that mistake and to prevent it from occurring again. *Punishment becomes a step in planning with boys and girls the things that can be done to bring about a more satisfactory relationship with the group.*

In this sense, punishment is not something that is autocratically imposed. The student has been in on all three steps of the disciplining process: (1) ascertaining what the behavior was, (2) getting at the causes of the behavior, and (3) planning for compensation and ways in which he can become a more effective member of the group in the future.

In any relationship with an individual student, his welfare and progress and that of the group should be primary considerations. Disciplinary action should be taken only in terms of improving his relationship within the group.

The foregoing statement should not be interpreted to mean that a pupil would be punished for a single misbehavior. Punishment is the outgrowth of unsuccessful counseling. Many hours may be spent in counseling and evaluation before punitive action is taken. Punishment is only the last resort.

Evaluation of Group Growth

Records of group activities and growth are as important as those of individual progress. The group, if it is to work efficiently, must evaluate its progress.

Class minutes are a valuable source of evidence of group growth. They are helpful in determining whether or not progress is being made in ways of working together. If a class can look at the minutes of a meeting in October and then at the minutes of January, and see that their planning and evaluation techniques have improved, they have definite proof that they are making progress.

Committee reports also provide significant evidence of group progress. If comparison is made of committee reports at the beginning of the year and reports later in the year, it is possible to determine whether or not the members of the group are learning better how to share the information that has been collected. Insight can also be gained into whether or not there has been an increase in skill in locating, collecting, and organizing material.

If the class is seeking to improve its reading, for example, records may be kept of the amount and kind of reading done. In one school of 1,000 students, 800 books were read during the fall semester. In the spring semester, after the library had been reorganized and teachers began to have pupils share reading experiences, 12,800 books were read. By looking at the reading record for the two semesters, the students in the school had dramatic evidence of the extent to which they were increasing their reading. Quantitative information of this sort can be supplemented if each student keeps a record of the titles he reads over a period of time. A comparison of these lists will enable the students to determine whether they are reading more mature books, or whether they are continuing to read at the same level. If a group continues to read the same type of book throughout a whole year, it is fairly safe to assume that the reading level and reading interests of the group have not improved.

A class diary enables the group to compare the types of activities undertaken by the class at different times. It also gives members of the class an opportunity to study the pattern of work they have followed and to compare the effectiveness of one pattern with another.

Having one student serve as class recorder is helpful. But keeping comprehensive records of class activities is a demanding, time-consuming job, and one pupil should not be made responsible for it over too long a period. Rather, it should be passed from one student to another so that all will have a chance to share in this responsibility and learn the techniques of keeping records for a group. Each member of the group should be willing to serve as group recorder, because of the contribution the records make to the group and because of the skill he will develop during the experience.

To simplify the task, the class recorder may set up a file in which he will keep a record of the aims the class has set for itself, minutes of class meetings, samples of committee reports, conclusions the class draws as a result of its study, and any other types of information that the group thinks are valuable.

To insure the success of this scheme, each member of the group should be willing to allow the group recorder to look at his individual records. Through analysis of individual records, the recorder will be able to compile a meaningful record of the work of the whole group. If he does not have access to individual records, his group record will necessarily be less accurate.

A file of class plans enables students to look back at their previous undertakings and to compare the thoroughness with which they have planned at different times. Since it also indicates the scope of the work previously done and reveals to the class the areas still untouched by its work together, the class file also serves as a guide in deciding on what steps should be taken next.

The tape recorder can be used to great advantage in sampling various class sessions. It permits students to review the ways they made plans, to evaluate types of participation, and to determine the level of enthusiasm with a greater degree of accuracy than do any of the other ways of recording behavior that have been mentioned.

In classes without access to a tape recorder, a flow chart will indicate the number and the general location of participants. It enables a class to see which pupils have withdrawn from various discussions, and, if this is a consistent pattern, it provides evidence upon which plans can be made for stimulating them into greater participation.

The group may also appoint one of its members to serve as an observer who will help obtain an accurate record of what is happening. An understanding of the purposes of the class and the use of the following questions as a check list will help the observer make his report comprehensive and meaningful.

General
Was the class meeting slow in getting started?
Was the atmosphere easy, relaxed, and comfortable?
Was the tempo slow, hurried, or satisfactory?
Was the interest level high?
Was the purpose clear to all?
Were members cooperative?
Was information shared?
Were members sensitive to one another?
Were tensions brought out into the open?
Was there evidence of feelings of superiority?
Were ideas forced on the group?
Was the group able to accept differences?
Was the group able to discipline itself?
Was any decision reached?
Was there resistance to group decisions?

Participation
Was participation spread throughout the group?
Was discussion centered for a long period in one portion of the group?
Was the discussion initiated by group members?
Were there difficulties in communication?
Was there a feeling of give and take?

Were members eager to speak?
Were certain members taking more than their share of the time?
Were members showing aggression?
Was the discussion limited to the topic?
Were members assuming responsibility for the success of the meeting?
Were members attempting to draw each other out?

Discussion Leadership

Did the leader help the group to establish direction?
Did the leader give encouragement?
Did the leader attempt to bring in nonparticipating members?
Did the leader volunteer more help than was needed?
Did the leader recognize those who wished to speak?
Did the leader dominate the meeting?
Did the leader manifest feelings of superiority?
Did the leader keep things going?
Did the leader bring the specialized skills of members to bear on the problem?
Did the leader summarize as necessary?
Did the leader try to give answers for the group?
Did the leader get a consensus?

In making judgments about group progress, steps should be taken to involve all members of the group.

When a project has been completed, a judgment concerning these aspects of the work is in order. "Have we accomplished as much as we had hoped? Have we been as thorough as we needed to be? Have we measured up to the standards we set for ourselves? How should we change our goals and our method?"

In evaluating class procedures, it is desirable to center attention on the "how" rather than on the "who." As a class looks back at an experience and discusses the mistakes that were made and ways to improve the process in the future, no specific individual action by the teacher or by a pupil should be isolated from the total procedure. If the pronoun "we" is emphasized, this result will be obtained. Helpful questions are: "What mistakes did we make?" "How can we improve next time?" "Should we change our goals?" These questions eliminate pointing fingers at individuals and leave people free to suggest improvements without fear of hurting anyone's feelings. Further, they leave the individual free to analyze his own participation without a sense of conceit or guilt. The emphasis in group evaluation is on group progress rather than on individual growth.

Pitfalls in Group Work

Teachers with wide experience in working with groups have pointed out certain pitfalls that can be avoided.

One of the most common pitfalls is not establishing a definite agenda. If the group does not plan ahead and establish an agenda for itself, chaos may result. The students develop a hopeless sense of drifting. They have no landmarks by which they can ascertain progress. They lose their sense of direction.

But simply setting up an agenda is not enough. An agenda does not give the course of action; it only states the topics that are to be taken up. Before a class undertakes a project, a plan of work should be formulated which outlines a procedure to be followed and specifies the responsibility of individual students. In the early grades this may be a very informal plan. The children will say, "These are the things we are going to do. John will collect the paints. Mary will water the flowers." But at the high-school level, the plan needs to be a written, step-by-step statement of the procedures to be followed, the results expected from each group, and the various responsibilities of each student.

Some teachers neglect to work out effective means of keeping posted on the progress of each work-group. When there are five or six groups working in a class, a teacher needs to know what each group is doing in order to decide where he can be of most help. As he moves from group to group, he needs some speedy method of reminding himself of just what each group is doing at any given time. The work plans of the various committees will usually provide the necessary information. They enable him to provide more help to each group by permitting him to enter its activities more quickly and with greater understanding. The plan of a work-group enables him to determine quickly what progress has been made. By checking the number of steps that have been taken and the number still to be taken and by comparing the status of one group with the status of other groups in the class, he collects the information that enables the planning committee to coordinate the class activities. If he doesn't have this information, he is unable to help the group as a whole to coordinate itself.

Another danger is failure to set up definite lines of responsibility and planning authority. Everybody's business is nobody's business. The direction of group activity will return to the teacher by default unless definite lines of responsibility have been established. A plan that some classes have found helpful is to establish a coordinating committee—sometimes called a planning committee or an executive committee—which meets frequently, perhaps every day, for a few minutes to talk through what is being done and what needs to be done to implement the plan that the total group decided upon before it broke up into work-groups.

Another difficulty that some teachers encounter is how to establish ways for the various groups to share their experiences with one another. The conclusions reached by one work-group may be very valuable to other members of the total class group. If some channel of communication has been established, perhaps through an executive or planning committee, it can serve as a clearing house for the sharing of information among groups. Such a committee can also arrange for the temporary halting of work in the various groups while progress is being shared.

Some teachers have insured the failure of group work by attempting to force the class to work on a project which it does not accept. Pupils will work as a group only on projects that they accept as important.

In group work pupils communicate with each other and express how they feel. They establish ways of combating the teacher if he is forcing them to do something in which they do not believe. They must resist if they are to have any integrity. Group work has a chance of succeeding only if the teacher and the class are working on things which all consider important.

Almost as disastrous is an attempt by the teacher to make the group stick to his preconceived plans. Since group work means bringing pupils in on the planning, the original plans that the teacher worked out cannot possibly remain intact as the work gets under way. And even the plans that the group makes for itself must undergo constant revision in terms of the thinking of everyone who has a part in the project. *Group work involves the sharing of the creative intelligence of all members.* If the pupils accept the work seriously, they will try to make their ideas a part of the plan.

Group work is often facilitated by simple physical arrangements—the way in which the furniture is arranged, for example. When a teacher keeps the chairs arranged so that all the members face in his direction, he decreases the possibilities of real group work. Group work involves communication among members of the group, and the furniture must be arranged so that they can see one another and work together.

Another pitfall pointed out by teachers experienced in group work is the failure to bring pupils into the record-keeping. If a pupil is to know where he stands at a given moment, he must be able to refer to some sort of record of what he has done. This need becomes even greater when pupils are participating in decision-making and planning. If the teacher keeps all the records himself, pupils are asked to plan without sufficient data. Group work demands methods by which both the individual and the group can keep records of progress.

Some teachers fail to help the group feel a sense of achievement. This is closely related to the preceding point. When students are directing their own activities, they need to feel that they are making progress. Otherwise, they will become discouraged and will react negatively to their experience. To prevent this breakdown of morale, the teacher watches for any indication that they have begun to doubt, to falter, or to lose sight of their purposes.

If students are brought into the record keeping, they know where they stand and they can see the progress they are making. If, in addition, the group from time to time analyzes what it has done, where it has gone and what achievement it has made, high morale is maintained.

As people can see that they are achieving, they gain confidence in themselves and become enthusiastic about what they are doing. With his greater insight into what group progress really means, a teacher can often help youngsters see the progress they have made when they cannot see it alone. They do not always recognize the evidence they have. If from time to time the teacher takes a few minutes to think with the group, to state with it the steps that have been successfully completed, the chance that the group work will be successful becomes much greater.

Other teachers fail to discuss with students how fast their progress should be. The students share in the planning of what is to be done, but they have no clear idea of how soon it should be done. The students lose an extra factor of security. If agreement upon deadlines is a part of total group planning, individuals and small work committees within the class will have a responsibility to the total class to complete their work by a certain date.

These mistakes are among those mentioned most frequently by teachers who have had long experience in teaching by the group approach.

SELF-EVALUATION CHECKLIST

Promoting Group Development

Do I:

1. Work in a group, not on it or for it?
2. Share willingly the leadership of the group?
3. Avoid use of "I want you to . . ."?
4. Use "we" and "our" rather than "I" and "mine"?
5. Discuss with the group the way members like to work?
6. Take time at the first meetings to help the group members become acquainted?
7. Get the pupils together in a social occasion early in their working as a group?
8. Propose an organization through which all can participate in planning?
9. Define clearly for the group the areas in which authority can and will be shared?
10. Invite pupils to assist in planning the work of the group and keep the invitation open until they are ready to accept it?

11. Propose a method of work and ask pupils to suggest improvements if they hesitate to participate in planning?
12. Plan several ways of starting work but be willing to change them?
13. Extend, as rapidly as possible, the range of decisions in which pupils participate?
14. Encourage the desire for self-direction as it becomes evident?
15. Praise the group for standing on its own feet and for solving its own problems?
16. Permit the class to experience frustration from time to time and to work out solutions to its problems?
17. Allow the class to make a mistake when the results will not seriously harm anyone?
18. Willingly play a dominating or recessive role as the condition of the group demands?
19. Refer my suggestions, as well as pupil suggestions, to the class for examination and decision?
20. Encourage students to work together on projects?
21. Agree with the group on a plan of work that will serve as a framework to give the pupils and teacher security and guidance?
22. Secure agreement on deadlines for the execution of the various phases of the plan?
23. Consider the plan of work as a contract that both students and teacher are to follow unless agreement to change is reached by the parties involved?
24. Suggest that group organization be flexible and subject to change in light of evaluation?
25. Recommend that individuals and small committees be responsible to the total class?
26. Use a planning committee responsible to the total group as a means of conserving time if the class is large?
27. Have one of the first meetings of the planning committee before the entire class?
28. Recommend that each work-group be represented on the planning committee?
29. Allow as many types of activities in the class as it is possible to supervise?
30. Encourage members to ask for evaluation sessions?
31. Assist the group to devise ways of collecting evidence of its progress?
32. Ask the class what should be done when an issue arises?

33. Stress what is right rather than who is right?
34. Suggest alternate solutions rather than give answers to a problem?
35. Serve as group or individual conscience when necessary in helping group members to live up to agreements?
36. Use departures from group agreements as learning stiuations and as opportunities to test the established policies?
37. Counsel, where possible, instead of punishing, in dealing with undisciplined behavior?
38. Seek agreement on facts, discover causes, and secure the pupil's recommendations if punishment is necessary?
39. Avoid group punishment?

BIBLIOGRAPHY

Promoting Group Development

Alpren, Morton, "Role-Playing: 'Misfires' and Successes," *Clearing House*, 26 (May, 1952), pp. 554–56.

Arnett, Glenn W., and Burton C. Tiffany, "I Liked Camp Because," *National Education Association Journal*, 41 (March, 1952), pp. 148–49.

Association for Supervision and Curriculum Development, *Group Planning in Education*. Washington, D.C.: N.E.A., 1945.

———, *Toward Better Teaching*. Washington, D.C.: N.E.A., 1949.

Bailey, H. H., "In this School there is Good Teaching," *Catholic School Journal*, 53 (October, 1953), pp. 241–42.

Baxter, Bernice, and Rosalind Cassidy, *Group Experiences—The Democratic Way*. New York: Harper and Brothers, 1943.

Benne, Kenneth, "More Learning Takes Place When Teacher and Students Understand the Various Roles in the Classroom," *National Education Association Journal*, 43 (April, 1954), pp. 205–08.

———, Leland P. Bradford, and Ronald Lippitt, *Group Dynamics and Social Action*. Freedom Pamphlet Series. New York: Anti-Defamation League of B'Nai B'rith, 1950.

Berger, Donald, "Planning in the Core Class," *Educational Leadership*, 8 (January, 1951), pp. 208–14.

Bradford, L. P., "The Pupil and the Group," *National Education Association Journal*, 46 (February, 1957), pp. 103–05.

Calhoun, M. L., *et al.*, "Experiment in Student-Centered Histology Teaching," *Journal of Educational Research*, 49 (May, 1956), pp. 709–13.

Coyle, Grace, *Group Experience and Democratic Values*. New York: Woman's Press, 1947.

Crenshaw, V. P., "Creative Participation in Class," *Progressive Education*, 34 (May, 1957), pp. 81–83.

Cunningham, Ruth, and associates, "A Group Creates Its Climate," *Educational Leadership*, 5 (March, 1948), pp. 358–62.

Cunningham, Ruth, et al., *Understanding Group Behavior of Boys and Girls*. New York: Bureau of Publication, Teachers College, Columbia University, 1951.

Daly, R. P., "Pupil-Teacher Planning," *Education Digest*, 21 (December, 1955), pp. 38–9.

DeHuszar, George B., *Practical Applications of Democracy*. New York: Harper & Brothers, 1945.

Educational Policies Commission, *Learning the Ways of Democracy*. Washington, D.C.: N.E.A., 1940.

Evans, Hubert (ed.), "The Problem-Centered Group and Personal Social Problems of Young People," *Teachers College Record*, 51 (April, 1950), pp. 438–59.

Farley, E. S., and Overton Harvey, "Improving Discussion as a Means of Improving Understanding," *The School Review*, 59 (October, 1951), pp. 403–09.

Giles, H. H., *Teacher-Pupil Planning*. New York: Harper and Brothers, 1941.

Gordon, I. J., "Class as a Group: The Teacher as Leader; Some Comments and Questions," *Educational Administration and Supervision*, 27 (February, 1951), pp. 108–18.

Grambs, J. D., "Using Group Work in High School Classes," *California Journal Secondary Education*, 26 (April, 1951), pp. 232–36.

Horace Mann Institute of School Experimentation, *The Teacher's Role in Teacher-Pupil Planning*. New York: Bureau of Publications, Teachers College, Columbia University, 1947.

McCowen, E. J., "Rich Learning Experiences in the Third Grade," *Elementary English*, 30 (October, 1953), pp. 343–51.

Miel, Alice, "A Group Studies Itself to Improve Itself," *Teachers College Record*, 49 (October, 1947), pp. 31–43.

Noar, Gertrude, *Freedom to Live and Learn*. Philadelphia: Franklin Publishing Company, 1948.

Raths, L. E., "Improving Classroom Discussion," *Educational Research Bulletin*, 24 (January, 1945), pp. 6–13, 28.

Rinker, F., "Subject Matter, Students, Teachers, Methods of Teaching and Space are Redeployed in the Newton, Massachusetts High School," *National Association of Secondary School Principals Bulletin*, 42 (January, 1958), pp. 69–80.

Rogers, Carl R., *Client-Centered Therapy*. Boston: Houghton Mifflin Company, 1951.

Schobey, M. M., "Sharing Responsibility in Instruction," *Educational Leadership*, 13 (December, 1955), pp. 157–61.

Sears, E. L., "By What Methods Do Pupils Think They Learn More?" *Ohio Schools*, 30 (December, 1952), p. 418.

Smith, M., and H. E. Benz, "What Effective Classroom Procedures for Training in Democratic Practices," *Bulletin National Association Secondary School Principals,* 39 (April, 1955), pp. 92–5.

Thelen, Herbert A., "Human Dynamics in the Classroom," *Journal of Social Issues,* 6 (1950), pp. 30–55.

Torrance, E. P., "Methods of Conducting Critiques of Group Problem-Solving Performance," *Journal of Applied Psychology,* 37 (1953), pp. 394–98.

Watson, G. B., "Evaluation of Small Group Work in a Large Class," *Journal of Educational Psychology,* 44 (November, 1953), pp. 385–408.

Welch, D. J., "Learning to Be a Part of a Group: The Teacher Helps," *Childhood Education,* 27 (April, 1951), pp. 365–68.

Zimmerman, W. A., "Small-Group Work?" *Clearing House,* 31 (September, 1956), pp. 42–4.

··· Providing for Individual Differences

If the learning environment is good, the difference in achievement among pupils will become greater the longer they remain. The students who learn more rapidly will move further and further ahead of those who learn more slowly.

To insure that the school program promotes the development of the gifted, as well as the less gifted, a teacher utilizes procedures which enable him to know each pupil; to counsel with each pupil; to plan with each pupil; to guide the learning activities of each pupil; and to help each pupil in the evaluation of progress.

UNSATISFACTORY TEACHER

This teacher doesn't bother to learn the names of all the students and doesn't want to know anything about them because this knowledge might prejudice his marking. He assigns the work to be done. The "good ones" do it, and they are given a passing mark. The "bad ones" can't or won't work at the required level and are failed. Everything is fair and objective. All are treated alike. All are given the same assignments. Each student determines his own fate. When students ask if they may study ahead of the class he refuses with the excuse that their added knowledge will make it difficult for the next teacher to work with the total class.

MINIMUM SATISFACTORY TEACHER

Although it is impossible to know all students, this teacher becomes acquainted with as many as time permits. When a pupil begins to experience real difficulty, time is taken to learn as much as possible about him.

All students follow the same course of study and work as a total class during each class period. Although all are given the same assignment, it is possible for a student to secure an adaptation of the task if it is requested and the proposed change seems proper to the teacher. When marks are being determined, pupils are permitted to supply evidence of progress which they think supplements that collected by the teacher in the tests.

8 · *Provision for Individual Differences*

Purposeful activity on the part of students cannot be obtained unless provision is made to accommodate their individual differences. If a teacher assigns the same reading to all the members of his ninth-grade class, he cannot expect the child who is able to read only at the fifth-grade level to find purpose in the work. The ninth-grade book will be almost as meaningless to him as foreign language text would be. And a uniform class reading assignment is as purposeless for the advanced student. To give a ninth-grade book with ninth-grade words and concepts to a student with college-level reading ability is to run the risk of convincing him that life is easy and the task not worth doing. The ninth-grade book is like a foreign language to the poor reader, but it is on a par with Mother Goose for the superior reader.

Failure to take into consideration other important types of individual differences may be equally disastrous. A fifteen-year-old boy who has been building radio sets as a hobby since he was eight will find very little challenge in reading a chapter on the elementary principles of radio, even though the material is included in the physics textbook. A high-school sophomore whose musical background and experience consist largely of participation in folk dancing or "all-night sings" of Sacred Harp music may find a study of *Carmen* meaningless. In one case the class work is a duplication of previous experience, and in the other the new topic is so far removed from knowledge already possessed that the child cannot make the necessary transition.

To insure purposeful pupil activity, it is necessary to use teaching procedures that make possible individualized instruction.

Certain Individual Differences Are Important

When asked how his school cared for individual differences, one principal said, "There is no problem of individual differences in my school—everyone follows the same curriculum. Everyone is treated alike and is subject to the same discipline. If a child does not conform, he is expelled." What that principal did not reveal was that each year his school contributed approximately twenty delinquents to the reform schools of his state. This unmentioned fact becomes all the more striking when it is known that the school is located in one of the best residential districts of the city.

Another example of the way some teachers feel about individual differences is indicated by the remark of a college professor of history. When asked whether he cared for individual differences in his class, he said, "Sure, I care for individual differences. On Friday of each week I give the students five minutes to ask questions concerning information they did not understand." Apparently the only difference he considered important was difference in lack of clarity on points of his lecture.

A high-school English teacher revealed how she was caring for individual differences by the following remark: "Wouldn't it be wonderful if all our classes were as good as the upper 20 per cent of the students we teach?" What she really meant was that she was providing for the type of student found in the upper 20 per cent. Until teachers become conscious of the important differences in their students and feel a responsibility for meeting individual needs, little significant change in teaching procedure will take place.

Individual differences are not equally important; nor do they all demand the attention of the school. For example, a teacher need not be concerned about whether Jack Black has blue eyes or whether Mike Loomis wears a size six shoe. But if Susan Jones is near sighted and can't see the blackboard from the back of the room, or if Earl Neal comes from a family of seven that lives in one room without adequate light or a place to study, acquaintance with these facts should lead to adjustments in the teaching procedure. Those individual differences that increase or decrease purposeful activity are matters of consequence to the teacher.

One of the most important differences that should affect teaching is home background. If one child comes from a broken home and suffers from insecurity, the most important contribution a teacher may be able to make to his life is to give him affection and help him acquire a feeling of belonging. This feeling of belonging will be necessary before efficient school work of the ordinary type can be expected. Another child, from a home where his every wish has been catered to and his slightest illness has been a cause of undue disturbance, may need just the opposite treatment. Pupils may be compared to a doctor's patients. The same medicine and the same bedside manner are not suitable to all. The treatment is varied in terms of the individual and his needs.

Another significant background difference is cultural level of the parents. One child may come from a home where the parents speak perfect English and talk knowingly about new books and plays. The parents of another child in the same class may mix tenses, mispronounce words, and read only wild west and movie magazines. Is the English teacher to treat these pupils alike and expect the same quality of work from both? The effect of differences in home culture is illustrated by the following incident.

> A boy in an education methods class went through the entire semester's work and said only a few words. When asked why he did not make more contributions to class discussion, he said, "My father and mother are Italian-born, naturalized citizens. In my home the only language I ever hear is Italian. When I start to speak in a large group the words do not come as fast as I think."

Economic conditions or social position of families affect the school work of children. A child from a poverty-stricken family may face school with the handicaps of poor nutrition, patched, "hand-me-down" clothes that give him a feeling of inferiority and insecurity, and a crowded, poorly lighted, noisy study environment at home. Or insufficient income may force children to come to school without needed books, pencils, paper, or even glasses and dental care. On the opposite side of the picture, an over-supply of money given to students by financially successful, well-meaning parents may lead to such a round of out-of-school pleasures that time for study will be inadequate. Or a child from a family of the upper social circles may feel so superior that he believes he should be favored by the teacher. One fifth-grade girl from a wealthy family demonstrates the point. She was generous on all except one point. She felt that she should be chairman of every committee on which she served.

Another important individual difference is the personal health of the students. A child suffering from malnutrition will most likely not appreciate *A Midsummer Night's Dream,* give full attention to a physics problem, or play a hard game of basketball. In some classes in certain districts one-fourth to one-half of the students lack energy for good school work because of malnutrition and other energy stealers, such as hookworm, anemia, and malaria. Other students, stimulated by an overactive thyroid, may find it difficult to remain as quiet as they are expected to in the classroom.

Closely allied to these factors are the handicaps suffered by school children as a result of physical defects. Estimates of the prevalence of serious deafness among school children are usually above 6 per cent. Defective vision seriously curtails achievement in schools which depend too much on learning by reading. Speech disorders such as stuttering, cleft palate, and thick tongue produce reticence or need for compensation in a certain percentage of the school population. And defects of bone structure affect participation in physical education classes.

In an ideal situation, all schools would provide health examinations for every child, and the pertinent reports would accompany the other records. Unfortunately, however, this practice is far from universal. Many school systems fail to give even vision and hearing tests. So if a teacher works in a school system where health records are unavailable, he must be on the alert for certain danger signals. Malnutrition shows itself in listlessness, pallor, and thinness. Signs of poor vision are squinting, frequent headaches, holding the reading material too close or too far away, skipping words when reading aloud, confusing common two- or three-letter words, such as "in" and "an," and complaining of difficulty in seeing the blackboard. Poor hearing is suggested by speaking too loudly, omitting syllables in new words, lip reading, constant asking for repetition of statements or questions, seeming inattentiveness, inability to follow group discussion, and unusual spelling errors. None of these signals mentioned is a sure indication of an eye or ear defect, but any one may serve as a basis for recommendations that certain pupils have their ears or eyes examined.

It would seem that any teacher would notice such obvious evidences of maladjustments, but not all teachers do.

> A girl from the county schools enrolled in an Alabama demonstration school. At the end of two weeks, all her teachers were concerned about her failing work. Most of the teachers felt the transition from a rural to an urban school had proved too great an effort. One day the mathematics teacher observed the girl, who was tall and slender, bent over her desk with her eyes only six inches above the paper on which she was working. Inquiry revealed that no record of poor eyesight had accompanied the girl's transcript of credit. When the mathematics teacher asked the student if she had ever had an eye examination, the girl, quite surprised at the interest shown in her, answered in the negative. Acting upon the advice of the teacher, the

girl had her eyes examined that afternoon. Next day she came to school with glasses, and from that time did successful school work. As if to make the lesson clearer, the very first day she wore glasses the child raised her hand near the end of the English period and asked permission to read an original poem she had written.

And this was the girl the teachers had expected to fail!

Emotional handicaps may also jeopardize a child's educational achievements. A timid child may be so afraid of the teacher or of participation in a large group that he refrains from contributing to class activities even though he possesses the necessary skill or information. A nervous child may find a long period of unbroken desk work unbearable. Thoughtless comments by the teacher or classmates may blight an entire day for a sensitive individual. Emotional instability resulting from a broken home or a recent tragedy will decrease intellectual efficiency, sometimes to the point of failure. Emotional disturbances may be manifest in other ways.

> An eight-year-old who had been a well-behaved, well-controlled youngster during most of the school year was unable to remain seated on a May morning. He would get up and go out of the room from time to time. When he remained in his seat he felt nauseated and did not take part in the activities of the class. When the teacher investigated the cause of his behavior, she found that his mother was being operated on that morning. His behavior was caused by his concern over the outcome of the operation.

When a teacher does not give students a chance to explain behavior, when he does not recognize that behavior is caused, when he does not accept youngsters as living up to the best that they know, he takes the kind of action that alienates youngsters and decreases his chances of ever being able to know them or to help them grow.

Another area in which important differences occur is native ability. Some children have much talent in music or art; others do not. Some children can run fast; others are poorly coordinated.

Differences in intellectual prowess represent the type of variation to which the school has devoted most attention. Although psychologists are no longer positive that individual intellectual ability does not change, and at least one study has shown that "intelligence tests" discriminate against children of lower socio-economic groups, still there is general agreement that potentialities differ from individual to individual.

Unfortunately, some teachers have placed too much faith in "intelligence tests," even to the extent of allowing the scores to influence their marking. At the present time those most familiar with such tests feel that their most important function is to aid the teacher to plan more intelligently the work expected of each pupil.

Care must be exercised in handling information concerning intellectual differences. Intelligence is an individual difference about which people are most sensitive. A teacher may tell a child that he cannot run as fast or write as well as other children in the class and he will not become angry. But if told that his intelligence is low, he may become discouraged and offended.

Differences in background information are also important. Some children, through travel, conversation with parents, hobbies, or out-of-school work, have built up vast stores of information. To expect them to go through elementary steps provided for children totally without background is to waste valuable time and to court discipline problems produced by sheer boredom. Other children, because of interrupted school attendance, find themselves without basic information. Their shortcoming cannot be ignored either.

The variety of past experiences produces diverse interests and ambitions in a group. A seventh-grade class was asked to tell what vocations they wished to follow. The list included aviator, fire chief, bareback rider, baseball player, minister, biochemist, nurse, beauty operator, and novelist. Imagine the difference in material that would appeal to the individual members of that class. And this class is not extraordinary!

Still another type of difference that is important in all fields is the variation in study procedures. Some children learn good study skills at home while others must be taught in school to use each tool and technique. One of the most essential study skills is reading. In an average class the reading ability extends for four grade levels on each side of the grade. For example, a ninth-grade class will include fifth-grade and college-freshman reading ability.

Children vary also in their desire for status leadership, even children within the same family. Two boys, a second-grade pupil and a fourth-grade pupil, illustrate the point:

> The seven-year-old boy came home from school saying he had been chosen to act the part of a "tree" in a class play. The following conversation ensued.
>
> "I get to be a tree and hold some leaves!"
> "Does the tree have the most to do?"
> "No."

"Do you like being a tree?"
"Yes."
"What part has the most to do and say?"
"The cricket."
"Why don't you try to be the cricket?"
"I'd rather be a tree."
"I wouldn't. I'd want to be the cricket."

The task of teaching participation and leadership and guiding these two youngsters in group participation presents two separate problems to the teacher.

From the foregoing description of the individual differences important in the classroom, it is evident that the same method of teaching will not reach all the children in any one class. Each child is an individual personality, and ideally each should receive individual treatment. However, since group teaching is an economic necessity and an educational asset, we are faced with the need for developing procedure that will allow us to care for important individual differences within a group. Effective teaching calls for developing a satisfactory method of caring for individual differences by helping the student to become aware of himself, his abilities, his strengths, his weaknesses, his needs, and his goals, and by working out a way of carrying on individual projects in a group situation.

Evidence of Concern for Individuals

No one plan will care for all individual needs, but a teacher can increase his effectiveness by recognizing that no two pupils are alike or have the same curriculum, that any attempt to have all students make the same growth in his class is doomed to failure, and that subject matter is primarily a tool to help pupils grow. If he understands that different types of growth will result for different youngsters from the same lesson, he ceases to regard his subject matter field as something to be mastered by all. Rather, he considers it an area in which he is competent to help pupils have experiences that will promote their growth in the ways that are important to them. This concept is basic to meeting individual needs.

If a teacher believes it is his function to provide for individual needs it is manifest in many small ways. He seats pupils according to the size of seats or according to their preferences, not in alphabetical order. Left-handed youngsters are provided with a work place in which they can write in a normal position. Nearsighted pupils are invited to sit near the center of activities, and farsighted ones farther away. Hard-of-hearing pupils are allowed to choose the spot in which they can hear best. The way he provides for physical differences and organizes the furniture in the room to promote work by small groups and individuals is an indication of whether or not he is really concerned about individuals.

The use he makes of individual conferences also indicates the extent to which he is attempting to care for individual differences. Does he hold conferences to guide special study, to outline work missed, to explain basic principles which the pupil does not understand, and to assist with reading difficulties? Does he use individual conferences to teach study skills, to help pupils discover the cause of difficulties, to guide the more advanced students and stimulate them to do more challenging work, and to help with personal problems?

A teacher who does not do these things usually protests that he cannot find the time with the load he has. But if he is really concerned, he can find opportunities to talk with individuals during study periods, free reading periods, a few minutes after school, during his planning period, or while the class is working in small groups or doing research in the library. During the preparation of reports, or while students are writing the results of their study, he can sit down with various individuals and talk with them about what they are doing and how they can do it more effectively. If he has established rapport, any spare moment is an occasion when he can talk with pupils about their purposes, plans, and progress.

Planning sessions can be opportunities for meeting individual differences if a teacher makes it possible for each pupil to make his wishes and preferences known. When the class suggests the things it believes it should do next, he has an opportunity to raise questions, both with the total group and with individuals, which causes individuals to explore the value of their present purposes and the efficiency of their work plans.

Accepting different types of growth and different means of expression is also a way of encouraging individual growth. By arbitrarily restricting the type of performance that will be considered successful in his classes, a teacher limits the extent to which he can individualize instruction. But by offering youngsters the opportunity to express their ideas in various ways, he encourages individual growth and the development of special talents. For example, after a trip to a canning factory, one youngster may write about it in prose; another may write a poem; a third may paint a picture; a fourth may sing a song that expresses the way he feels about the experience; a fifth may compose a dance; a sixth may write a play; a seventh may make a model of the canning plant. All are legitimate expressions of an individual's reaction to an experience. All provide an interpretation of that experience which gives the teacher cues concerning the type of help he can give the individual.

The general objectives for the class may be supplemented by individual objectives established for each pupil. For example, in teaching American history, a teacher may seek to have the entire class gain an understanding of present social problems, but he may also attempt to improve the reading of Mary Adams, who reads at the ninth-grade level. If he has sufficient information about each pupil, he is able to guide each child in some type of self-improvement in addition to the regular class work.

A teacher meets individual differences by varying the amount of work undertaken. He could never hope to have pupils accept willingly greater amounts of homework simply by assigning it to them, but if he creates within his class the type of situation in which the students may select different tasks in terms of special abilities, and plan together what is to be done and how it will be done, different programs of work emerge. Individual differences can be met through group planning.

Group work accommodates another type of individual difference. It gives pupil leadership and initiative a greater opportunity to function.

To conduct a class in a way that cares for individual differences requires a variety of materials. For instance, one text is not enough. Since the range of reading abilities within an average class is great, it is obvious that one text, suited to only one grade, is too difficult for some pupils and too easy for others. Textbooks for several different grade levels, and supplementary reading materials that include related fiction, autobiographies, references, pamphlet and magazine articles, visual and auditory aids, and illustrative materials are all necessary. The richness of the collection of materials is one of the best measures of the extent to which a teacher is trying to care for individual differences.

Provision for a variety of activities and work areas in the class is another way of caring for individual differences. If an elementary teacher wants to provide the kind of learning situation in which a wide range of abilities and potentialities can be served, he needs to provide for reading, for art, for crafts, and for dramatics within the classroom.

A wholesome emotional climate, which has been mentioned before, is a way of meeting certain individual differences. Although some children are able to succeed in an emotionally tense classroom, others require more careful treatment. If tension is decreased in the classroom, nervous or emotionally unstable children will find themselves able to work more efficiently. The old rule, "Treat all children alike," is a dangerous one. Creating different emotional relationships between pupil and teacher is just as much a part of caring for individual differences as providing different materials. The process of helping pupils to become concerned about each other, and to begin to plan together how each can assist the other, described fully in another chapter, is a part of individualizing instruction.

The way a teacher uses drill will reveal whether or not he is concerned with individual differences. Not all learning can be a totally creative experience. In certain types of learning it is necessary to reemphasize the patterns already discovered. The spelling of a difficult word or the fingering in typing may be examples. If the teacher insists that all students practice the same pattern at the same time, he is not organizing his class to meet individual needs. Students learn at different rates and have attained different levels of achievement. The teacher who is providing for individual differences will have each pupil drill on the procedures and patterns which have been identified as his individual weakness.

If a teacher wants to work individually with students, he has them help him by keeping many of the records themselves. He will not be able to record all the types of learning that take place. He will not be able to build up an adequate fund of evidence concerning pupil growth by himself. The only person who is in a position to make a fairly complete record of his work is the individual student himself.

If a teacher must give marks, he tries not to stress the comparisons they imply. When he begins to compare one student with another, the discrepancies in abilities and purposes become so apparent that the students with least purpose and intelligence fall into the background and become discouraged. It is far more effective to talk with students about their progress on an individual basis than on the basis of class standings. In marking, it is advisable, also, to use more than one index in determining any mark. Some students speak well, others are more fluent with the written word, and still others express themselves best through pictures. To consider only one type of expression handicaps certain students. A particularly vicious practice is the custom of basing marks on final examinations. In addition to being a direct invitation to cheating, the mark based on a final written examination imposes an unfair handicap on the emotional child or the child who speaks better than he writes. Any marks assigned should be based on many records of behavior which sample a variety of activities and skills.

Types of Individuals

Even though a teacher follows the procedures suggested in this section, certain children in a class will continue to be problems to the other group members and the teacher. Some will not succeed as well as the others. A few will seem to lack any interest in the work. Others will disturb the group by being overly aggressive. And a small percentage will withdraw from group activity.

Each child is unique. Each case is different. But there are certain steps we can take that will be helpful in meeting each type of problem.

The Underachieving Pupil

Some children do not learn what the teacher hopes they will learn in his classes. He may be tempted to call them "nonlearners" or other derogatory names, but name-calling does not help them or relieve his sense of failure.

As long as a pupil continues as a member of a class, the teacher cannot afford simply to classify him and stop trying to help him.

The most important step is to discover the cause of the pupil's failure to make the growth it was hoped he would attain. Through study of school records, conferences with the pupil, home visits, and discussions with other staff members, the teacher should check the following points:

Is poor health responsible for his failure? When a student is not in top form physically, he will not acquire information as fast as he would otherwise. His attention is focused upon his physical disturbances. Or if he lacks sufficient food, his hunger may serve as a barrier to his acquiring the information and skills expected.

Are unmet emotional needs responsible for his failure? A child wants to belong, to be loved, and to have security. When neither the school nor the home nor the community provides these satisfactions, the child is so concerned about the lack that he is unable to make the progress that is expected of him.

Is a conflict in values responsible? When a student finds that his parents' beliefs conflict with those of his teacher, he may become confused. He doesn't know which to accept, and in his confusion he fails to take the steps that the teacher hopes he will. Value conflicts may also arise between the pupil and the teacher. They belong to different age groups and have different purposes. In such a situation, any attempt to override the pupil will probably result in open rebellion or withdrawal. In an attempt to meet the situation, the pupil refuses to learn what is required.

Another source of value conflict may develop between the pupil and other members of the group. When a youngster comes from a home with strong beliefs concerning certain types of behavior which are in conflict with the beliefs held by the other boys and girls in the class, he is caught between the desire to be accepted by the group and his allegiance to the values he has learned at home. Out of this disturbance may come interference with the learning the teacher desires.

Is it an intense worry? When a child worries about his hatreds, or whether or not he is like other people, or about the relationships in his family, he may not do well in his school work. If there is a divorce pending between his parents, or if his father is in jail, or if there is a drastic conflict between the boy and his stepfather, the focus of his attention is on other than school subjects.

Is it overload? When different teachers confront a youngster with unreasonable demands that call for more time than he can give to school work, he does all his work in a sloppy, haphazard manner. Or he may simply say, "What's the use," and quit altogether. Or the overload may be physical. The student may come to class so weary from outside activities or a job that he cannot give the school work his attention. His learning efficiency will necessarily be reduced.

Is it lack of background information or skill? Inadequate instruction in a previous class may have made his foundation in the subject being investigated so weak that he has great difficulty in understanding the concepts and words used.

Is it poor study conditions at home? Some youngsters come from homes in which there are no books, no newspapers, not even a radio. Such pupils suffer unjust handicaps when they are required to carry out the class work.

Is it the social-class structure? When parents find themselves relegated to unsatisfactory economic and social strata, their attitude of frustration is transferred in some degree to their children, who bring this attitude to school. If a pupil shares his parents' lack of hope, his motivation is decreased and his learning in school is less efficient. If the student from a less-favored home is sensitive to discrimination on the part of the other students, and feels that his teacher favors certain youngsters and rejects the group to which he belongs, this feeling of rejection will reduce the amount of desirable learning that he derives from a given experience.

Is it unreasonable standards? The imposition of unreasonable standards on boys and girls blocks their attempts to learn. When people are continuously unsuccessful, they lose their motivation. They may still want to succeed, but they feel that success is impossible in the situation. Eventually, they stop trying.

Is it overprotection? Some children have been so protected by their parents that they hesitate to go beyond the familiar. They want to check with the teacher on each step. They want someone to whom they can turn. Since they have been cautioned time and again to do only what they are told to do, they are incapable of getting the greatest benefit from new experiences.

Any one of these factors may cause a child to be less successful than he could otherwise be. Each of these difficulties requires different treatment, but they all require that the teacher know each child, plan with his parents, and adjust the requirements and the way of working to his individual problems. It does no good to assert that all pupils will be treated alike, or to threaten a child with dire consequences if he does not change his behavior, or to tell him that he must adjust to the school. The teacher's task is to help each pupil to live up to his potential, and it can be done only by adapting the program to his needs through joint planning with pupil and parent.

The "Less-Developed" Child

The term "less-developed" is used deliberately here. It refers to a physically normal child who for the time being appears to be retarded. The variation in rate of growth sometimes causes difficulties for the child who develops slowly. He may be smaller, slower in acquiring his second teeth, later in entering adolescence. He appears to be retarded when in reality he is following his normal pattern of development.

> Two famous tennis stars, both twenty-two years old, illustrate the point. One was six feet six, a potential national champion, and the other was six feet three, a former national champion. The six-foot-three youth said, "You would never guess it, but when we were fourteen, I was six inches taller than he was." The ex-champion at twenty-two had matured faster in size and coordination, but his friend had become a taller person.

Growth patterns vary. Some children mature earlier than others. In any group some children who are markedly less developed than others may be smaller and less coordinated. They may not write, or run, or dance as well as others. They may not be as interested in the opposite sex. Any of these conditions may handicap them in their social dealings with other members of the group.

This problem is particularly acute at the junior-high-school level, when children are entering adolescence. Some students grow rapidly in early adolescence, while others develop later. In junior-high-school classes, youngsters of the same age may vary as much as six or eight inches in height and exhibit vast differences in body contour and in weight and muscular development. The problem is accentuated by the fact that some of the youngsters who find themselves less developed than the rest of their fellows at this age have, prior to this time, been physical peers in their group. They have not learned any of the techniques of meeting the problem involved in being smaller than their fellows.

Establishing good human relations in the class is the first step in helping the less-developed child. If a teacher can get the group to accept the idea that each member has a contribution to make, that each has a responsibility for helping the others grow, he creates an atmosphere in the class where differences in size, skill, or ability do not prevent acceptance and harmonious relations.

A second step to take is to encourage each youngster to make his own special contribution to the group. Discourage the underdeveloped child from competing with his classmates in areas in which he is always sure to lose. To make this approach requires opportunity for varied activities which permit youngsters with different types of skills to make their own special contributions. As competitiveness within the group is reduced, differences in physical development become of less concern to youngsters.

The Uninterested Child

Some children appear to be uninterested. They sit in the classroom and say little. They watch what is going on, but as far as can be seen they show very little reaction to it. When they are asked to offer suggestions they make no reply. They take up seat space, and that is about all, it seems, that they are contributing to the classroom situation.

Sometimes, as these youngsters are followed into the community, it is found that they display the same lackadaisical attitudes in their relationships with other boys and girls in out-of-school activities. If they are on the playground, they have to be forced to take part in activities. What can be done for an uninterested child?

Any hope of helping him is based on two beliefs: One is that all children want to take part in what is going on around them. The other is that his seeming lack of interest in out-of-school or in-school activities may have come about as a result of so many failures that he has lost any hope of success. Making these two basic assumptions is the starting point in helping the uninterested child.

One of the first steps is to put the child at ease. If he has failed so many times that he has lost confidence in himself, the task of anyone interested in his progress is to convince him that other people are anxious to help him and want to see him succeed. Much of the responsibility for developing this type of atmosphere in the classroom rests with the teacher. If he can demonstrate these qualities in his relationship with the pupil and not evidence his discouragement or dissatisfaction, the pupil may gradually build the willingness to venture. If stress is placed upon profiting from mistakes as well as from successful achievement, additional encouragement is provided. When uninterested boys and girls begin to feel that they are accepted and that they can learn from mistakes as well as from successes, they will gradually move out of their self-imposed isolation and become active in the group.

These first steps may take a long time.

> In a class in California, boys and girls were grouped together who had been unsuccessful for the first ten years of their school career. The teacher, who adopted the procedure just outlined, worked four months before any of the group began to respond. The youngsters had developed such a distrust of teachers and such a lack of faith in teacher sincerity that they refused to let down their defenses, even though the teacher tried to give them every sort of assurance—verbal and otherwise. It took four months before they accepted the truth of this teacher's statements and actions sufficiently to display an interest in class activities.

Once the uninterested student has advanced to the stage where action becomes possible, the teacher's function is to encourage him to decide for himself what activities will be most rewarding for him. He faces an uphill battle to gain self-confidence, and it is necessary for him to take his first steps in an area in which he feels most confident of success. The teacher can't determine this area. Nor can other students. The impetus must emerge from the desire of the uninterested youngster himself and his belief in his own potential. Under no circumstances should the teacher ask him to undertake tasks beyond his ability.

The third step is to let him participate in the evaluation of what happened as he took the action. This evaluation may be no more than saying, "It was fun," or "This is something I learned." Or he may simply remain silent, with perhaps an implication that he will try again at another point. In any case, refrain from exhibiting any negative reaction, or from pretending that his performance was good if it really wasn't. Encouragement is a much more satisfactory type of teaching activity than giving false statements concerning the success of an action. Wait and stress success when it is observed, no matter how small it may be.

As soon as the student has advanced far enough to derive satisfaction from sharing in class projects, other members of the class should be encouraged to welcome him into the group.

At no point during this process of working with an uninterested child does the teacher attempt to stimulate him in the ordinary sense. He has received stimulation all the years he has been in school. He has been threatened. He has been pleaded with. He has been encouraged. He has been chastised. He has borne the brunt of many attempts to motivate him and to interest him in various topics. And to all of them he has failed to respond. These efforts have succeeded only in driving him further within himself. The only hope is to create an environment in which he feels free to let himself grow, in which he is not afraid to try.

The environment should also provide assistance to the youngster in becoming a more social person. Most uninterested youngsters have failed to achieve social success in their relationships with their fellows. As a teacher works with the class in improving social skills and in sharing these skills with one another, he creates an environment in which the rebuffed child, the shy child—the uninterested child—can gain the confidence that will permit him to move out toward the frontiers that have formerly threatened him.

The "Aggressive" Child

It is no trouble to spot the aggressive child. It can't be avoided—he makes himself known to the teacher and to the group. He strikes other children. He makes sarcastic remarks, he attempts to exclude other youngsters from certain situations. The teacher is afraid he will hurt another child, is concerned about his monopolizing teacher time and energy, resents his attacks on the more submissive pupils. It would be easy to feel justified in punishing him and preventing him from injuring the feelings and the physical well-being of others.

The studies of Dollard and others, however, reveal that aggression is the result of frustration. With this understanding, the aggressive child is viewed in a new light. He is unable to achieve satisfaction by approved methods of behavior. He is seeking ways of building his ego and gaining the type of satisfaction that is necessary to his own well-being. The teacher finds himself confronted with the problem of how to deal with this need for ego satisfaction and how to work with the aggressive one in such a way that he can attain it without injuring those about him. A way must be found of treating him that will enable the teacher to continue to exist as a balanced person with wholesome relationships with other youngsters. Teachers are not superhuman, and they resent, as do the other members of the group, the actions of the aggressive child. By accepting this fact, it is easy to see that the problem of teaching the overaggressive child is as much a problem of dealing with teacher sensibilities as it is of dealing with the child himself.

The big problem with the overaggressive child is to help him discover that he can gain satisfaction from situations in which other people are enjoying themselves too. The emphasis is on helping him understand that the only way to true satisfaction is when other people around him are enjoying themselves and gaining satisfactions from the situation. This is not an easy concept for anyone to acquire, and is far more difficult for a child than it is for an adult.

One of the first steps is to let the child know that he is loved. No one is selfish in a situation in which there is plenty of everything. Persons are selfish about the love of others when love is not abundant enough to go around. Children are selfish about their toys and begin to demand other people's toys when there are not enough for everyone. One of the first steps is to let the child know in many little ways —through glances, through a touch of the hand, through private conversations, and by doing things together—that he is loved and accepted.

As soon as the child is sure of affection, the teacher can gently but firmly insist that he engage in no action that is detrimental to other children. Simply diverting his attention is not enough. It may be necessary to take him by the arm and lead him aside to talk with him. The teacher has a responsibility to the aggressive child and to the other members of the group to say, "This is a type of behavior that, even though we love you, cannot be accepted in this group. It is harmful to the other members of the group."

The overaggressive child is helped by participation in the process through which the total group sets up standards of behavior. As the group members discuss satisfactory ways of behaving and agree upon certain criteria by which to judge behavior, the decisions reached are impersonal. But at the same time he is afforded an opportunity to learn the types of behavior that are socially acceptable. Youngsters can be taught far more effectively through group action and opinion than they can through an expression of like or dislike by an adult.

Aggressiveness decreases as there is opportunity for group work. Any situation that gives the aggressive boy or girl a chance to work with others is a learning situation in social relationships. His skill in living with others will be increased if he has a chance to analyze his experiences with a teacher who is sensitive to his problems and who helps him devise more effective social techniques at his request. Both factors are important—*opportunity to work in a group and assistance in analyzing his behavior.* If the group experience is not followed by analysis, the student may continue to make the same mistakes that he has always made and continue to grow more and more aggressive.

This process of guiding the aggressive student in his integration into the group is not easy. If a teacher conducts group work in a free atmosphere, the aggressiveness will probably grow worse before it gets better. The child will not believe what he finds and will test it out with even more violent behavior. Understanding, quietness, firmness, love, patience, and time are the only answers. Attempts to suppress him simply increase or divert his aggressiveness.

Another way of working with the aggressive child is to develop with him ways to utilize his aggressiveness. Some teachers make definite provision for boys and girls to work with clay or metal so that they will have an opportunity to pound and hit, thus working out their aggressiveness in a socially acceptable way. If the school has a good intramural sports program, all students have an opportunity to use their competitiveness to help the group achieve standing in the school. The aggressive child who can help his homeroom team win a school championship or bring the team through to victory in a crucial situation realizes that there are ways in which he can use his aggressiveness for the benefit of the group in which he is working. Another outlet is opened through working on the construction of stage and room properties. When a child has a chance to hammer and nail and wrestle with pieces of equipment that are large and cumbersome, he works off some of his desire for physical aggression.

In dealing with the aggressive child, it is well to talk over his difficulties with him. Physical punishment simply multiplies the symptoms that he already feels. When he is punished physically, he feels even more that he is inadequate and that he has to fight back. But if he has an opportunity to discuss his problems with a sympathetic, understanding teacher, he gains a different impression of the way other people feel about him. He begins to learn that he has someone to whom he can turn for understanding and that he need not resort to the use of his fists in order to solve his problems. As a check on the classroom environment, the teacher should review his own behavior to see if the child's actions are reflecting the teacher's behavior. Do his harsh commands to other children echo the type of directions he has heard given to youngsters who are not behaving? Does his hitting of other youngsters duplicate the teacher's use of physical contact with youngsters to get them to do what is desired? A teacher who hopes to help youngsters overcome aggressiveness must be sure that his own behavior is not aggressive.

It will be necessary to talk with the child's parents to find out what conditions at home may be responsible for his behavior. Is there a great deal of emotional disturbance in this home? Does he see his parents bickering constantly? Does he feel that he is not loved and wanted? Any of these factors could lead to strongly aggressive behavior at school. Or do the parents overemphasize the importance of getting ahead and make him unreasonably anxious to excel? Do they insist that the child always be the leader, the champion, the contest-winner? This type of parental pressure can make a child determined to seize the advantage in every situation. What are the manners in the home? Is the child encouraged to fight for his rights and get what is coming to him regardless of the consequences to others? Are the parents and the other children in the home well mannered toward one another? Perhaps what has been aggressiveness in the child is simply ignorance of what type of behavior is acceptable.

In any case, it is necessary to determine the cause of a child's behavior before deciding on the most helpful and beneficial way of working with him. Discover what the child's needs are—love, attention, a feeling of greater adequacy—and then satisfy those needs as effectively as possible in the class situation. How much can be done will depend upon how successfully an atmosphere of cooperation is created in the classroom, how much time is given to work with him and the extent of physical endurance and emotional stability of the teacher.

The "Withdrawing" Child

Withdrawal, like aggression, is an attempt to meet a situation for which the child has not found a satisfactory solution.

First, it is necessary to determine the causes of withdrawal. It will help to talk with the parents and with teachers who have had the child before to see what has been done to help him overcome his tendency to withdraw.

With the withdrawing child, however, there may be a greater reason for giving the child an opportunity to work with the teacher. Make it easier for him to succeed and increase his self-confidence. Avoid trying to force him to become an active participant in the group. When force is applied to the withdrawing child, he withdraws even further. Provide an atmosphere in which the child can relax and work amid encouragement, respect, and advice when it is asked for. Encourage the child's friendship with one or two other pupils in the group who can be of help to him. If he can be helped to form a friendship with even one other child, he will gain tremendously in confidence and security. All of these steps are ones the teacher can take.

Work in small groups is also an effective way to help withdrawing children gain confidence. Many children who are afraid in large groups find themselves drawn into a discussion in small groups by the enthusiasm of the other members. In a large group of twenty-five or more, the participation of all the members is not continuous. Five or six pupils may talk more than the others and some may not speak at all for as long as twenty or thirty minutes. But in a small group of three to six, everyone participates frequently in the conversation and even the withdrawing child gradually begins to participate more easily.

The teacher will want to observe the withdrawing child closely to identify special contributions that he can make and special skills that he possesses. Once certain unique abilities that will be of value to the group have been spotted, situations in which his contributions will be recognized by his fellow students should be used. When a promising situation arises, turn to the withdrawing child and ask if he would like to make a contribution. But never say, "This is the time for you to do the things that you can do so well." Instead, simply provide an opportunity that he can accept or decline as he wishes. Even though the child does not respond on the first five or six occasions, continue to present similar opportunities. Gradually, he will begin to open up and will finally take the first feeble steps in the direction of active participation in the class.

The "Gifted" Child

Gifted children constitute a precious resource of a society. They represent the chance for advancement, the opportunity for improvement. Although most could educate themselves well enough to succeed, the problem for the teacher is to discover ways to challenge them to more nearly fulfilling their potential.

If no provision is made for individual differences in the teaching procedure, giftedness is penalized. It is no challenge for the gifted child to compete with the average. When the same assignment is given to all, the gifted lose interest, seek devious means of occupying themselves during school, or become openly rebellious. Whatever the behavior chosen, the result is the failure of the gifted to make the growth desired.

The teacher's first concern in working with a gifted youngster is to avoid the procedures that will retard his progress. Lockstep assignments, total group activities for all of the period or school day, marking based entirely upon position in class, use of learning materials of only one level of difficulty—all will interfere with the gifted pupil's progress.

If individuals within a class may follow different plans of work, the major problem of providing a good learning environment for the gifted will be solved. If, as a class undertakes a project, group planning results in individuals or groups working on special phases of it, the gifted pupil can find activities that challenge him. His participation in the small group or committee will provide opportunity for leadership. His work on a special phase of the problem will enable him to avoid what he has already examined and investigate areas of learning that are new to him. As the teacher plans with him, individual goals, plans, assignments, deadlines and methods of keeping a record of progress can be established. Elaboration of the techniques of accomplishing these results are presented in the next chapter.

The teacher will want also to utilize resources outside of the classroom in providing the learning environment for the gifted child. A portion of the day may be designated for individual study. It may be used to work with other pupils who have similar purposes and ability, or it may be used to do research or secure special experiences with other teachers who have greater competencies in the area of the gifted child's concern.

If a part of the problem of providing for the gifted is his emotional disturbance or his feeling of rejection by his age peers, the chapters dealing with human relations should be applicable. Gifted pupils have the same emotional problems and secure the same satisfaction and growth from being accepted and valued by a supporting group.

To provide for all the gifted, it is important that the teacher examine his concept of giftedness. If it is narrow and limited to quickness in problem-solving or manipulation of abstract symbols, much of the giftedness in creative expression and human interaction may be allowed to wither in his class.

Conclusion

Meeting individual differences is not a technique; it is a way of living. It includes accepting others, respecting their contributions, working for the kind of group operation in which each individual knows he has a part, and encouraging each pupil to give his best in each situation.

9 · *Instruction for the Individual*

A teacher's success in meeting individual differences is conditioned by his approach to teaching. It is not a technique or a trick that can be applied when a pupil who is markedly different from the others in his class is discovered. It involves getting to know each pupil, helping him discover his strengths, weaknesses, purposes, and values, planning with him what he should study, and helping him organize and evaluate his learning.

Procedures for Learning to Know Pupils

To be of real assistance to the individual, it is necessary to get to know him as a person. Learn his name. Become familiar with his family and his background. Study his school record. Talk with him about his interests and concerns, and how he feels about people and school.

Start at the very beginning of school. Techniques recommended for promoting good relations on the first day help the teacher to become acquainted with his pupils. Have them introduce themselves and tell about their summer vacations, hobbies, books, movies, or sports. As pupils learn one another's names, faces, and interests, the teacher does too.

An examination of the cumulative record of each pupil may provide valuable information. Such records usually give the test scores that the pupil has made on the various standardized tests used within the school system. They reveal the level of achievement of the pupil at the time the tests were given. By comparing the intelligence test scores and the achievement test scores in various areas, the teacher can get some idea of the extent to which a student is living up to the development that might be expected of him. When an eighth-grade pupil with an IQ of 100 is reading at the sixth-grade level and has arithmetic skills at the fourth-grade level, it is evident that study of the child to determine why he is not living up to the achievement that might reasonably be expected should be undertaken. Test scores do not tell what is wrong. Rather, they are indications that the pupil may need help.

From the record, it is possible to discover the father's occupation, the approximate family income (which can be estimated from the type of work and location of home), other members of the family, and the pupil's personality and social poise as indicated by his behavior record and participation in activities. If the record includes a case history, even more information can be gained.

But if the school does not maintain pupil records, a teacher is forced to move more slowly and to rely upon the use of indirect questionnaires, playground and classroom observations, and informal conversations.

A pupil's creative products are to some degree indicative of the type of person he is. The pictures that he paints, for example, reveal how he feels about certain things and some of the ideas and symbols that are important to him. Interests and needs are easier to determine at the elementary school level than at the secondary school level, because the younger children are more direct and a single teacher spends a greater portion of time with the same children.

> A first-grade boy spent all his free art periods drawing pictures of horses and cowboys. His scenes ranged from prairie to mountains, but they always included horses and cowboys firing at one another. Obviously, the boy's interests were centered on cowboys and the Old West. But equally important was the indication that he was not of a passive nature. All his pictures revealed action and, in most cases, conflict. His art work suggested that one way to relate class work to the boy's motivation would be through references to the West and, secondly, that he would be striving for leadership and authority within the group in which he worked and lived. Such data, like test scores, provide a teacher with clues, but they cannot be interpreted intelligently without supplementary information.

The stories that a youngster writes record his interests, his fundamental skills, his creativeness in the expression of ideas, his awareness of color, and his observation of the inanimate objects of the environment. They suggest the features of his environment to which he responds most strongly. Since all persons respond to any situation in terms of their background, much information can be gained about the values, the goals, and the past experiences of youngsters through their creative interpretations of their experiences.

Youngsters provide many significant clues to their personalities as they talk informally with one another about their hobbies and their reactions to world and community events. By listening to what they say in such sharing periods, much can be learned about their ambitions, fears, and interests. *If a teacher wants to teach boys and girls in terms of their individual capacities, interests, and needs, he must be willing to listen to them.* Many effective teachers have found it helpful to keep for each pupil a 3 x 5 card on which revealing comments are recorded verbatim.

Another technique for adding to the store of pertinent information about youngsters is to observe them closely as they engage in exploratory activities. A free period a day in which pupils may work on projects they choose, or a free reading period in the library in which they are free to select the stories or books that interest them will lead to increased understanding of interests and needs. *A pupil constantly reveals himself through the free choices he makes.* It is almost impossible to learn anything but superficial facts about pupils if the teacher insists on having them perform a program of activities arbitrarily decided upon by him. Unless freedom to use the classroom facilities in their own way for a portion of the school day is provided, a teacher limits his opportunities to observe and know pupils.

Home visits, where possible, are also helpful.

> An Oklahoma teacher was teaching two sections of ninth-grade English. By the end of three months, one group was so far ahead of the other that she became concerned enough to investigate the causes. At the beginning of the year, she had tried to arrive in the community early to get acquainted with the town and with her students. But she had been able to visit only the homes of one section of her ninth-grade English classes. The students whose homes she had visited were those in the class that had been making the exceptional progress.

Obviously, method is not limited to activities in the classroom. Anything a teacher does that gives him more understanding of pupils and lets them know that he is concerned about them contributes to the development of individualized programs.

Promotion of Pupil Self-Understanding

The foundation stone of individualized instruction is helping each pupil to see himself honestly and realistically. Unless a pupil will accept himself and his present status as the starting point, it is very difficult for anyone to provide individual assistance.

A pupil must be able to talk freely about his emotions, beliefs, and attitudes. In order to do this, however, he must be able to accept himself as he is and to know that the other person accepts him too. If the teacher doesn't accept him, he cannot be honest. If judgments are pronounced about his behavior or answers given to his problems, he withdraws and is denied the opportunity to know himself better.

An eleventh-grade student in an English class wrote:

> But if you don't listen—
> Who will? . . .
> I can say what I want,
> Just like I've always
> Wanted to . . .
> And I can tell you
> How wonderful I feel
> When you said
> I could continue to write
> Like this—
> If I was honest with myself.

His teacher was in a position where she could help him know himself because she had his trust and had convinced him that she was willing to examine with him his deepest thoughts. Sometimes the teacher may be shocked and repelled by what he sees and hears, but he cannot help if he shies away from an unpleasant situation. To help a pupil clarify his confusion requires encouraging him to state his beliefs, listening while he talks about himself, reflecting what he says and thinks and feels so that he can understand himself. The teacher may state implications of his present point of view which he may never have considered.

A teacher of five-year-olds followed this procedure:

> In my kindergarten, one child came to school after losing her grandfather during the summer. During the first two weeks of school her grandmother died. This child's relationships with both grandparents had been very close and the loss of both of them by death built up a tremendous fear of death and a great sense of insecurity. The child hurt inside and in the kindergarten became a disruptive force. She kicked and hit other children. I had to be continually on guard to prevent her from physically injuring another child. Finally, one day after the little girl had kicked another girl in the face, I asked her to remain after the others had left. I looked the little girl directly in the eye and said, "I know why you try to hurt other people. You hurt inside and you want other people to hurt too. You have lost your grandparents and because they are gone you hurt and you are trying

to make other people unhappy. It can't work that way." Then I began to talk with her as to how she could work off these feelings of hurt in a way that would not bring similar feelings to other people and as we talked we decided that whenever she felt that she just had to kick or to hit something she would go to the cot in the nurse's room and lie down on the cot and kick until she had had her fill of kicking or until the hurt was gone for the moment. This procedure worked. The little girl continued to be a disruptive influence in the kindergarten, but she no longer physically hurt other children.

At a higher level the teacher would probably have been less willing to verbalize the difficulty for the child. Further talks would be necessary at any age level to tell whether or not the procedure was working as well inwardly as outwardly.

Situations in which youngsters can identify themselves with other persons and analyze how they would have reacted in a similar situation provide them with an opportunity to examine and analyze themselves. Many youngsters are too shy in a class group to state their beliefs or their problems openly. But a timid student will often discuss the behavior of a character in a movie, a socio-drama, or a play and in so doing will make valid analyses of his own emotions and convictions.

A group of ten-year-olds were planning a Christmas play. They decided to do Rudolph, the Red-Nosed Reindeer. When it came time to cast, the teacher asked for suggestions and volunteers. Sammy, a boy with 150 IQ who had been belittled and rejected throughout the fall, volunteered to play Rudolph because he felt like Rudolph. All members of the class voiced approval. This occasion was the first in that class in which Sammy had verbalized his feelings about himself and his interpretation of the situation.

The approach to teaching being outlined makes it impossible to set up stereotyped assignments to which all the youngsters must react in the same way. It does away with telling pupils what to do and how well they have done it. It makes teaching, instead, a process of sharing experiences and then encouraging students to interpret and analyze their experiences in terms of the values that were involved. Teaching, then, becomes a process of helping pupils understand their experiences, and is conducted largely through encouraging them to talk out their reactions. *Teaching involves (1) setting the stage for experiences and (2) creating a situation in which those experiences can be analyzed.* Subject matter is organized by each student on the basis of the conclusions and generalizations he draws from his experiences; it is not presented in an organized form to which the individual is supposed to accommodate his purposes and his interpretations.

When a pupil finds he can be honest, the teacher is in a position to help him clarify his goals. A pupil's goals are the basis for judging his status, his strengths, and his weaknesses! Talking with him about his ambitions, his daydreams, and his wishes is a phase of teaching. Questions that help him decide which of two alternatives he wants or to see more clearly the implications of his hopes for present action serve an essential educative function.

If a student asks for help with his plans the teacher can assist him to obtain a realistic picture of his needs.

Standardized tests provide one means by which he can learn to know himself. Performance on tests for which group norms have been established provide him with a reference by which he can make more intelligent judgments on his own status and progress. As he secures the results of such tests he has an opportunity to form a more objective picture of his standing in relation to others and to decide for himself what steps need to be taken. Pupil-teacher analysis of his pattern of work and his products is another source of data concerning his present status.

It is not the teacher's function to make the judgments about the evidence obtained. If he allows himself to move into the position of judging, he prevents the pupil from knowing himself because the pupil focuses his attention on how to present strengths for approval. The teacher's task is to assist in the inventory of skills, knowledges, and attitudes, and the development of the understanding that strengths and weaknesses are not absolutes, that they are determined by the outcomes sought.

A sense of security and increased confidence will be obtained by many students from the knowledge that all people do not need to judge themselves by the same standards. For example, a pupil seeking to become a musician does not need to consider lack of skill in library research as a weakness. Neither must a boy planning to be a chemist obtain skill in writing poetry or painting. The needs of the individual are determined by a contrast of his present status with his present hopes.

As a student begins work designed to help him achieve his purposes, the teacher serves as a resource person who helps him locate the facts and materials which will make it possible for him to formulate his own conclusions, generalizations, and interpretations. The emphasis is on individual learning and individual interpretation. Only by exploring a problem on his own, by testing data for himself, and by arriving at his own conclusions and interpretations can the individual pupil discover himself.

A student's self-knowledge is furthered by teaching the technique of self-evaluation: how to decide on purposes; how to record progress; how to judge the evidence recorded in terms of the criteria established; how to revise plans in terms of the judgments made. Through help in his constant self-evaluation of his day-by-day performance, the student gradually becomes capable of making a valid analysis of his strengths and weaknesses. This analysis is not something that is accomplished in a day or a week. It is a continuous process. Teachers help by working with boys and girls in such a way that they say to themselves, "What are my goals? What are my strengths? What are my weaknesses? What activities should I undertake in order to become the kind of person I want to be?" These questions will be phrased in different language at different grade levels, but the pattern of evaluation is the same for all students.

The Pupil's Decision

In planning with a youngster what he should study, the teacher needs to discover what his goals are and to utilize them as a starting point in his learning experience. How can his goals be learned? Sometimes, just by listening to him talk. Or by bringing him into the planning so that he can express his goals. By giving him an opportunity to say, "These are the things I want from this unit." Basically, the technique consists of starting with the assumption that pupil purposes are as worth while and important as those of the teacher.

A pupil is not always sure of his purposes. He may be accustomed to doing what he is told. Or he may want to do so many things that he finds difficulty in making decisions. We can be of help by raising such questions as, "What do you like to do?" "What types of activity give you satisfaction?"

These questions bring out into the open short-term purposes at least. Some of the paper-and-pencil devices such as the *Wishing Well* for elementary school children and the *Kuder Preference Checklist* for secondary school pupils are also useful in helping boys and girls identify or isolate their interests. Each pupil's answers give a starting point in planning with him.

But immediate interests are not enough at all levels. Questions should sample long-range purposes as well. "What kind of person do you hope to become?" "What do your parents want you to be?"

One of the teacher's functions is to help each student extend into the future the goals that he has. As he comes to identify his long-range goals, his purposes become more worth while.

An effective contrast between immediate interests and long-term purposes permits the youngster to form a clearer picture of his needs. He can see that his ambition to be an engineer is not furthered by his constant interest in playing basketball and in dating. If he continues to make such comparisons over a period of time, he will increase in his ability to make wise decisions.

He may determine his purposes by finding how his present status differs from his picture of himself.

> In one eleventh-grade class, pupils were accustomed to follow only immediate interests. As a part of a state-wide study of secondary schools, however, they took some achievement tests in the fields of social studies, language, arts, science, and mathematics. They ranked at the 11th percentile, the 9th percentile, the 51st percentile, and the 65th percentile on the four tests. Yet their home environments and intellectual abilities should have put them all in the upper percentiles, had normal progress been occurring in the areas measured by the tests. Should the teacher tell youngsters how they scored on the achievement tests? He decided in the affirmative. When the students found that they were not achieving at the level that they believed they should, they revised their class program and made provision for individuals to concentrate on the areas in which they were doing poorly. In this case, test scores revealed a need of which the pupils had not been aware. They were not measuring up to their concept of themselves and their abilities. The recognized need, not the test scores, motivated them to plan their work. Tests simply describe present status. The difference between *what a student is doing and what he expects of himself* is the most fruitful area in which to start individual work plans.

Of course, there is one major limitation in planning exclusively in terms of pupil purposes—the teacher's lack of knowledge and skill. Pupils should be made aware of the boundaries within which a teacher can be of assistance. The teacher helps if he indicates the subject-matter areas within which he is capable of providing guidance and his special competences and background. Then the students can determine for themselves how they can best relate the class to their own purposes. This process of connecting the pupil's purposes and goals with the range of experiences available in the immediate situation is essential.

Naturally, not every one of a student's goals can be accommodated within a given class. A girl may be concerned with increasing her charm, but it would not be within the limits of the algebra class to assist her in working for that goal. A boy may want to be a star baseball player, but it would not be the function of the teacher of social studies to work with him in developing such skills. But any teacher can assist each pupil to determine which of his goals can be furthered by the work at hand.

This limitation is not so drastic as it may seem, since every pupil has a wide variety of purposes.

At times a teacher may be so intent on a limited range of goals that he fails to recognize a pupil's purposes or to see the full potential in his proposed activity.

> John, who has a "reading block" that we are working on, still has not become interested in reading for pleasure. He will listen when read to, but then his attention span is short. As for finding something himself and reading silently, John is not interested. His real interest is electricity. But it's hard or impossible to find something about electricity—the real intricacies of it—written on John's reading level (second-grade). He busies himself drawing complicated diagrams. During a regular library period, John very rarely even looks at a picture book. He has been the challenge of the year! We have succeeded in building up other abilities, but not reading.

When the pupil's purpose, whether he be a second-grader or a high-school senior, is constructive, the teacher promotes efficient learning by working with it rather than against it.

Some teachers have attempted to relate all the school experiences of a student to a particular vocational goal. But that is only one of the multitude of goals that every youngster has. The wise teacher will help each student identify several of his goals and then will help him decide which of them that teacher can help him attain.

There are other limitations, too, on how fully pupils can implement their desires. Both time and resources are limited. For instance, although it would be very desirable to help a pupil undertake a long-term study of electronics, the school may not have the money to buy the necessary equipment. And the necessary reference works may not be available either in the school library or elsewhere in the community. In such a situation, it would be unsatisfactory planning for the student to set up a complicated study in the area of electronics. Such a plan would lead only to frustration.

Limitations should be applied cautiously, however. They may be cases of self-deception.

Free and inexpensive material is available in large quantities. Librarians can help discover it or the teacher may locate it by examining listings such as those prepared by such agencies as H. W. Wilson. The resource people and the possible experiences in the community should be explored thoroughly before ruling out a study on the basis of lack of material. It is much easier to secure material for study by one pupil than for an entire class, and an interested student may tap the resources of the community as part of his homework.

Time is a major limitation. The primary question for the individual is how he will best use the time he has available in the class. Actually such a situation is good because it causes the student to sift his purposes and decide what is really important for him.

In brief, a teacher assists the individual to decide what to study by determining his goals, contrasting his immediate interests with his long-range purposes, ascertaining the resources available, and selecting the activities which he can carry to successful conclusion in the situation.

The Pupil's Plan of Work

After helping the pupil select the project he is to undertake, the teacher has the responsibility for assisting him to formulate a plan of work that will attain his purposes.

One of the first steps is defining sub-problems. This can be a very simple operation, in which the child simply states his questions. One question posed at the beginning of the study may be enough, but it is more likely that he will continue to ask questions over a period of time, as he delves further into the topic. At any rate, it is necessary for the student to make a clear statement of his problem and to list as many of the sub-problems as he can identify at the very beginning of the study.

Secondly, the teacher helps the student survey available resources: what books are in the library; what material is contained in the textbooks; what free materials are available; what people in the community can provide information; what places should be visited to learn more about the problem. In making this survey of resources, neither we nor the pupil can identify them all. Other people will certainly be able to help. The librarian, for instance. Each student should become acquainted with the vertical files of clippings and pictures which the library maintains. He should also become acquainted with the various sources that list free materials so that he can collect and bring to school anything that will be valuable to his study. And other teachers may be asked for suggestions on ways of getting information. That means, of course, that the teacher will need to know the backgrounds and experiences of his fellow faculty members. Another source that the student will want to tap in gathering materials will be other class members. The skillful teacher encourages boys and girls to share their materials and to ask one another to contribute materials that will be useful in conducting individual researches.

As a student undertakes a study, he will need to develop a plan, to state the questions that are to be answered, and to outline the procedure and materials that will be used in finding the answers. This plan of work becomes the blueprint of the study, the design of the research. By writing out the plan of the study, the student has a means of knowing, at any point along the way, where he is and what remains to be done. The written plan becomes a source of security to both the student and the teacher. The use of written plans enables a teacher to supervise many activities simultaneously. They permit him to refresh his memory on individual projects and guide him as he helps each pupil to evaluate his progress and plan his next steps.

Not all the research can be conducted in the classroom. Sometimes pupils will want to work in the library or at other places outside the classroom. If the schedule is too rigid for individual research during a class period, the teacher may need, as a temporary measure, to plan with students ways of carrying on individual research during out-of-school hours in their home. In the meantime, he will work for a change in school policy that will recognize the importance of individual work.

In planning individual work with a student, time should be spent in thinking with him about how he will share his experience. Some of his findings may be valuable to other people, or may represent a special contribution to his class or his school. This emphasis on sharing the results of one's labors with other people and with the school constitutes one of the important learnings in developing citizenship in boys and girls. It needs to be a part of any planning between the teacher and the individual student.

Pupil Organization of Learning

Since no two students can have the same experiences, and since the most useful organization of subject matter is one that the individual creates from his experience, each student will have to master the techniques of consolidating and organizing his own learning.

A feeling of achievement is promoted by organizing the results of an experience. If the teacher does not help youngsters arrive at some sort of organization of information, he leaves within them the feeling that the teaching has been haphazard, the learning without purpose, and the achievement limited. But when he does help them formulate their own generalizations, he increases their sense of progress and heightens the usefulness of their learning.

Keeping a scrapbook or a log often helps a student to work out his own organization. As he pulls together the experiences that he regards as meaningful, he has an opportunity to see whether they present a hodgepodge or a definite pattern. He begins to organize his learning. This organization is his own and expresses his own interpretation of what he feels and knows.

The teacher makes possible individual organization of knowledge by permitting many different patterns of record-keeping. When he prescribes in detail the kind of material that is to go into a log and the form that is to be followed, he prevents students from devising the types of organization that are most significant for them.

He also helps by asking youngsters to review, from time to time, the generalizations they have reached, to see whether or not any basic conflicts exist among them. When he asks a student, "But how does that statement tie in with the one you made yesterday?" he is inviting him to analyze the relationships that are developing in various areas of his learning. Questions that get at the internal consistency of beliefs expressed, that challenge the implications of a conclusion drawn from one experience as it applies to a different situation, that force a student to see possible applications of the proposal that he is making, all assist the student to organize the information that he has gained into a meaningful pattern.

Generalizations formed should be functional. One outcome to be sought in the organization of knowledge is the formation of standards by which to judge future experiences. As a student deals with various types of source material, the quality teacher encourages him to formulate for himself criteria by which he judges movies, books, radio programs, art, speeches, or research. Through his life in class and community, and through contact with reference material, the teacher strives to get the student to organize his beliefs about human relations into definite criteria that he will be able to apply in evaluating the quality of living in a given situation.

Knowledge is often clarified and organized by the very act of sharing it with other people. Consequently, if the teacher can create situations in which pupils have an opportunity to share the results of their learning with other persons or with other groups, he assists them to clarify and organize the information they have gathered.

The evaluation process itself assists in the organization of information. As a teacher says to a group of students, "What have we learned?" "How far have we come?" "What are the next steps?" he is helping them formulate an information structure satisfactory to them. By asking them to state at the end of an experience the ideas that have been most significant to them, he assists them to analyze and classify the conclusions that have emerged from their experience.

Conclusion

Individualizing instruction involves helping people learn about themselves. It is a process of helping a person ask himself the questions he needs to ask to answer the conflicts that he has. It is a process of suggesting answers, several possible answers which the individual can evaluate for himself in terms of the data that he has. No teacher can know as much about a student as the student knows about himself. Thus, we raise the questions with the student which help him interpret the data that he has about himself.

To help individuals learn efficiently requires that a teacher study them—their abilities, their interests, their backgrounds, their attitudes, their values, and their problems—and plan with each a program adapted to his purposes and needs. He does not need to be concerned if all pupils do not have the same curriculum. They could not, even if he tried to give it to them.

SELF-EVALUATION CHECKLIST
Providing for Individual Differences

Do I:
 1. Study the cumulative record of each pupil?
 2. Compare his achievement scores with the indices of his ability?
 3. Visit the homes of many of my students?
 4. Listen as pupils talk for comments that reveal their purposes and problems?
 5. Help the pupil to state his purposes, immediate and long-range?
 6. Examine the creative products of pupils for clues to purposes and problems?
 7. Help each pupil learn as much as he can about his values, attitudes, purposes, skills, interests, and abilities?
 8. Share with each pupil information available about his present status?
 9. Help each pupil establish personal goals in addition to the class objectives?
 10. Know the types of individual differences that are important in my teaching?
 11. Seek to increase the differences in levels of pupil achievement?
 12. Use more than one textbook or study guide with each class?
 13. Provide materials on several reading levels for each class?
 14. Use a variety of materials—books, films, pamphlets?
 15. Assist pupils to secure chairs and work locations suited to their physical condition?
 16. Bring pupils in on planning the class activities?
 17. Provide opportunities for each pupil to suggest activities, ways of work, and individual projects?
 18. Provide opportunity for individual choice of at least a portion of the activities?
 19. Encourage each pupil to develop his plan of study?
 20. Vary the amount of homework expected of pupils in the class?
 21. Use group study periods as time for individual conferences?

22. Encourage pupils to help one another?
23. Recommend that each pupil collect and share materials?
24. Accept different types of growth and expression by class members—analyze with pupils their interpretations of their in-class and out-of-class experiences?
25. Base judgments about pupil growth on a variety of types of evidence?
26. Secure the help of the pupil in recording his individual progress?
27. Use his record-keeping as a way of helping the student to organize his learning?
28. Talk with pupils about progress on an individual basis instead of comparing them with other pupils?
29. Study the history and home of each pupil who is not succeeding as well as he should?
30. Treat each pupil differently?

BIBLIOGRAPHY

Providing for Individual Differences

American Council on Education, *Helping Teachers Understand Children.* Washington, D.C.: The Council, 1945.

Arnold, M. B., "Motivation and the Desire to Know," *Education,* 77 (December, 1956), pp. 220–26.

Association for Supervision and Curriculum Development, *Toward Better Teaching.* Washington, D.C.: N.E.A., 1949.

Baker, Janet Bassett, "Personal Error Charts: How a History Teacher Used Test Papers," *Clearing House,* 25 (October, 1950), pp. 85–8.

Cowell, Charles C., "Diary Analysis: A Suggested Technique for the Study of Children's Activities and Interests," *Research Quarterly,* 8 (May, 1937), p. 158–72.

Elkins, Deborah, "Students Face Their Problems," *English Journal,* 38 (November, 1949), pp. 498–503.

Espy, Gladys, "A Description of Attempts to Meet the Mathematical Needs of High School Pupils," *The Southern Association Quarterly,* 7 (August, 1943), pp. 319–31.

Ferguson, Evelyn B., "A Method for Getting to Know Your Pupils Quickly," *The Elementary School Journal,* 50 (February, 1950), pp. 341–45.

Haigh, G. V., and W. H. Schmidt, "Learning of Subject Matter in Teacher-Centered and Group-Centered Classes," *Journal of Educational Psychology,* 47 (May, 1956), pp. 295–301.

Hanszen, M. W., and W. G. Hollister, "Teaching Human Relations Through Spontaneous Pupil Play," *Understanding the Child,* 25 (October, 1956), pp. 103–10.

Hefferman, Helen W., "Each Child Is a Custom Job," *Childhood Education,* 30 (November, 1953), pp. 109–12.

Hicks, Leon, "A Program for Individualizing High-School Science," *High School Journal,* 24 (February, 1941), pp. 63–65.

Hoyt, K. B., "How Well Can Classroom Teachers Know Their Pupils?" *School Review,* 63 (April, 1955), pp. 228–35.

Jensen, B. T., "Instruction and Personality as Factors in Student Performance," *Journal of Educational Research,* 47 (March, 1954), pp. 529–35.

Keliher, Alice, "The Freedom to Be Different," *Child Study,* 28 (Spring, 1951), pp. 3–5.

——— "You Are a Good Teacher If . . . You Consider Each Child's Individuality," *Grade Teacher,* (November, 1954), p. 101.

——— "You Are a Good Teacher If . . . You Understand Readiness," *Grade Teacher,* (February, 1955), p. 101.

McDaniel, J. W., "Improvement of Instruction by Planned Teaching," *California Journal of Secondary Education,* 31 (December, 1956), pp. 487–91.

Mary Amatora, Sister, "Forced Learning May Be Harmful," *Understanding the Child,* 26 (January, 1957), pp. 8–12.

Merrill, K. G., "Teacher Made the Difference," *National Education Association Journal,* 43 (October, 1954), pp. 413–14.

National Council for the Social Studies, *Adapting Instruction in the Social Studies to Individual Differences,* Fifteenth Yearbook. Washington, D.C.: N.E.A., 1944.

National Education Association, "High School Methods with Slow Learners," *N.E.A. Research Bulletin* (October, 1943).

——— "High School Methods with Superior Students," *N.E.A. Research Bulletin* (September, 1941).

O'Day, Labera, et al., "They Said It Couldn't Be Done," *National Elementary Principal* (April, 1955), pp. 33–35.

Rose, Elizabeth, "An Experiment with Non-Academic Boys and Girls in Senior English," *High School Journal,* 24 (November, 1941), pp. 319–29.

——— "Changes in My Teaching of English Since 1935," *High School Journal,* 24 (January, 1941), pp. 5–11.

Schiff, Samuel, "Developmental Reading Program," *Clearing House,* 26 (April, 1952), pp. 466–68.

Skeen, Bernice, "When a Difference Is a Difference," *Educational Leadership,* 14 (January, 1957), pp. 217–21.

Snyder, A., "Stage for Learning," *National Education Association Journal,* 43 (April, 1954), pp. 231–33.

Standlee, L. S., "Dynamics of Students Teaching Themselves," *Progressive Education,* 31 (February, 1954), p. 112.

Tipton, Gladys, "All God's Chillun," *N.E.A. Journal*, 39 (February, 1950), pp. 128–29.

Trail, Mabel Cay, "Agassiz and His Log Again," *The Educational Forum*, 19 (November, 1954), pp. 55–56.

Van Meer, L., "Tellin' Ain't Teachin'," *Michigan Education Journal*, 31 (October, 1953), pp. 89–91.

Vroman, Mary Elizabeth, "See How They Run," *Ladies Home Journal*, 68 (June, 1951), pp. 40, 100–02, 105, 107–09.

Wood, Helen C., "Children Who Move with the Crops," *N.E.A. Journal*, 47 (March, 1958), pp. 170–73.

••• Stimulating Intellectual Growth

Every person has at birth the potential for many types of growth. Some lie dormant throughout life. Others are developed in part. The determination of which possibilities are realized, and the degree to which any one is fulfilled, is a function of the environment.

If it is hoped that children will develop their intellectual potential, society must provide an environment that is intellectually stimulating and in which achievement of an intellectual nature is respected and nurtured. Within each school provided by a society which seeks to develop the intellectual resources of the population there must be teachers who, through their scholarship, stimulate others to search for greater truth.

UNSATISFACTORY TEACHER

The teacher does not know the field or the type of pupil growth sought. He can only follow the textbook. His assignments are the readings of certain specified pages. Class periods consist of the pupils' closing their textbooks and the teacher's questioning them about the details of the pages they were supposed to have read. The correctness of an answer is judged by the exactness with which it repeats the textbooks. No child may question or think for himself. School activity of pupils consists of memory, recall, drill and conformity.

MINIMUM SATISFACTORY TEACHER

The teacher has the minimum numbers of hours for certification in the field and follows the textbook to make uniform assignments for all members of the class. During class periods, pupils may question. They may suggest ideas that are not in the text and the teacher will examine them with the class.

If a paper is assigned, the student may choose the aspect of the topic he will emphasize. Products of student work are displayed and marks do not depend entirely upon ability to recall the facts in the book. Some credit is given for being able to express the idea in the student's own words.

10 · The Creation of a Stimulating Intellectual Climate

A stimulating intellectual climate is one in which people are searching for truth. It consists of a belief in creative activity and contact with ideas and information which challenges and tempts the individual to explore.

Fostering Creativity Essential

In a world in which change is certain and the present transition is rapid, new answers must be sought. New information about the physical world changes our conception of it. New issues and new problems arise. Conformity to convention, custom or hereditary commitments cause confusion and contradiction.

Hypotheses concerning ways to live in the emerging world must be formulated and tested. If schools are to aid society face the challenge of the day-by-day crisis, creativity must be stressed in the classrooms. Many teachers must assume that the encouragement of creative activity is one of their major functions.

The events of the past few years emphasize the importance of helping pupils become more creative. The atom bomb and the hydrogen bomb have forced all thinking people to reorient their concept of living and of the world. Missiles which bring all men of the world within minutes of one another eliminate the sense of security that comes through being far away from the things we fear. Satellite launchings and other ventures into outer space have outmoded mere global thinking.

Change is the most significant characteristic of present-day society. Old answers and former ways of doing things are no longer satisfactory. Problems are different. If the world situation were stable, trust could be placed in routine and dogma; but, in a world in which new relationships are dynamic and emerging, the present and coming generations must creatively and individualistically work out solutions to current and future problems.

Creativity is the method of progress. Conformity and the learning of present ways of doing things are only ways of maintaining the status quo. In reality, nothing is ever quite the same. As long as the rate of progress was slow, people were able to make the minute adjustments which gave them a feeling that most things were constant and that current conclusions could continue to be applied. But, with the present rapidity of change, it is easy to recognize that society is emerging and in it values and ways of living must be continually re-evaluated.

In addition to the pressure produced by rapid cultural change to stress pupil creativity, teachers have new information from the field of psychology that underlines the importance of stressing creative activity in the classroom. Studies of perception indicate that each individual perceives uniquely in terms of his background of experiences, his purposes and his needs. It is no longer safe for the teacher to assume that all youngsters will learn the same thing from reading the same assignments, from the same field trip, or from the comments of the teacher. It is necessary for the youngster to have the opportunity to creatively express his perception if the teacher is to know what the pupil has learned. If the pupil hands back answers in the words of the text, the teacher cannot be sure what the pupil has learned. His answers can be mere repetition of nonsense items memorized.

But if a youngster has the opportunity to creatively express, in his own words, his understandings and his feelings, the teacher can know more accurately what has been learned. Provision for creative activity by the pupil is essential if a teacher is to be sure what he has taught and to be able to evaluate adequately the teaching he is doing.

Barriers to Teaching for Creativeness

A short time ago a supervisor in a large mid-western city was asked what she had seen recently of teachers' efforts to promote creativity on the part of youngsters. She replied: "It's embarrassing to try to answer that question. Teachers are so busy taking care of teaching the skills and covering the syllabus that there is little time left for creative activity. Even in the best schools the major emphasis is on the promotion of other types of growth than creativity. It's not that creativity is unimportant—it's just that other things seem to have priority. The administration and the public are more concerned about other types of pupil growth."

This pattern, from the point of view of the supervisor, was prevalent throughout the city. Why, in a world of rapid change, is the emphasis on learning to memorize, to conform, and to carry out directions rather than on the development of creativity?

A child is creative. He is constantly seeking better answers to the problems that confront him. From infancy he tries to find ways of getting the help he wants from his parents and siblings. He explores, he puts things together, and he tears them apart. He babbles, talks, and connects words and ideas. He expresses his glee, his hate, and his scorn. He learns by trying out his ideas.

He brings this method of solving problems, of learning, to school with him. If he were free to operate in a normal manner he would continue to be creative. But some teachers attempt to prevent it. They conceive of gaining knowledge as memorizing answers to problems that someone else has solved, or someone else's interpretation or organization of that knowledge. They fail to value the answers, interpretation, and organization that the pupil formulates for himself.

Creativity is something that all children have potentially. It may be cultivated or curbed. In some schools children are told to follow patterns. They are forced to conform. Their assignments consist of directions to do something and the way to do it. Answers are judged by the extent to which they coincide with those in the textbooks. Opinions are evaluated in terms of the extent to which they conform to the teacher's. Even in some art classes, youngsters are required to perceive, draw, and paint animals, flowers, and clouds in the same way that everyone else does. If a child colors a turkey purple and the teacher has only seen brown turkeys, the child is asked to change his interpretation.

Some teachers are afraid of creativity. They are not creative themselves. They never venture. They read only the best sellers. They wear what everyone else does. They express only the opinions that are approved. They would dread being called an experimental teacher. Security, as they see it, is found in conformity and children who question, who have ideas that challenge majority opinion or do not follow the accepted form of behavior are anti-social and should be taught to adjust. Such teachers could not be expected to foster creativity. They stamp it out whenever they are able.

Creativity is curbed in a school with too rigid a curriculum where teachers interpret guides and syllabi as directives. It is hampered in classrooms in which teachers are afraid or are unsure of their competence or their ability to form their own answers.

Actions Which Promote Pupil Creativity

But many teachers promote creativity. They recognize the fundamental importance of contributing to the creativity of children and they seek to create the conditions in which it is fostered. How do they do it?

They establish regulations that cover the routine of the classroom. Some people feel that regulations will stifle creativity. It doesn't work this way. Unless a person is freed from the burden of continually thinking through routine decisions, he does not have the time for creative thought and action. If a man had to stop and think through how to tie his tie or how to button his shirt each time he did it, it would be a much more time-consuming process with less opportunity for the solving of more important problems. If the decision as to how to spell a word has to be made each time the word is used, there would be very little opportunity for creative written expression. If energy and effort must be spent in dealing with the routine, the amount for creative activity is decreased.

They are permissive enough to enable the student to be honest. If the teacher penalizes points of view that differ from his own, students will be unable to express new thoughts and consequently will be afraid or will not take the trouble to develop them in that class.

> A graduate student was working on a paper on the philosophy of teaching art. When asked if he would really deal with creativity as a possibility in many areas or would restrict his interpretation of creativity to the field of art alone, the student replied: "My teacher does not see creativity in any area other than art. If I hope to make a good grade, it will be necessary for me to write in terms of my teacher's interpretation."

Coercion to accept the answers the teacher holds on questions of belief, interpretations, or hypothesis, quenches the spark of creativity. Value judgments about the quality of an interpretation are avoided if creativity is sought. If judgments are made about the quality of interpretation, fear begins to enter and creativity is stifled. Grading creative effort hinders the development of types of creativity that conflict with the vision of the teacher.

They avoid giving their interpretations of events and materials to children. Too frequently the teaching process consists of the teacher attempting to interpret. Many teachers do not see their role as helping youngsters interpret, draw generalizations, and formulate hypotheses based on facts examined. These teachers view their role as scholars who have the responsibility for sharing the judgments they have made.

As a young man preparing to teach political science stated it:

> I am gaining mastery of my field so that I can tell my students what is right and wrong. My job as a teacher is to interpret the political events and issues to my students.

Contrast the viewpoint of an elementary school teacher who was effective in promoting creativity. If creativity is sought, the teacher's role becomes the opposite. As she put it:

> Creativity requires identification with the children at all times. I seek to blank out my maturity as we seek answers. My experience and knowledge are put into the situation as resources as I attempt to help children make their interpretations. Promoting creativity takes empathy on the part of the teacher. He must constantly seek to feel and to see as children feel and see.

When an adult attempts to give his interpretation to children, they withhold theirs.

They take class time to give children opportunity to express their interpretations.

> A fifth grade class was beginning to write poetry. When children asked what type of poetry the teacher expected, she read the following poem once, again, and a third time very slowly:
>
> > Does the pear tree say to the apple tree:
> > 'I hate you 'cause you're not like me?'
> > Does the green grass ask the sky so blue:
> > 'I'm green, why aren't you green, too?'
> > A rose smells sweet, 'cause it's a flower.
> > An onion tastes strong, a pickle is sour.
> > They're different, yet they get along
> > And no one seems to think it's wrong.
> >
> > Must I be a chicken or a goose?
> > Can't I be a churkendoose?
> >
> > You know, the cow says: 'Look, I give milk.'
> > The silkworm answers: 'I make silk.'
> > The horse says: 'Look how strong I am!'
> > The piggie answers: 'I give ham.'
> > 'My skin makes leather!' snorts the bull.
> > The sheep replies: 'I give wool.'
> > Each one has its special use
> > And I'm sure there's one for the churkendoose.

The children were asked to interpret it. One boy said, "Everyone is proud and tries to say he is good for something." Another spoke up, "Each was jealous because he didn't have a job to do." A little girl spoke up, "The churkendoose can do anything, 'cause he's bragging like all of us and he is in the middle." Another girl said, "They think that each person has something good and different in his heart but that other people are afraid to come out and say he's good." The teacher asked if this poem had any application outside of class. A third girl replied, "The Negro is just as smart as the white man but his skin is different and the white man doesn't want to admit it." A boy added, "We don't want Negroes to do well because we are afraid they'll get ahead of us and take our jobs." The conversation switched back to the class. A little girl who felt she was an isolate said, "The churkendoose felt and knew that nobody liked him but he said to himself, 'I want to be what I am but I can't and live peacefully.'"

The teacher was dealing with two kinds of pupil interpretation. She had made it possible for the youngsters to begin to probe their own feelings and their own interpretations of a poem as she had begun to help them think through what kind of poem to write. She was stressing the importance of personal feeling and without saying it she was attempting to make clear that when we write we are attempting to share our feelings and our interpretations of life.

They are concerned about the feelings, hopes, and aspirations of their pupils. Encouragement of honesty and creativeness is important when it comes from persons who are close to us and persons we value and trust. It doesn't matter much if a person who withholds himself from us attempts to give encouragement. His praise and his judgments have little real meaning for us. If a teacher hopes to encourage youngsters to be creative, he cannot be withdrawn and unfeeling as far as his students are concerned. He must strive to create the kind of atmosphere in which there is warmth, friendliness, and acceptance. We are only willing to share our innermost thoughts and our real interpretations with those we trust. What teachers do and say in their day-to-day relations with students when they are not attempting to stimulate creativeness will limit or enhance any actions they take to promote creative activity at a definite point in the schedule.

They help students value feelings and emotions. Many times in the process of growing up people are made to feel ashamed of feelings. They are told many times that a mature person does not reveal his feelings, that he keeps them to himself. As this experience is multiplied, students come to be ashamed of their feelings, to withhold them, and to cover them up. The teacher who values creativeness will need to take steps to help youngsters realize the importance of honest emotion in creativeness. He will not succeed with all students but his own use of his emotions will have a telling effect in freeing children to use their feelings. A teacher must be willing to share his own feelings, his insecurities, and his concerns. If he poses as a person with all the answers, a person without doubts, disturbances, anxieties, and unfulfilled desires, he will seem so infallible that children will be afraid to expose their feelings. When a teacher admits to a group, "I was in this type of situation—I didn't know what to do. What would you have done?" he is opening the door to creative thinking. He is removing the barrier that comes out of the impression that many adults give youngsters that they have all the answers.

They are willing to wait for pupils to arrive at their answers. They do not rush to give pupils their shortcuts or organization.

Creativeness does not always appear at the exact second the teacher thinks it should. Sometimes when teachers are in a hurry, they don't feel that they have the time it takes to allow youngsters to think their way through problem situations. They do the thinking for children in order to get a particular task accomplished in a hurry and deprive children of the opportunity to use their creativeness.

> Although the ninth grade was to give one of the skits in the pre-homecoming celebration, they had not been told until three days before the production. Mr. Brown, a new teacher who wanted to make good, was frantic. When he started planning with the class what they could do, the responses were unrelated. Ted wanted to use a football scene. Sue proposed a ballet. Jerry outlined a fantasy. No one seemed to agree. When the homeroom period was almost over, Mr. Brown couldn't stand it any longer. He said, "We have talked about this skit long enough. Evidently none of the ideas is very good because you can't agree. I guess I'll have to use the one my fraternity gave when I was a senior in college. Be on stage in the auditorium fifteen minutes after the end of the last period and I will tell you what do to and what costumes and equipment to get."

Planning is the phase of production in which pupils can be creative. The actual performance itself is the end result and usually a routine part of a production. As children think together how best to stage, how best to interpret, how best to accentuate, they are engaging in creative activity. If the teacher takes over, rather than seeing his role as a stimulator and coordinator, the opportunity for creativeness is lost.

They stimulate creativeness through brainstorming sessions. The procedure was developed in industry. When a group of people face a problem, they sit down together and advance ideas as rapidly as they can state them. No one attempts to criticize any of the ideas. No suggestions are evaluated. The main purpose of the time spent is to get a large number of possibilities out into the open. Later each point is examined and analyzed. Time spent in visualizing, in attempting to foresee possibilities and in generating ideas is one of the ways that creativity is fostered. The creativity of each participant is strengthened through the emphasis on imagination.

Putting a value on being able to imagine is something that happens too infrequently in many classrooms. Work is definite, fixed and the answers are already established. The pupil's task is to seek to find the given answer, not to create and test new hypotheses. Planning of projects, activities, organization, operation, and ways of communicating are all opportunities for the teacher to release the imagination.

They help youngsters with the recording of their feelings. Creativity and the teaching of communication skills can be conducted together. Many activities in the early grades can serve the dual purpose.

> In a kindergarten the teacher hoped to develop creative expression. She combined art and human relations. When a youngster was ill the other children sent their drawings to him. If any child wanted to, he dictated a story to accompany his drawing. The teacher assisted by writing the story as it was told. The practice of dictating a story to accompany the pictures became a habit and the children increased in their ability to express their ideas. One of the more imaginative girls drew a picture of a cat and her kittens. The cat and the kittens wore many diamonds. The girl dictated:
>
> This is a story about Mrs. Cat and her babies (kittens, you know).
>
> Mrs. Cat doesn't have a husband. She did but he went to the Army.
>
> Mrs. Cat is all dressed up. She has on a beautiful watch, a diamond ring, a diamond watch, a diamond bracelet. She and her babies (kittens) are going to see their daddy.
>
> He doesn't know them still so when he sees them he starts shooting. He has been in the Army having a good time and that's why he forgot them. (That happens, you know.)
>
> Mrs. Cat tells him who she is and that these are his children. She takes him back home and he never gets to run around and have a good time again.

They provide first hand experience with concrete and live objects. It seems that the further away people get from reality, the less creative they become. If all of a child's experiences with things are through reading about them in books, he will not have much to share because he has not experienced deeply. Children who have read books about frogs have less desire to write poems about them or to draw pictures of them than a child who has gone as a part of a class to collect frogs. This association of creativity with first hand experience is illustrated by another story written in the same kindergarten.

> The child who had drawn a picture of a man on a cloud dictated: "This is a picture of a man who got sick and died. God let down a strong rope and pulled him up to heaven. This is his picture in heaven. God gave him a nice, soft, bouncy bed with a pillow. He never got bitten by mosquitoes in heaven and he had plenty of food."

Needless to say, this child was frequently covered with mosquito bites, did not always have enough food, and wanted a more comfortable bed.

The teacher contributes to the creativeness of children as he recognizes the importance of developing creativeness: (1) as he provides first hand experiences which youngsters are free to interpret, (2) as he stresses the validity of emotions, (3) as he encourages students to use and value their own feelings and interpretations, (4) as he withholds value judgments concerning the interpretation that others make, (5) as he provides a variety of channels for the expression of interpretations, (6) as he conceives of his role as an encourager, coordinator, and stimulator of action rather than an interpreter of life, (7) as he emphasizes visualizing, foreseeing and postulating rather than comparison and evaluation, (8) as he establishes an atmosphere in which diversity is valued and disagreement is permitted, and (9) as he values each youngster and helps the youngster to value himself.

Contact with Scholarship Essential

Association with teachers who are scholars in their field is an essential ingredient of an educational process which fosters the development of the intellectual potential of youth. If teachers are not scholars, if instead of giving honor to scholarly attainment and seeking it themselves, teachers belittle intellectual pursuits and label those who engage in them as "eggheads," students acquire the same attitudes. Unless some teachers are scholars, able to think for themselves, and concerned with increasing their knowledge and that which is available to the world, pupils receive little intellectual stimulation in the school. Intellectual curiosity and the spirit of investigation are developed by being in association with persons who find intellectual search a satisfying activity.

The scholars on a school staff help to surround the pupils with ideas. They bring many types of information. They question. They define and examine issues. They challenge current beliefs. They share information of current developments in their field. They promote the purchase of additional reference material. They share their investigation of problems. They supply explanations which can be examined.

The interpretation of scholarship will affect the way the faculty is able to promote creativity. If scholarship is conceived of as acquiring a mass of information by examining a record of the past, creativity will flourish in only the limited area of different organization and interpretation. But if scholarship is interpreted as the search for more truth or the collection and use of available data to improve living, creativity will flourish.

The presence of the second type of scholarship will enhance the creativity of a student body. It is possible to make a creative approach to planning and preparing for a bridge party. But greater intellectual development will result if the creative urge is utilized to formulate a social proposal or a scientific theory. The content contacted in one creative experience can be the basis for more insight as to problems and procedures for future creative ventures.

Contributions of the Scholars

It is difficult to designate which teachers are scholars. Most elementary and secondary teachers modestly deny that they are. Almost any honest person would feel humble about laying claim to the title. But the scholarship contributions of teachers to the school program can be recognized.

They supply information beyond that available in the textbook. Because of past experience or study, they are able to evaluate the text and support portions of it and to question others. They supply stories and illustrations which give meaning and add interest to the facts and generalizations presented in the text. For example, a biology teacher who has been a forest ranger can supply information about animals and plants from his own experience. His anecdotes give a sense of reality to the classroom. A business education teacher with a background of office experience knows what a student needs to be successful, can specify essential skills and knowledges and can give illustrations from his own background when desirable.

They possess and share a wealth of illustrative material. The French teacher who has been in France may return with menus, travel posters, theatre programs, and other souvenirs which he uses in his teaching. A history teacher may have a collection of newspapers published during World War II which pupils may read to gain a sense of the emotional tone of the period. During the years, a mathematics teacher may have made models and visual aids which students handle and discuss in gaining a better understanding of mathematical concepts. All of the illustrative material a teacher uses enriches the intellectual climate of school, and the teacher who collects and shares items which stimulate interest or increase understanding is going beyond the minimum level of instruction.

They know their field well enough to be able to make a variety of organizations of it. A teacher with only a surface knowledge in a field must depend upon the organization of knowledge presented in the text. If he allows the students to stray from the text, he will not know what is correct and incorrect, what is important and what can be overlooked, what concepts depend upon understanding others, or what is the significance of various information. For example, what would a teacher who is not a student of American history do with a student's proposal to spend a week studying the Whiskey Rebellion? Is it important? Is it as significant as the Alien and Sedition Acts? On the other hand, a teacher who knows his field well enough to know the basic principles, concepts, generalizations, and skills is able to make many organizations of the class work. He provides a higher quality teaching because he will be able to teach in terms of the purposes of pupils.

> A sixth-grade teacher had a course of study which called for teaching world geography. She found that her pupils were interested in travel. And the movie *Around the World in Eighty Days* came to the local theatre the first week of school. After seeing the movie the pupils began talking about going around the world. The teacher wondered what a person could see and would want to see in going around the world in eighty days in 1958. The class was intrigued and began to explore the idea. Enthusiasm mounted and the project expanded. Travel folders, timetables, steamship schedules, airline and railway maps, travel regulations, and geography books began to appear. Parents became so enthusiastic and involved they began talking about going around the world in eighty days at their bridge parties. The idea became the central theme of the geography work for the entire semester and spilled over into other areas—costs, budgets, customs, passports, religion, art, and dramatics. Since the parents had become so interested, the concluding activity had to be a pageant of scenes and experiences encountered on the trip.

The teacher was able to work in terms of pupil interest because she knew her geography well enough to make an entirely new organization of the knowledge. She did not have to worry about covering the rainfall, the principal cities, and the mountain ranges of each continent because she knew sufficiently well the basic concepts she was trying to develop to make the approach to the geographic information that was most meaningful to the pupils. A business education teacher who helps a group of children develop and operate a Junior Achievement Corporation or the English teacher who is guiding the class in the preparation and production of a series of radio programs are providing the same type of quality teaching because they know their content well enough to use it to promote desired pupil goals. *Content is the servant of the quality teacher, not the master and director of his steps.*

They produce in their fields. If a teacher is an active contributor to the advancement of his field, boys and girls know they are working with a person who can do what he is talking about. Just as an instructor who had been in battle, other qualities being equal, carried more weight in the training of recruits than the officer who had not, so the teacher who produces has greater respect from his students. The speech teacher who has been successful as an actress or a director of plays has a distinct advantage over the teacher who has never earned his living by his skill in the field in which he is teaching. The teacher who regularly sells short stories or has had a novel published starts the teaching of a creative writing class with greater respect and acceptance than a teacher who is compelled to turn to the textbook as the authority. As pupils work with a teacher who is constantly demonstrating his scholarship by his production, they see scholarship as a way of life, not a withdrawal from reality, and are stimulated to write, experiment, or seek truth by other types of study.

A teacher of French who spends his summers in countries where people speak French comes to his classes with an assurance on pronunciation and idiomatic usage that is evident and influences his pupils. He does not hesitate and wonder if he is right. He knows. He can enrich with stories of real life situations in which language problems arose.

They are able to apply the knowledge they possess to the improvement of daily living. In a small high school in Alabama the chemistry teacher led his class into the production of cosmetics. A home economics teacher in the same school helped pupils study the food pattern of their homes and develop a system of food preservation and storage which permitted change in the nutrition of the families of the students. When a teacher helps a class make application of the knowledge its members are gaining to the improvement of living in their families and community, learning acquires much greater importance.

They search for new knowledge. He conducts research in his laboratory or in the community. When students have the privilege of working with such a teacher they have the opportunity to discover that knowledge is not a static body of information which has already been discovered. They gain the understanding that new knowledge is being sought and formed each day by scholars all over the world, that the world is being changed constantly by the knowledge obtained through the search, and that each person can be one of the searchers if he chooses. If a student acquires this understanding by his work with a teacher who is an active scholar, it changes his way of life.

They know which portions of the field are complex and confusing. He will have studied the research and determined which processes and concepts cause the learner's difficulty and what procedures of teaching have proven most effective. With this type of preparation the teacher has an added value to his scholarship; he is able to interpret his field to pupils in the manner which makes it most meaningful to them; his scholarship is more functional for teaching.

Probably no single teacher makes all of these scholarly contributions. The scholars on a staff will be different combinations of these qualities but all will be concerned with increasing their own competence in their field and with stimulating the curiosity and competencies of pupils.

The combination of content and creativity is a necessary blend if the classroom environment is to be intellectually stimulating. Neither can be allowed to outweigh the other. Stress on acquiring knowledge without the opportunity to use or interpret it dulls the excitement of learning. Stress on creativity without attempting to increase the range of knowledge and experience which the learner can use results in shallowness. The teacher who makes a major contribution in stimulating intellectual growth continually seeks to produce creative scholars.

SELF-EVALUATION CHECKLIST
Stimulating Intellectual Growth

Do I:

1. Experiment in my own reading and teaching?
2. Attempt to increase the creativity of each child?
3. Give assignments which permit pupils to make an individual selection of ways to fulfill requirement?
4. Encourage pupils to express interpretations and points of view that differ from my own?
5. Avoid giving my interpretation of events and materials to pupils?
6. Use class time to give pupils an opportunity to express their interpretations of life and literature?

7. Stress the validity, importance, and use of personal feelings?
8. Show concern for the feelings, hopes, and aspirations of my pupils?
9. Show warm friendliness and acceptance for my pupils?
10. Share my feelings, fears, and aspirations?
11. Let pupils know I am still seeking better answers?
12. Use brainstorming sessions to secure a variety of ideas for the class to examine and test?
13. Give credit and honor to scholars?
14. Seek more knowledge about the field I teach than the textbook contains?
15. Collect information about topics not included in the course of study?
16. Try to obtain summer experiences which will provide illustrative material for my classes?
17. Collect souvenirs and documents which can be used by my classes?
18. Study the research concerning the problems of learning associated with special phases of my field of specialization?
19. Vary the organization of the content I teach as I work with different classes?
20. Conduct research in my field?
21. Produce new organizations or interpretations of the content in my field?
22. Assist pupils to apply the information they acquire in my classes to the improvement of their living?
23. Demonstrate my belief that new knowledge is being constantly discovered?
24. Encourage each pupil to believe he can discover new knowledge?
25. Share the research techniques I possess?
26. Demonstrate enthusiasm for scholastic activity?
27. Recognize the scholastic achievement of members of the class and student body?

BIBLIOGRAPHY

Stimulating Intellectual Growth

Association for Supervision and Curriculum Development, *Toward Better Teaching*. Washington, D.C.: N.E.A., 1949.

Nesbitt, M., "A Creative Approach to Learning," *National Education Association Journal*, 47 (January, 1958), pp. 14–16.

Zirbes, L., "What Creative Teaching Means," *Childhood Education*, 33 (October, 1956), pp. 51–54.

• • • Developing Self-Direction

The determination of group direction and policy is based upon the individual decisions of group members. If the society is to improve, or even sustain itself, its individual members must be able to make wise decisions. Each must be able to decide for himself what he values, what he wants, and what is the best method of obtaining it.

Thus, in a democratic society, the school must place a major emphasis on helping the individual become self-directing.

UNSATISFACTORY TEACHER

The teacher tells pupils what to do, how to do it and how well they have done. He defines the task to be done, gives the solution and does not allow questions. No viewpoints that conflict with those held by the teacher may be expressed. Pupils are forced to conform by punishment and the use of marks.

MINIMUM SATISFACTORY TEACHER

The teacher plans what is to be done by the class but members are allowed to propose supplementary activities and to suggest additional questions they would like to have considered. A few minutes are allocated each day to discuss questions that have arisen in the mind of the pupils, and on occasion a pupil may state an opinion which is in conflict with that held by the teacher. Marks are determined by scores on teacher made tests, but if a pupil does extra work he may submit it for consideration. From time to time the teacher holds a conference with a pupil who is having difficulty to see what plans can be made to increase the pupil's effectiveness.

11 · *Guidance in the Formulation of Goals*

The individual acts to secure something he wants. The effort may be made to satisfy a sudden whim, a passing interest, a long term goal, or an ideal. Or the end desired may be an escape from fear, discomfort, or pain.

As a teacher works with pupils he is concerned with helping them formulate the goals that will guide their behavior. He seeks to help them establish purposes that are strong enough to insure sustained effort and to discover values which will serve as the basis of choice among purposes.

All Pupils Have Purposes

A father sits in his study. Jack, his six-year-old son, yells outside the window. The boy attracts the man's attention. The father looks out the window and sees that his son is playing with a snake. His parental interest is aroused and he watches. He questions Jack about its length, its color, and the shape of its head. They talk for a few minutes about snakes and then the son asks his father to help him build a pit to keep the snake in. But the man shakes his head and turns back to his writing.

Much teaching is like that situation. The teacher brings in a device to get the students' attention, like Jack's yelling. The pupils look and talk with the teacher, as the father did with Jack, and are then ready to go back to their other pursuits. When the teacher asks them to do something about it, they have no greater desire to do it than Jack's father did to help Jack make a snake pit.

But the teacher has something that Jack did not. He is bigger than the pupils and knows more ways of appealing to their pride, curiosity, good sportsmanship, and other sources of motivation. He also can use force—marks, isolating the pupil from friends, detention, derogatory remarks on the permanent record which may hinder future life activities. Whether he uses entreaties, blackmail, or physical force, the teacher does not create real motivation. The pupil is going to sneak away from the task as soon as he dares—just as the father would if Jack could have forced him to help him with the pen.

But suppose Jack's comments have confirmed the father's sneaking suspicion that the snake his son was examining was a coral snake. He would have bolted from his chair, grabbed a hoe, stick, or gun, and gone to kill the snake despite his distaste for the job. After he had killed the snake, presuming he was the successful gladiator, he would have searched the yard for still other snakes. All this action, even entering a dangerous fight, would have been undertaken to do something he thought was important, to preserve the safety of his child. *A person takes action without artificial stimulation and keeps at it without supervision or reward when he believes there is something important to do.*

All pupils have purposes. They have vocational goals, they are attempting to establish certain human relationships, and they are seeking to attain certain material objects. Just because some student purposes may not coincide with the purposes of the school is no reason to conclude that the students lack motivation.

Jack could have looked at his father when he did not respond to the invitation to help build the snake pit and could have decided that his father was lazy, shiftless, and unintelligent. Jack could have said that his father had no purposes, or motivation, because he was not concerned about the snake pit too. Some teachers make exactly the same type of judgment concerning the pupils they teach because of an inadequate understanding of motivation.

A teacher can strengthen pupils' motivation by helping them to recognize and implement their socially acceptable purposes, rather than by trying to create an artificial interest in activities that they care little about. New purposes, and thus new interests, are developed as pupils widen their horizons while pursuing present purposes. For example, while learning how to make a bow and arrow he wanted, David, age seven, learned about spears and knights in armor and for a time became deeply interested in studying about castles, moats, and how people lived in Robin Hood's time.

To be skillful in promoting self direction involves a study of the background and environment of pupils. It requires knowing enough about each pupil to discover his purposes and values.

Pupils approach any situation with many distinct purposes. They may look upon an English class as a terrific bore, but they may at the same time have an intense desire to get to college. As a result of the value that they attach to becoming a college student, they will put up with what they consider the useless activities of the English class in order to achieve the college career they value. It works the opposite way too. A student who is concerned about being accepted by the boys in the gang, all of whom belittle English, may make fun of and refuse to participate in studying a poem or play that he might otherwise be inclined to enjoy.

Not all the purposes an individual has operate with equal power in a single situation. His desire to belong to the gang may conflict with his desire to win teacher approval. Although both purposes are real, *the purpose that is of greatest importance to the student at the moment is the one that is the motivating force in the situation for him.*

Group motivation has been achieved when the class agrees to undertake a project. As long as the ideas or plans belong to the teacher, he is still in a position of attempting to arouse interest. When pupils have decided that a task is worth doing, have participated in planning and have committed themselves to its completion, the teacher is in a position to ask individuals who change their purpose, "Did you make an intelligent decision? Can you improve it? Are you living up to your agreement with the class? How can you do so more adequately?" The burden of proof and explanation is on the shoulders of the student.

The members of the class assume responsibility at the moment they decide on the project to be undertaken and the methods to be followed. From this point on, the teacher's role is that of a consultant and a resource person, until it is time for further evaluation and planning.

Motivation cannot be achieved in fifteen minutes. When a teacher talks to a student about his failure to exert effort in class, he too frequently makes the error of assuming that the interview must lead to a commitment from the student. Such an assumption decreases the chances of success. If a teacher tries to crowd a student into doing something, the student becomes defensive. The interview degenerates into a battle of wits. As it becomes a game or battle, the teacher loses his chance of helping the pupil find how to work in terms of important purposes in the class.

Of course, students should not be permitted to do nothing at all. No student should get the impression that he will get something for nothing. He should be made fully aware of the consequences of inactivity. A student who refused to exert any effort should not receive credit or be passed. In interviews or group planning, this point should be made clear, but a teacher makes a mistake if he attempts to make decisions for the pupils or force them into action.

His job is to help them examine their behavior and its consequences and to suggest other possibilities as he sees them, and then wait for them to move. Motivated action involves their deciding that it is important for them to do something, and their identification, sometimes with teacher assistance, of the activity they consider worthy.

There are various levels of classroom motivation. Ray Simpson, of the University of Illinois, has identified them as follows:

1. Works because of fear.
2. Works for extrinsic rewards (credits, marks) without understanding the purposes of the teacher.
3. Understands the purposes of the teacher, rejects them, but works to obtain the extrinsic rewards.
4. Understands the purposes of the teacher, accepts them without having any part in forming them, and works for them.
5. Establishes goals with necessary guidance and works to achieve them.
6. Is able to clearly define goals and work for them wisely with a minimum of help from others.

Some children's purposes are influenced by their relationships with their parents. For example, a parent may want his child to go to college. If the child is anxious to please his parent, he may select a college preparatory course and try to learn the content of the course, even though he isn't interested in it. Another child may be attempting to show his parents that he really has certain abilities that they refuse to recognize. In either case, the relationship of the child to his parents is an important factor in his motivation.

A child's age-group will also determine his purposes. He wants to be accepted; he wants to belong; he wants to be recognized. The ideas, the goals, and the attitudes of his gang will be directly responsible for many of his purposes. He will try to do those things that will give him status in his own age-group.

On the other hand, older friends outside the age-group help to create his purposes. The comment of an older cousin, the approval of the gang leader in the block, the attitudes of his heroes, all influence him. If a boy wants to be a second Mickey Mantle, he will attempt to do the things that Mickey Mantle says are important. If a girl wants to be a movie star, she will try to copy the way her favorite movie star dresses, the way she combs her hair, the way she walks. Any attempt on our part to belittle or deride the recommendations of the hero is, in the mind of the child, an attempt to destroy his purposes. The child will fight back and will attempt to retain and carry out the purposes he had when he first entered the classroom.

PURPOSES ← PARENTS / COMMUNITY LIFE / MOVIES / TV / NEWSPAPERS / FRIENDS

Movies, radio, and television all significantly affect the way children attempt to attain their purposes. Situations portrayed as desirable in these media will often be accepted as desirable by the children who see them. They seek to attain success in the ways they have seen it attained in the movies and on television programs. The early 'fifties saw a sweeping demonstration of the influence of movies and television on children's purposes. Boys and girls who had never seen a cow or a horse, or plains or mountains, suddenly wanted cowboy hats, cowboy guns, cowboy equipment of all kinds. Why? Because motion pictures and television had built up a "two gun rootin' tootin'" cowboy as the acme of success and enjoyment. Teachers were faced with the problem of what to do with youngsters who came to school with high-heeled boots, toy guns, or even real guns. They couldn't ignore the motivation of the pupils; they could only work with it.

Community mores influence the purposes of boys and girls. They want to be accepted and they are motivated to behave in ways approved by the community. If members of the community say "ain't," boys and girls will find it hard to start saying "am not." They want to be accepted by their parents, by their older brothers, and by their heroes who say "ain't." Any teacher who attempts a different pattern of behavior is confronted with the task of discovering purposes as strong as the desire to be accepted by the gang, family, and community.

Community issues also lead to strong motivation. When children see the adults of the community divided on certain issues, they wonder why and they begin to ask questions. The intense emotion displayed by their parents and friends increases their desire to find answers.

Pupils' purposes are also influenced by the statements and behavior of their teachers. The strength of this factor depends on what they think about their teachers. If they believe that a certain teacher is a fine person, a person they like, a person they enjoy being with, they give serious consideration to his wishes. If they respect him for his scholarship, reputation, or knowledge, they may want his respect. A teacher may demonstrate poor human relations and still be able to get boys and girls to work in his class simply because of an excellent reputation. If another teacher without the reputation practices the same behavior he would find himself ostracized by his students. A teacher's influence on pupil purposes often depends more on what pupils think about him than on what he actually does.

The impact of all these influences and others determines the purposes which pupils bring to school, and these purposes constitute the basic motivation with which he works.

Boys' and girls' purposes are revealed in many ways. During a sharing period, when pupils are talking about the things that interest them, a pupil may casually mention something that he wants to do. Or someone may say, "That's something I wish we could improve." Sometimes the entire class comes into the classroom bubbling over with excitement about some project they wish to undertake. The alert teacher is waiting for these opportunities and is ready to go along with the purposes that are in line with the objectives established for the school program.

Not all purposes are alike or of equal value in a learning situation. A child might pay close attention to the reading of *As You Like It* and do the homework faithfully each night without feeling that the play was worth reading. Such a child undoubtedly has a purpose. Probably the purpose is to get a good mark in English to please mother, but it is not to gain a richer understanding of human nature or a deeper appreciation of Shakespeare's beauty of expression. Another child in the class may read his homework because he finds enjoyment in the outlook on life held by some of the characters. His purpose is to enjoy himself. No prod by mother or the teacher is necessary to get him to work. A group of boys building a boat does not need adults to urge them to work faster or to praise them for the "A's" they receive in woodworking class. Rather, they are impatient when they encounter difficulties.

Purposes are easy to discover but sometimes difficult to utilize in the classroom. All pupils have desires, things they want to do, information they want to obtain.

Motivation, when considered as a teacher problem, is closely related to discipline and guidance.

A disciplined pupil is one with a purpose strong enough to enable him to ignore or fight off the distracting features of his environment. If the purpose is one that coincides with the purposes of the school, self-discipline is recognized. If his purposes are not satisfactory to the teacher, he may be labeled undisciplined.

Attempts to deal with the pupil called "undisciplined" by telling him that he must forget his purposes and accept those of the class will be unsuccessful. No one changes purposes because someone else tells him to. He may seem to acquiesce until some purpose stronger than his desire to please comes along. Or a trick may be able to arouse his interest for a few minutes. But if any teacher is going to deal with real pupil motivation, it is necessary to discover why the pupil refuses to accept the purposes the school thinks are important. Such knowledge is obtained through guidance and counseling procedures.

The development of adequate motivation is assured when pupils are given an opportunity to organize their experiences around the problems that to them seem vital. If they can say, "These are the things we want to know" or "These are the things that are important to us," motivation takes care of itself. By stating their concerns, students identify the motivation that is present in the class. It will only be broken and dissipated when the teacher, in organizing the experiences with the class, creates the kind of situation in which students are unable to carry out their purposes.

A successful teacher must take the time to talk to students, to discover their real purposes, and to analyze any lack of motivation to do the things the school considers important. But he will discover nothing unless he creates a situation in which pupils feel free to talk, unless he is willing to listen to them, and unless he is aware that their purposes are not necessarily the same as his.

A teacher should not expect students to be enthusiastic about the same things that he is. But this is probably one of the most common mistakes. He assumes that because his previous experience with Shakespeare or with clay-modeling has been satisfying, other people will respond in the same way. This is not true. Expect students to be interested only in the types of things that they have experienced and have found good. They may *acquire* enthusiasm for the things about which he is enthusiastic, but they don't necessarily *start* with his enthusiasm.

TEACHER AROUSED INTEREST = [figure] MOTIVATION = [figure]

Some teachers make the mistake of assuming that motivation is a simple process of arousing interest. They think they are motivating students when they arouse enough interest to secure the pupils' willingness to talk with them for a little while about a certain idea. They write lesson plans in which they indicate the devices by which they will motivate. Each plan for each period contains a "motivating device." These teachers aren't really creating motivation; they are simply stimulating interest. And often the interest is very superficial. They don't go beyond the interest-arousing stimuli. They merely hope that by getting youngsters to talk with them for a few minutes, they will succeed in bringing about real and valuable learnings.

True motivation goes much deeper than that. It involves the basic drives and purposes of the individual. A teacher promotes self-direction as he helps a class or an individual recognize and focus the motivations they have. Any simple surface interests that he can create are not really the motivating forces in their lives.

Motivation is closely associated with the values that a pupil holds. His values determine whether or not he will put effort into a project. If he can see that the things that he believes in and wants will be furthered by the project or the activity, he will engage in it wholeheartedly, with no question about the amount of effort expended. But if he is not really motivated, if his interest has been artificially stimulated by the teacher, his reaction will be, "Well, how much work do I have to do?" "Is this enough?" When he is truly motivated, however, he never thinks about whether he has done enough to satisfy his teacher. Rather, he asks himself, "Have I done as much as I can in the available time?"

When a person believes something is important to do, he is motivated. He has a purpose and will do his best to fulfill it. A motivated student is one with a purpose. An interested child may not have purpose. Interest may be mere whim—a short-lived response to a passing stimulus. *Purpose is being concerned about accomplishing something.* If the purpose is strong enough, it will control behavior.

If students want to learn a particular skill or certain information, teaching is a very simple process. It is nothing more than helping them find the necessary materials, or explaining to them what we already know about what they want to learn, or demonstrating and providing opportunity to practice the basic skills that we have and that they want to acquire. It is no trouble to teach most girls how to use make-up, for example. They want to learn. The problem in teaching comes when we attempt to get youngsters to learn something that they are not interested in or actually don't *want* to learn. If we are the only ones who want something to happen or who want students to learn certain things, we have a difficult time transferring that "want-to" from ourselves to the student.

Teaching for self direction means the teacher places his emphasis on helping students discover and work in terms of their purposes rather than on ways of motivating students to do what the teacher wants.

The Clarification of Values

As the individual works for the things or way of life he values, he establishes the day-to-day purposes that control his behavior. Any teacher concerned with promoting pupil self-direction through the formulation of goals must be concerned with helping them clarify the values they hold.

> An eleventh-grade girls' health class was discussing the bone structure of the body. A redheaded girl, seemingly paying little attention, gazed out the window. Suddenly she turned, waited for a break in the conversation, and commented, "You know, what I really want to

find out is whether I day-dream too much." Five or six other girls exclaimed, "I do too," and the entire class became attentive. The teacher recognized that a teachable moment had arrived. She asked how many felt that day-dreaming was a personal problem of theirs. Every hand was raised, and the class proceeded to discuss for the remainder of the period the amount of day-dreaming that each did and to try to determine what was typical. As the girls left, many commented to their close friends that they had been worried but had concluded during class that they were normal.

After the first comment that was not on the topic, the teacher had had to make a decision. She had to decide whether continuing with the planned lesson was more important than exploring the question raised by the student. Because she believed that helping pupils understand themselves and their feelings was of fundamental importance, she took the time to explore their concerns and beliefs with them.

A teacher cannot avoid helping pupils formulate values. He teaches by the way he lives, by the remarks he makes, by the points he emphasizes, by his reactions to ideas, by the arrangement of the room, and by the interpretation he makes of his role as the teacher.

It may be negative teaching. If the pupils dislike the teacher, any values he expresses will be outwardly rejected by the class. Boys and girls will want to show their resistance to the teacher's authority and will assume values contrary to his to show their independence. If the students like their teacher, his wishes, hopes, and expressed beliefs are absorbed by them. In their desire to please, they accept and assimilate some of his values.

To be effective in the teaching of values, a teacher should clarify and classify his own values. What does he believe about himself? What does he believe about others? What does he believe about how human beings should relate to each other and their environment? What does he deem a desirable social organization? If a teacher is confused in his own thinking, if the values he holds are in conflict with each other, if he has not identified the areas in which he is uncertain of his convictions, he will be less able to provide assistance to pupils in exploring what they hold dear. He may add to the pupil's confusion. If he is timid in exploring and discussing his own values, he may influence pupils to feel that class work is for the learning of facts, but not for the exploration of the implications of facts for human behavior. A teacher is less secure in helping pupils explore the values they hold unless he has had the courage to examine his convictions.

The teacher who recognizes his responsibility in teaching values scrutinizes his behavior. Is it consistent with his professed beliefs? Does he give verbal support to freedom of speech? If so, is he willing to have pupils challenge and attempt to refute his arguments? Does he lay claim to valuing diversity and try to secure homogeneous grouping of his classes? Does he advocate respect for human personality and take action which makes some of his students feel less adequate and less worthy? Actions and words that conflict leave the pupils disturbed or convinced that the teacher is a hypocrite or unintelligent.

In the classroom values are taught by the way the group lives together. Although in American society there are many values on which people disagree, others are held in common by most of the members of the community and it is desired that the young acquire them. Parents, the local media of mass communication, and public officials all support the common values and boys and girls absorb them. These values are incorporated into the group living of the school and usually are not questioned. The learning occurs without the pupil knowing it, with only the exceptional child challenging the ideals held by the adults.

A major step in helping a pupil to develop a satisfactory set of values is to encourage him to determine what his current values are. Many times a pupil lives without ever being fully aware of the values that guide his behavior. He needs to have an opportunity to talk through with someone who is understanding and sympathetic the types of values and beliefs that he displays by his actions in a given situation. Questions can be raised in class discussion or in individual conversation that help a youngster to look at himself and what he believes. When the student hands in a written project, for example, he can be asked by what standards he has judged his work. If his paper is sloppy, with misspelled words and poor grammar, if it reveals antisocial attitudes, he can be asked if this piece of work really measures up to the standards that he holds for himself. The effort is made to help him see that a person's values are manifest in his beliefs and the standards he sets for himself.

Pupils can be helped to develop their own values by encouraging them to investigate the values their fellows hold. In a population as cosmopolitan as the American, every classroom includes youngsters from families with a wide variety of backgrounds. Out of these backgrounds come different values, revealed in different beliefs and different standards. As youngsters have an opportunity to talk together about the standards and beliefs that are held in their own homes, each youngster has a wider basis for determining the quality of his own values. However, care must be used in examining the values pupils hold.

> For example, in a school in New York City, a teacher found that one boy was making book on the horse races. The teacher was faced with the decision of what to do. As he began to inquire into the situation, he found that the boy's father was also a bookmaker.

If the teacher had said to the boy, "Your values are all wrong. They are antisocial and unworthy," he would have been condemning the boy's father. The boy would have been torn between loyalties, loyalty to his teacher and loyalty to his family. It is easy to guess which allegiance would have won out. If the teacher had told the boy before the class that bookmaking was wrong, he would have destroyed any chance he had of helping the boy to revise his values in a positive direction. The boy's values would only be changed positively as he had an opportunity to contrast them with other values in a situation where he and his family were not threatened.

Change cannot be secured in an individual's values by telling him that he is wrong. Such an approach forces him to defend what he believes and to deride and reject other values without a sincere examination.

If a teacher wishes to affect the values held by the pupil, he has to be willing to have his own values questioned. If pupils are not free to question and challenge, the teacher will not know what pupils believe. The only comments he hears will be those which support and supplement his own. He will be unable to probe the values of boys and girls because he will not know what they are.

Even if he did not need to be permissive in order to know the values held by his class, he would find a permissive attitude and mutual respect the only way to work in the area of values. Coercion can produce conformity but it will not develop allegiance to values. Commitment is a personal decision, voluntarily given because of sentiment or intellectual analysis.

It is important that a teacher makes clear to the group what values he holds. This does not mean telling the pupils what values they should accept. It means rather that the teacher is honest about the values he regards as worth while just as he expects children to be honest about theirs. He explains his reasons for holding certain values and gives the pupils a chance to explain their reasons for holding theirs. He makes no claims about which values are superior. The superiority of given values is ascertained only by the group as a result of its own analysis. If boys and girls do not decide to accept a teacher's values as a result of examination and trial, he cannot force them to do so by authoritarian procedures.

An example of the difficulty that a teacher encounters in the area of values is found in a community in which there are many religions.

In one Long Island community, the school population is divided almost equally among members of the Catholic, Jewish, and Protestant faiths. Suppose a teacher goes into that situation and tells boys and girls that there is only one true religion. What chance does he have of acceptance? What chance does he have of getting boys and girls to examine freely and openly the values that they hold? It is easy to see in this situation the lack of possibility for the teacher really to influence the values of boys and girls when he takes a dogmatic position and tells them what they should believe. To make the contrast still more evident, suppose a teacher in a city in which there is a strong labor organization goes into the classroom and tells boys and girls that labor organizations are detrimental to the welfare of the population. Suppose he advocates the abolition of labor unions. What are his chances for changing the attitudes of boys and girls?

As the members of a class have opportunities to think through together the issues that confront them, each individual student develops his own values. If certain youngsters reject the values that are commonly accepted in American society, the teacher can work and talk with them on an individual basis to discover if they see the full implications of their values. He can't go much further. Force may win compliance but it will not win acceptance. Persuasion may win verbal acceptance but not valid commitment. Pupils can be made to repeat answers mechanically, but they cannot be made to believe them. It is easy to see the ineffectiveness of attempting to "give pupils the answers" where local customs are involved. A teacher may tell high-school boys they should bow when they ask a girl to dance, but they will reject the statement once they see that their older brothers are successful with girls without bowing. An English teacher in a rural community tried for two years to convince pupils that they should not say "ain't." But on the playground they continued to use "ain't" constantly. In the classroom, out of deference to the teacher, because they liked her, they said "am not," but in other situations they followed the customs of their family and friends. Chances of changing deep-rooted values simply by telling people they should change are even slimmer.

If the teacher takes a position in opposition to accepted patterns, he may lead the students to reject him. A refusal to examine open-mindedly the beliefs and ideas of adolescents has caused many teachers to be labeled "outdated" and out of touch with reality. When this condition exists, he cannot hope to be effective in helping pupils formulate their values.

Each class will have pupils who hold conflicting values on some issue. These may be examined with honesty and without harm if the values held in common are recognized and emphasized. The common values provide the cement which holds a group together while it explores the differences in viewpoint.

If the previous experience of an individual student has given him little opportunity to become aware of the social values of his community, his school experiences should help him obtain this information. Suppose a first-grade boy comes from a home in which stealing is accepted. He needs to discover that the community as a whole regards stealing as unacceptable. He needs to come into contact with the standards of honesty which prevail throughout the rest of the community and to recognize the implications of taking a stand in opposition to the community and social standards. Values are raised only as individuals and groups become aware of new values which promise to make life richer than the ones previously held.

Sometimes the experiences of certain members of the class will suggest to the others new values that they have not previously experienced in their community.

> A third-grade boy who had previously attended a school in which racial intolerance was completely unknown moved to a community that excluded Negro children from the school he attended. One day, as the boy was playing with one of his classmates in the schoolyard, a Negro boy passed by. One of the other pupils yelled out a derogatory name

that was offensive both to the Negro and to the boy who had never before experienced such attitudes. The new boy promptly hit the offending pupil.

What should the teacher have done? How could she have helped the new boy recognize the difference in standards and the implications of his act? What future behavior should she have advised him to follow? What should she have said to the boy who called out the offensive name? What opportunity did this incident provide for the entire class?

Two sets of values were in open conflict. The teacher was presented with a made-to-order situation. By her questions she could encourage each pupil in the class to examine his own standards, to compare them with those of his fellows, to contrast the standards of the group with which he lives with the standards of other groups, regions, and authorities, and then to determine the values that were acceptable to him.

The analysis that is made will differ in length and intensity from grade-level to grade-level and from incident to incident. No single analysis stands alone. Developing values and self-direction is a long-term proposition. Comfort for the teacher lies in the recognition that the values that a group or an individual formulates at any moment represent only their present experience and insight and are satisfactory only when they are kept open to revision in light of new experience. Helping pupils see and verbalize the values they live by is not easy, but helping them to formulate new values is even more difficult. If the values which seem preferable are in conflict with those of their age-group or of the community, the teacher can help by bringing them into contact through discussion, movies, radio, television, or the printed page with persons who hold different values. If the difference raises questions in the mind of the pupils, that is the opening wedge.

The teacher can set the tone for careful analysis and honest evaluation. A major contribution is the way he handles opposition to his own ideas. If he seeks to win by argument when he finds someone who differs, he influences others to do likewise. If he listens as intently and as openly to persons who disagree with him, he makes clear his valuing of exploring and testing values.

The teacher who takes seriously the task of helping pupils clarify values cannot stop with the experiences of the class or local community and feel that he has performed his function. In the area of social, political, and economic values, boys and girls should have an opportunity to come into contact with points of view that have been taken by religious authorities, by philosophers, and by social scientists. As they examine the values held by people who have had more experience than they, each class member has a more adequate way of judging his own values. Let's consider values at the level of standards by which we judge writing. If an English class is studying literature and rejects every type of literature except the comics and pulp magazines, the class should also have an opportunity to come into contact with the values and standards held by authorities in the field of literature. The class members may reject these standards. They may refuse to accept the standards of authorities as values for themselves. But if the school is to be a richer learning environment than the home and community out of which the boys and girls have developed their own standards, the pupils must have contact with a greater number of standards. Failures in the areas of conflicting values come as teachers attempt to tell pupils the answers. Success comes through skill in impartial consideration with pupils of the conflicting values that bear on the problem being solved.

When a class investigates values held, pupils will find that each individual has beliefs that conflict with others which he accepts. This lack of consistency should be seen by the teacher as an opportunity. He helps the pupils identify the conflicting values within themselves and raises questions that will lead them to probe the sources of their beliefs and why they hold contradictory views. *As pupils discover discrepancies in their beliefs, they should be assured that they are not unique, that they reflect the conflicts of our culture, that all people growing up in a civilization with heterogeneous values have these conflicts in their thinking until they evaluate, sort, classify, and develop a consistency in values which is the mark of a mature, thinking moral man.* The teacher can affirm that the examination of conflicts discovered in our pattern of beliefs is the doorway to new insight. Instead of being dreaded or denied, the conflicts should be looked upon by the learner as opportunities to seek the truth.

A heterogeneous class, one that contains children from families of different social, economic, religious, national, racial, and political backgrounds, offers a rich resource for the development of greater consistency and commitment in the area of values. *If the teacher is permissive of difference and can help boys and girls to accept and examine difference, a desirable learning environment is created.* As they talk together, students will discover a range of values related to a single issue or type of behavior.

A teacher helps pupils examine values by recognizing that there are more than two viewpoints toward any issue. As long as a person thinks there are only two answers or ways of action, they fall into two categories: ours and the wrong one. But when it is discovered that there may be many ways of looking at a problem and a variety of solutions, the situation shifts from defending a position and discrediting the opposing one to intelligent selection by careful examination of positions and the differences among them.

As an individual's vision is increased by discovering a greater number of possibilities, he is in a position to make a more intelligent choice. If pupils are encouraged to ask who should hold these values, under what conditions and with what consequences they are held, the teacher is going as far as he can. Testing any value by these criteria is the way a person examines and refines his values. As he subjects his values to the test of honest comparison with the values held by others, he increases his commitment to those that stand the test. He discards those found to be inferior. He revises those which he finds can be improved and eliminates obvious conflict. The process is continuous throughout life if he can contrast and compare in an atmosphere of mutual respect and permissiveness. If on the other hand, someone, teacher or colleague, attempts to belittle or discredit his beliefs or attempts to prove the superiority of his point of view, the learner is threatened and clutches his values to his heart and defends them with intensity, enthusiasm, and the most effective rationalization he can produce. If pressed hard, he defends by beginning to criticize the values held by his opponents.

Much of the difficulty in dealing with difference in opinion and values in the classroom comes from inept handling by the teacher of situations that arise. If pupils are free to react explosively, without an attempt to understand the other person's feelings or point of view, the exploration of difference may result in increased prejudices and rejection of values. *If the teacher, however, will help the class define the problem, state the issues involved, determine the variety of beliefs concerning it, and consider the implications of the application of each belief, he provides the stability and structure which make the experience educative.* If the teacher guides this process during the first controversial situations it will become habitual and the class will follow the same procedure with new problems that arise. The teacher cannot be a passive factor. He must see his function as sharing with pupils his ability to examine differences. It is not his function to attempt to provide the evaluation of a given value but to guide the evaluation process intelligently.

Not all consideration of values comes from controversy. Values are derived from the analysis of experiences. After a class has taken a trip, completed a unit, produced a play, or finished any project, the teacher has the opportunity during the evaluation session to focus attention on values. In addition to making judgments concerning achievement and process the teacher can raise questions concerning satisfaction with goals and the ways of living and working together. As a pupil says, "I like the way we worked because it gave me an opportunity to know more people" he is stating a value. As another says, "I was unhappy during the time Sally chaired our group because she made all of the decisions," he is verbalizing a way of life he has come to dislike. Out of such discussion can emerge statements of beliefs and codes of behavior which the group establishes as guides.

Much of the work with values will be individual teaching. Pupils will bring their personal problems to receptive teachers in various ways. In an eighth-grade class Evelyn, an intelligent girl who is thinking of the future, will say, "I want to be a teacher. Do you think I will be a good one?" Junior, a boy whose father left home three years ago, shyly questions, "Why do fathers and mothers quarrel? Is a stepfather as good as a real father?" Jackson, a big good-looking boy, two years older than his classmates because he lived as a child in a mountain district in which school attendance laws were not enforced, questions, "Coach, why do some of the kids think they are better than I am? I can whip any of them." Paula, a girl more physically mature than her classmates complains, "Why don't you notice me the way you do Sue and Milly? You are always busy when I want to talk to you." All of these comments were opening remarks of pupils who were seeking answers. Most would never have been asked in class.

Being willing to take the time to listen, to ask the sincere, interested questions that lead to the pupil's stating the real concern that lies behind the opening remark, is a part of helping pupils clarify and refine values. *Listening, reflecting, restating, asking about consequences but not judging or condemning are the actions of the teacher who is skillful in helping pupils clarify values.* Being a person who is understanding and trustworthy is the basic ingredient. Taking the time to talk when the student is ready, not when the teacher wants to schedule a conference with him, is a second contribution. Unless the teacher is willing to listen when the pupil is ready to expose a portion of his deepest beliefs or concerns, the student will conclude that this adult is not really helpful, and will re-establish the defenses behind which he hides his important values.

The teacher who considers helping students clarify their values will be willing to interrupt class plans when a teachable moment arises. The occasion may be produced by a comment like that in the eleventh-grade health class. It may be produced by a dispute between two boys. A pupil's observation may lead to it.

> In a Louisiana school a class of fourth-graders was looking at some covers on *Saturday Evening Post* issues as a step in getting ready to write some stories. The picture was of a football hero surrounded by admiring girls. To the side and away from the fans were two youths, a boy with a heavy load of books and an unattractive girl. They both appeared dejected, dissatisfied with themselves, and not interested in anyone else. A little girl in the class who had not made an observation suddenly pointed to the girl on the outside and blurted out, "I know how she feels. She feels like hell. I know because I feel like that too." The teacher, somewhat shocked, turned to the girl and said, "One of the things we are working on is good ways of expressing ourselves and good choice of words. Ginny, will you think about it until tomorrow and see if you cannot find a word that more accurately describes how the girl in the picture feels?"
>
> The next morning during sharing period, without any prompting by the teacher who was probably hoping the incident had been forgotten, Ginny announced: "I've been thinking about the girl in the picture. I was right. She does feel like hell. I feel like that when my brother beats me when I try to follow him. He is an s. o. b."

The teacher could have condemned her for the language or the antagonism toward the brother. But she did neither. She accepted the observation as an accurate contribution to the discussion of human relations.

> A five-year-old girl in a kindergarten dictated a story about a little boy of three who continually teased his sister until she slapped him and made him cry. Her last sentence was "The girl is sorry she slaps her brother and I'll bet he likes his sister."

Clues like the two above give the teacher direction concerning the ideas to explore and the type of comment that can be made.

If an administrator, a parent, another teacher, another class, or the minister objects to an activity of the class, it provides an opportunity to analyze values. Rather than giving in, resisting, or ignoring, the protest gives the teacher an opportunity to ask the class to rethink its position. Why do we think it is important to engage in this activity? Why would anyone else object? Are there consequences that we are ignoring? How are our purposes and values different for the person objecting? Should we revise any of our values or our actions? If the pupils widen their knowledge of positions held by contemporaries, if they gain more understanding of the position they hold, if they revise their beliefs or course of action, the challenge from outside has served a valuable function.

As a class works together, it will want to develop symbols which represent their values. Phrases, key words, and mottoes are ways of reenforcing by repetition the agreements pupils have reached about the way they desire to live. Emblems, flags, and objects which can be seen serve as reminders of agreements reached concerning desired types of achievement. The important point for the teacher to remember is that these symbols should grow out of the experience of that class. Such symbols have a relatively common meaning for teacher and pupils.

Throughout all of his work with values, the teacher is seeking to have a pupil develop the ability to state his values, increase the consistency among the values he holds, act in terms of his values, exhibit the same value-pattern in dissimilar situations, and gain knowledge of the relative importance he assigns to the various values he holds.

12 · *Promotion of the Ability to Make Intelligent Decisions*

Self-direction consists of knowing one's purposes and values, skill in implementing them, and the ability to evaluate and revise. The preceding chapter has discussed ways to assist pupils to formulate their goals. Chapter 9, "Instruction for the Individual," treated the development of pupil ability to plan and execute. This chapter suggests ways of helping pupils grow in the ability to make judgments and revise goals, plans, or procedures.

Any individual or group is confronted daily with many choices concerning what is important to do and how to do it. The courses of action selected may be determined on the basis of whim, prejudice, emotion, physical condition, or by flipping a coin. But such decisions may not be intelligent.

The wisdom of a decision increases as the ends sought are more clearly defined, as more of the pertinent data are considered, and as more people who will be affected by the outcome participate in the process. Teachers concerned with improving pupil ability to make intelligent decisions will work to increase pupil skill in taking these steps.

Emphasis on making more intelligent judgments can be the essential feature of a teacher's work. Whenever a decision is being made, the teacher may see the process as his opportunity to develop the problem-solving skill. What is most important to study? How shall we work? How shall we arrange the furniture to facilitate our work? What conclusions can we draw from these data? What application can be made of these principles?

Not only does the teacher who strives to develop his pupil's ability to make wise decisions work through the total group situation, but he takes the same approach in his guidance of the work of individuals. He asks, "What do you need to do? What do you hope to become?

How can work in this class further your goals? What is the problem? What data are needed? What are the possible courses of action? Which action holds most promise? Is the progress being made satisfactory? What changes should be made in goals or procedures?"

The teacher's effort with the group and with individuals is to get them to assume responsibility for action by making decisions. He helps them make wiser choices by clarifying problems and procedures, but, at the same time, he constantly encourages the student to become more independent and self-directing.

It is common practice in many classes to try to "get by," to go into the class and determine the minimum quantity of work that will be acceptable, instead of seeking the greatest possible growth that can be made in the class.

As long as judgment-making remains a function of the teacher, it will be accepted seriously by the students only as it either endangers or advances their personal objectives.

The judgment-making process gives the teacher the opportunity to get students to take school work seriously. When a teacher gives them a share in deciding what is best—and, through that participation, assuming responsibility for the success of the decision—he increases the probability that judgments concerning their growth will be meaningful to them. Judgments made are in terms of pupil purposes, previous status, ability, interests, and assets and liabilities. The judgment is not a mechanical comparison of one student with another, or of a class with a national norm. Behavior that is considered unsatisfactory for one student may indicate real progress for another. For example, a teacher once made the following statement to her professor after four class sessions in which she had been working on a committee composed of four white pupils and three Negroes: "You know, some of these Negroes are as intelligent as I am. I have never had an opportunity before to associate with such Negroes." This girl was not willing to admit that the Negroes in her home state were as intelligent as she was, but she had progressed to the point where she felt that some Negroes, in the proper environment, could be. This new awareness marked real progress for her. But such an attitude might have represented retrogression for other students on the same committee.

Judgment-making is a device for helping an individual or a class to become self-directing; it consists of the establishment of definite goals, which in turn serve as criteria for judging change; it provides techniques for collecting evidence on which to make judgments; it is the foundation stone for further planning. By helping students master the process, the teacher helps them become less dependent on adults.

The essential point is the assumption that the process is a tool for helping the individual or group to control and improve their environment.

The Definition of Goals

When a student enters a class, at least three people are concerned about his goals: the pupil, the teacher, and the parent. Every pupil has purposes. He may not see a way to further them by participation in the class activities. In fact, achieving them may seem to call for resistance to the program the remainder of the class is undertaking. The teacher has goals; he wants students to make certain types of growth in his class. And parents have hopes and expectations for their children.

If judgment making is to be realistic, the purposes and concerns of all three must enter into the establishment of criteria to use in making judgments about pupil progress and study procedures. If pupils are not involved in the goal-setting, they will not take either the goals or the judgments seriously. If they see no value in the standards by which an experience or growth is judged, they will reject the judgment made and the judge as well. If teachers face reality, they have to admit that many students, particularly in high school, have very little respect for their judgment. They reject teacher judgment in matters of clothing, records, movies, cars, dance bands, and many of the other items that they feel are really important in their daily lives. They are willing to accept teacher judgment only in matters relatively remote from their everyday experience. Listen to a group of high school pupils discussing the marks they have received. "I got a 'C' but you know how Miss Brown is. If she happens to like the way your hair curls you get an 'A,' but if she doesn't you know what happens."

One of the major reasons that students accept teacher judgments is that teachers have control over something they want. In the secondary school, the desired objective may be a diploma, entrance to college, or making the honor roll, for which the student will receive a certain amount of prestige. If these motivations are strong enough, the pupils will seek to obtain a high rating. If these drives are not strong, the students will make little effort to secure a favorable judgment from a teacher.

Teachers cannot withdraw from participation in the goal-setting. It is their legal and professional responsibility to foster certain types of pupil growth, one of which may be more intelligent decision-making.

Parents, too, must have a part in establishing the criteria by which progress is judged. Their desires, attitudes, and feelings condition pupil learning. If they participate in establishing the criteria, they are more likely to subscribe to them, thereby enhancing the learning situation. But if they have no part in the planning, they may resent or misunderstand the criteria that are set up. Although they cannot participate in the evaluation of each activity, they can be brought into the planning of the types of pupil growth sought during the year. And these agreements represent the parents' point of view in any specific evaluation.

All persons involved in the situation being judged should have a part in establishing the criteria by which it will be evaluated.

The success of judgment-making depends on a thorough understanding and acceptance by the persons involved of the criteria to be used in making judgments.

Actually, the purposes that an individual establishes are the real criteria by which his work should be judged, but it may be necessary to formulate even more specific standards for analyzing progress. Defining objectives in terms of observable pupil behavior is a helpful step. As long as goals are stated only in a generalized way—such as improving citizenship—judgment-making remains haphazard. But it is possible to be more definite. For example, citizenship can be defined in terms of such observable behavior as:

1. Taking part in student government.
2. Volunteering to serve on committees.
3. Assisting in the planning of class work.
4. Contributing to school welfare collections.
5. Serving as a member of the school safety patrol.

When citizenship is defined in such simple terms, it is easy to ascertain whether or not progress is being made by any individual. If his participation is increasing, it is evidence that he is growing. By defining the type of growth desired, concrete evidence of his growth can be observed and recorded.

When objectives are defined in terms of behavior, it becomes clear in many cases that evidence can be obtained by means other than paper-and-pencil tests. For instance, if a pupil is seeking to promote more harmony among races and religions, it is not easy to evaluate his success by finding out how much he knows about the cultural contributions of other races or religions. The phrase "promoting more harmony among races and religions" must be defined in such terms as (1) working effectively on committees, (2) exhibiting friendliness toward members of other races or religions, (3) giving recognition for accomplishments of others, and (4) working to decrease discriminatory practices in the school and community.

After stating a goal sought, an individual with the aid of the teacher needs to go further and describe varying degrees of the attainment of it. For example, if he wants to become familiar with the music of the world, learning songs from the current popular and semiclassical selections and the folk songs of several countries is a higher attainment than learning the same number of folk ballads of one country. Or, if he is attempting to apply the scientific method, using the method in solving personal problems, school problems, and science problems represents a higher level of proficiency than following the scientific procedure in the science laboratory alone. Of course, these gradations may be defined differently by a student and his teacher. Their definition is the one they should use to determine the desirable direction of growth.

It is difficult to interpret evidence unless the pupil and teacher agree on the degree of attainment represented by various types of behavior. For example, the teacher is seeking to develop ability to live harmoniously with others at the fourth-grade level and sees the following behaviors:

—Jack voluntarily accepts responsibility for bringing books for his committee from the library.
—Jane volunteers to wash the blackboards for the teacher and the class.
—Michael stopped a fight between two boys on the playground.
—Sam stopped and let the girls enter the cafeteria before he did.
—Larry suggested that a hostess be appointed to greet visitors.

Which indicates the highest attainment? Is engaging in a wider variety of these activities what is sought? Is having pupils do one of them more frequently the goal? Does stopping the fight represent greater insight and skill than suggesting the appointment of a hostess? A part of defining the behavior sought is agreeing with the pupil on the degree of attainment various actions indicate. Establishing certain categories of behavior which represent degrees of progress toward a goal enables the teacher to interpret anecdotal records and to determine the stage in development a pupil has reached. However, in evaluation these standards do not remain fixed. As a group gains more understanding and insight, it will redefine the standards it sets for itself and its members.

It should be pointed out that making judgments concerning progress does not mean classifying the pupils. Suppose a teacher is striving to get eight-year-old pupils to assume responsibility for keeping the room clean without being told. Tommy cleaned up his work area three times out of ten last week and four times out of nine this week. Is Tommy a failure, a success, or what? It is not necessary to label him.

The evidence provides a basis for joint judgment-making.

The Collection of Data

Intelligent judgments are based on as much evidence as it is possible to collect.

To know how much desirable growth is taking place, it is necessary to know what pupils were like when we started the work. What a pupil is as a teacher begins work with him constitutes the baseline for evaluation, and changes from this baseline constitute the evidence on which judgments are based.

What pupils say about themselves, the autobiographies they write, the information in their cumulative folders, the samples of their work during the first weeks in our class, the purposes they state, the skills they exhibit, all are baseline data. Information collected the first few weeks with a group is essential to wise judgments.

In working with youngsters in a classroom, it is not difficult to locate evidence of the learning that is occurring. The difficulty lies in how to isolate, how to collect, and how to interpret it. Every movement of a child, every action he makes within the group, is an evidence of learning that is in progress, because learning occurs in every experience a youngster has. It may be the learning that is hoped for, or it may be learnings that are completely opposed to the teacher's purposes and objectives.

It would be impossible to record all the learnings that occur in any situation. And it is difficult to record even those learnings that are in the direction of the type of growth sought. Anyone would be overwhelmed by the quantity unless he designated the particular types of growth desired and then devised techniques for recording and interpreting the changes that occur.

Merely stating the growth desired is not enough. It is necessary to go further, and discuss the kinds of behavior which represent that growth. The behavior will vary from grade to grade. If skill in collecting information is the type of growth sought, a third-grade class may agree that they want to learn how to get a book out of the library, how to use the index of a book, how to ask questions, how to read better. A ninth-grade class with the same objective might decide it means improved skill in reading the newspaper, greater discrimination in weighing contrasting reports of the same events, or more rewarding techniques in interviewing persons in the community. Without these definitions of purpose in terms of behavior, neither the teacher nor the pupils may recognize progress when it actually occurs.

The faculty of a twelve-year school described getting pupils to assume responsibility in the terms of the following behaviors:

> First Grade—Ball from playground rolled into school garden and knocked down a stick used to mark the radishes. Boy went after the ball and replaced the stick.

Second Grade—The play period had not gone well. The leaders of the small group games came to the teacher and asked if they could talk over their physical education period.

Third Grade—Students accept responsibility without being told. Examples are:

"I cut enough book marks to last for a long time."

"I saw these scissors in the wrong box and changed them."

"I'm late because I saw the ball outside and brought it in."

Fourth Grade—A boy volunteered to lead the class devotional.

Eighth Grade—Class continued work alone when teacher was called to the doctor's office.

Ninth Grade—A committee working on recreation in the community found some information they felt the class should have. They prepared a bulletin board display and put it on the board without consulting the teacher.

The class became concerned about attitudes of county commissioners who opposed establishment of a juvenile court. Began to plan action they could take.

Tenth Grade—(Home Economics) Pupils participate in planning the class procedure. A central planning committee, composed of one representative from each work committee, plans with the teacher.

Eleventh Grade—(Science) A book was mutilated. Teacher called the problem to the attention of the class and left. When he returned the class had collected money to pay for the book.

In this school the behavior examples cited indicate that the faculty saw at least seven gradations of responsibility.

1. Carrying out directions of teachers.
2. Doing things that need to be done and claiming credit.
3. Volunteering for service to the group.
4. Seeing something that needs to be done and doing it without telling teacher or claiming credit.
5. Going ahead when teacher is absent.
6. Establishing regular channels for planning and administration.
7. Becoming concerned about society outside the school and planning what needs to be done.

These different degrees of growth did not become evident to the faculty until it began to list behavior which it considered assumption of responsibility at the various grade levels.

In beginning evaluation it is helpful to spend a portion of the class time in discussing situations in which evidence of growth may be expected. The third-grade class mentioned above could actually check on their trips to the library to see whether they had increased their skill in getting a book. They might undertake some role-playing in which they could create test situations for themselves.

Only through the collection of many and varied samples of a pupil's behavior are sound judgments to be made about his growth. If it were possible, the most valid evaluation of a student's growth would involve a description of his total activities and an application of the criteria established for judging behavior to his total behavior. Since a complete description of a person's behavior is manifestly impossible, it is necessary to sample intelligently.

The samples taken should be determined by the type of objectives for which the class or individual is working. An attempt to measure all the types of pupil growth sought is made, no matter how difficult the process. Samples may include products such as drawings or themes, statements, test scores, indications of attitudes and interests, and descriptions of behavior.

Once agreement has been reached on the type of behavior sought, the next step is to decide upon situations that will reveal either the presence or absence of that behavior.

> The . . . High School in Alabama sought to develop the pupils' ability to plan their work. The core teachers and pupils decided that a pupil should be able to plan his own work and to plan with a group. In determining ways of evaluating this type of growth, records were made of a pupil's actions in his own planning and in class periods when the group planned together. Minutes were kept of the group planning sessions and each pupil maintained a file of his individual plans. By examining the minutes and the individual plans which were collected during a year, it was possible to obtain evidence of each pupil's growth in ability to plan.

It is not always possible to determine the results of a learning experience immediately. For example, a ninth-grade pupil sees a movie such as *Grapes of Wrath*. The results of his experience may not become evident until many years later, when he decides to vote in a certain way. On the other hand, it may result immediately in a strong attitude change of very short duration.

Indication of the out-of-school carry-over can be secured by devising with pupils ways of recording their home behavior. Tooth-brushing charts, logs of radio listening, and diaries are samples of such techniques.

Records Kept by Pupils

A teacher enhances the chances of success in evaluation if he encourages each student to take responsibility for collecting evidence of his own growth.

Teachers aid pupils in collecting evidences by helping them decide on the type of growth sought, define the types of behavior which represent desired growth and establish ways of sampling and recording the behavior exhibited. Paper-and-pencil tests may be one device, but it is just as feasible and as valid to help pupils utilize such techniques as anecdotal records, interviews, diaries, records of activities, pupil and class products, and tape recordings.

If records are kept to assist the pupil, he should have a part in planning the type of records to keep, how they will be kept, and how they will be used.

If records are used as the basis for decisions on improving the school experience, rather than as the basis for value judgments about pupils, they may be kept by the pupils, by the teacher, or even by the parents. The teacher's function then is to help pupils decide what is important to record, to devise efficient ways of keeping records, and to join with them in making judgments based on the records.

Bringing pupils into the recording process makes possible the use of a greater number of techniques. One technique is to have pupils keep folders of their work, including specific plans and final products. If a youngster can examine the work he did in November and compare it with his products in September, he will be able to determine for himself whether or not his experiences have resulted in significant progress. He can say, "These experiences have been satisfactory," or "These experiences have been largely futile and pointless." In either case, he can use the evidence in the folder as a basis for planning his next steps.

A folder of samples is an easy sort of record for pupils to keep. The only work involved is the actual selecting and filing. It does, however, lead to an added sense of responsibility on the part of each student.

The folder is a record of *his* work, and *he* is responsible for choosing the samples wisely and selectively. Naturally, this process also leads to the gradual development of self-imposed standards of performance.

A Problems of American Democracy teacher in Connecticut describes her results as follows:

> I bought a single, letter-size, cardboard file drawer. I placed separators for each class in the file, such as Period 2, 4, 5, and 6. Each student contributed two cents to defray the expense of the Manila folders. In the upper righthand corner of each folder is the student's name and class. Each folder is filed in alphabetical order behind the proper class separator. The students have a choice of keeping an Annotated Bibliography or notes in outline form on their readings.
>
> So far, the new system of record keeping has accomplished the following:
> 1. Students progress at their own speed.
> 2. Students are doing their own reading and filing their reports.
> 3. They are filing their own reports and seem to have a greater sense of responsibility and accomplishment.
> 4. For those students who are test shy, it gives them a prop—they know they have that grade to their credit.

The contents of the sample folders may vary from class to class. In an English or social studies class the pupils may maintain a *log* of books they have read, movies they have attended, or radio programs they have listened to. In an art class, actual samples of paintings or sculpture may be supplemented by a scrapbook of pictures or descriptions of new techniques. A boy in an industrial arts class might record the repairs he has made at home. A girl in home economics could include some before-and-after pictures of her room decoration, or a record of her attempts, successes, and failures in cooking at home. A typing or shorthand student can easily maintain a progress chart. Certainly one of the primary records will be the statement of goals the group or individual formulates. These will give guidance in record-keeping and will serve as criteria in judging the evidence collected.

Records of the way a pupil plans and works are as important as the final products themselves, and they can also be included in the sample file. *Individual and committee work plans are valuable sources of evidence.* If the pupil draws up a written plan of his proposed activities, including his purposes, methods, sources, and evaluation procedures, he can compare his first plan with others that he develops later in the year as evidence of improvement in self-direction.

Work plans of committees throw light on the way a pupil works cooperatively. Some students do excellent work by themselves, but are inept when they work with others because of shyness, selfishness, prejudices, or lack of appreciation of the value of cooperation. Samples of the type of work plans produced in a group or committee constitute one source of evidence of the student's ability to work with others.

But the final plan of a committee may give a false impression. When possible, it is desirable to obtain descriptions of the way the committee or group arrived at the final plan. One type of pupil-kept record that gives such information is the minutes of the committee or class meeting.

One worthwhile pupil record is a *diary of the ideas and questions* that develop as a result of his experiences and reading. This sort of record has been used as a valuable learning experience and record of growth from the fifth grade through graduate school. It provides evidence of increased insight and understanding. One of the advantages of the diary is that it enables the pupil to have a record of his thinking as well as of his activities. If the entries are really free responses which indicate the thinking and feelings at any given moment, they will permit a youngster to trace the growth of his own ideas and beliefs. Used in this manner, a well-kept diary proves effective in helping him develop a sense of direction and a pattern of values.

But a word of caution should be added here. If the teacher makes judgments about a diary or puts a mark on it, he destroys its value. He creates a situation in which the pupil becomes concerned about putting down the ideas that will win the teacher's approval rather than tracing his own thought pattern. Teacher assistance should be in terms of raising questions about how to record in a more easily read form, how to record more accurately, how to resolve conflicting viewpoints, and how to recognize the implications of the beliefs stated.

Records and reports can be combined by having each pupil write letters to his parents, telling what he has been doing and describing his strengths and weaknesses. Such letters develop the pupil's skill in self-analysis. They also serve as a record for persons outside the class who are interested in class progress. They can be used as the basis of conferences between pupil and parent or between parent and teacher, or among all three.

Throughout this discussion, the assumption that a pupil will have access to his records has been implicit. When teachers bring pupils into the judgment-making about pupil growth, easy access by a pupil to his records becomes imperative.

Records Kept by the Teacher

Teachers need to keep records to supplement those maintained by the students. When a teacher's record of pupil growth is mentioned, the "grade book" immediately comes to mind, and it is hard not to think of recording scores on quizzes and examinations, or the ratings given to pupil work. But quiz scores are not part of the evaluative process. Rather, they are *final ratings of certain portions of the activities a pupil has experienced in a given class*. In evaluation, a shift is made from recording *a series of final ratings to recording a series of samplings of behavior*.

One sampling of pupil behavior is a diagnostic test which helps the pupil determine the area in which he is weak. By administering the same test at the end of a period of study, the teacher and pupil have a record of the amount of development the pupil has made while working in the specific course.

Recording of diagnostic test scores by parts of the test instead of as a total score gives a better picture of pupil growth. Diagnostic tests recorded in this manner make teaching more effective because they direct attention to the areas in which the student needs help and give evidence of the effectiveness of the method used.

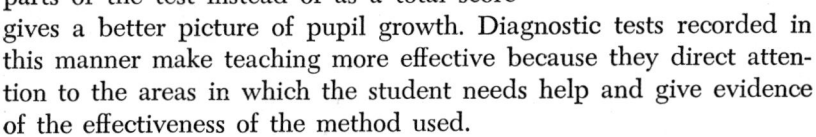

Of equal value with tests are records of significant observed behavior. For example, if one of the objectives for which a pupil is striving is to develop critical thinking, it is important to record that he brought to class an advertisement which he had analyzed to discover propaganda techniques. Another piece of such behavior that might be recorded would be his collection of editorials designed to stimulate a reader to accept a viewpoint without making an analysis of necessary data. The collection of such materials may be evidence of the pupil's growing awareness of propaganda techniques and their use. Records of observable behavior have proved particularly helpful in recording emotional development, social development, and improvements in the techniques of social interaction.

Teacher records of observed behavior are of many types. One form is the anecdotal record of an incident which demonstrates growth or lack of it. When it is observed that a pupil either succeeds or fails in carrying out some important purposes, the teacher describes the event on the card and files it until it is time to discuss his progress with the pupil or with his parents. Or a brief chronological record of behavior exhibited by a pupil may be maintained by jotting down any bits of evidence of growth together with the date on which the behavior was observed. For example, the card for Ralph Jones in a social studies class might read as follows:

RALPH JONES

9/10—Argued that all Jewish businesses should be boycotted

10/1 —Refused to work on committee with a Japanese

10/11—Argued that voting privilege should be restricted to persons whose families had lived in U. S. over 100 years

10/31—Strongly supported right of KKK to organize

11/5 —Volunteered to study anti-lynching bill before Congress

11/16—Questioned right of citizens to take law into their own hands.

Examples of behavior as widely scattered as these might easily go unnoticed among thirty-five pupils unless objectives are clearly defined and some chronological record is kept. If a teacher expects to rely upon anecdotal records, he must be aware of two shortcomings. Keeping them is a time-consuming process, and his interpretation of what happened may not be an accurate description of what actually occurred. A teacher's perception is conditioned by his own needs and purposes.

Interviews also provide important information about pupil status and growth. They may be conducted with parents, pupils, or any other persons who know a pupil and his activities. Such interviews may deal with the pupil's success or failures, his strengths or weaknesses, his selection of a college or a vocation, or his personal, social, or scholastic problems. Each interview gives important insights into pupil motivations and relationships, which are important data to record. It is as vital to know that a parent insists that Ralph become a doctor as it is to know that Ralph's greatest abilities lie in color and design. Interviews with parents are also a means of securing a record of out-of-school behavior, where the most significant growth may be occurring.

The Pupil's Judgments

It is not the teacher's function to make judgments about pupil growth. Instead, it is his job to assist individuals in the class to analyze the situation and formulate plans for improvement.

In the process, the teacher does not ask leading questions designed to convince others of his point of view. He gives his opinion if it is called for and offers suggestions when they are asked for. He is there to help the pupils grow in self-direction and maturity, rather than to increase their dependence on his judgment.

> Each member of a fifth-grade class was asked to keep a folder of his work. Each student placed in his folder samples of his work of which he was proud. In January, near the end of the first semester, each student was asked to formulate a list of the ten things that he needed to work on most during the second semester. Note that this was not a list of what he *wanted* to work on but a list of what he *needed* to work on. Number one on Jimmy's list was "work on my 8 tables." His arithmetic level was at the third-grade level. No one had to tell him that this was a fundamental weakness. He put it at the top of his list of things he needed to do. When he listed this as one of his projects, no one had to insist that he work on his 8 table. If the teacher had done so, it would have been her responsibility and not his. Number seven on his list was "cut down on my cussing." Such an item on a list is indicative of the kind of relationship that existed between the teacher and the student. He saw in his teacher a person who was concerned with helping him work through all types of problems he faced, not just the problems in the textbook.

The final judgment was in the hands of the student. With his teacher he had planned the type of growth he expected to make in the fifth grade. The ideas accepted had guided Jimmy in the selection of materials to include in the folder and had been used by him in deciding on his shortcomings and what he needed to do next.

His analysis and proposed set of goals were discussed with his teacher and his parents. Their reactions also became data for him to use in making his final decision. If the teacher and parents were wise, they did not tell him he must revise his plan and priorities. They merely expressed ideas and asked questions which would supply a broader base for decision.

In applying the evaluative process to individual growth, all the persons concerned have a part in making the decisions. Pupil-teacher conferences provide opportunity for both to examine the record, to make judgments in terms of the criteria, and to formulate new plans. Teacher-parent conferences or pupil-parent conferences or reports to parents which provide space for parent reaction are other opportunities for joint judgments about the work.

> In one parent-teacher conference the teacher of a second-grade youngster said, "Your son likes to paint. His pictures all feature Indians and cowboys—usually fighting. He has read five books. He has learned to add single digits. He gets along well with the members of the class, even though he fights occasionally to retain the leadership among the boys." No attempt was made to pass judgment. Instead, the teacher asked if the boy's behavior at home followed the same pattern. After the parent had supplied additional information, the teacher and the parent agreed on steps that each should take.

If parents or pupils are unrealistic about the amount of progress that can be expected, the teacher may need to acquaint them with the typical achievement of youngsters of similar ability and maturity. His purpose is not to say that any pupil must measure up to such a standard. It is merely to provide additional data which can be used to make a more intelligent decision. In most cases, the parent will ask for this information. Sometimes it is so hard to keep parents from concentrating so much on the norms that other factors are given enough consideration.

Even though it is possible in most situations to arrive at agreement concerning pupil progress, it may be necessary at times for the teacher to register a judgment that differs from that of the student or his parents. Such judgments should become a part of the pupil's record so that he may consider them in future planning. If the teacher wants to continue to work with the pupil, he should agree to test his judgment in future situations. If both agree to try to gain more evidence and to review judgments at a future date, the disagreement does not become a barrier to cooperation. Rather it becomes a common problem two people are exploring together.

It helps if pupil and teacher keep in mind that any judgment is an individual matter. The amount of growth that is good for one pupil is not satisfactory for another. Any judgment must be in terms of the potential and the limitation of the situation and the persons.

At the end of the time a teacher works with a student, a final judgment must be made. The teacher has the legal authority and responsibility to make it. The chances are great that there will be no disagreement among pupil, parent, and teacher if all have planned and evaluated together frequently. But it should be recognized that this judgment is of a different nature. The teacher is marking—perhaps failing or promoting. Where possible, he should make it in a way that will enable the parent and pupil to re-establish the evaluative process with the next teacher.

But this judgment is not a part of the process of helping the pupil grow in judgment-making. It is a classifying, administrative decision, not an instructional process. If possible, however, it should be made in a way that will not discourage the pupil and parent from sharing decisions willingly in the future.

Inclusion of the Parent in the Judgment-Making

The teacher who attempts to promote intelligent judgment-making seeks a method of bringing parents into the process. He hopes that his reports to parents will enable them to know of their child's progress, give them guidance in assisting the child's education, stimulate them to offer advice, and help them counsel the child concerning his future plans.

In addition to having a part in the formation of individual and class goals, the parent should be brought into making judgments about the amount and rate of progress and the procedure. Let's look at typical reporting procedures to see if they serve these functions.

Reports to parents are, for the most part, in the form of report cards listing courses in which the pupil was enrolled, his average mark in each course for the period, days absent and times tardy, plus an estimate of his citizenship. Although the exact procedure varies from school system to school system, administrators, teachers, parents, and pupils have come to expect descriptions of pupil progress expressed in terms of some symbol—either percentages or letter marks. The extent to which these symbols have had the same meaning for teachers, pupils, parents, and administrators depends upon the extent to which persons involved in each situation have discussed the symbols and their meanings.

In recent years, there has been a definite trend away from the use of percentage marks in reporting pupil progress. The impossibility of making distinctions so fine that a teacher can classify students in 101 different categories has been proved by research and has become widely recognized. In fact, only 15 per cent of the senior high-school report forms throughout the country use percentage marks as the sole form of report to parents.

Letter marks such as A, B, C, D, and F are little better in communicating with parents concerning pupil growth, even though most schools use them. *Letter marks tell parents only that their children conformed or did not conform to a set of unknown standards held by a variety of teachers.* Even when the school states that a certain mark represents a certain average of work, parents do not receive descriptions of the situations the teacher averaged to obtain the mark. Nor are parents told that the same action by a student will receive widely different ratings from different teachers.

Marks indicate class standing. The parents know that a pupil receiving an "A" is at the top of the group being rated. But that's all. It obviously tells them nothing about what progress the child is making, nor does it suggest ways in which they can help in his education. What does the fact that their child is first in his class each month really mean? Only that he is at the head of a group which may be inefficient, lazy, and unintelligent, or brilliant, hardworking, and effective. Or suppose the pupil's standing is always the lowest in the group. Does it necessarily mean that the child is a poor student or lazy? Not at all. He may be a good student who tries hard, but who has been placed in the best group in the school. He may be getting more valuable educational experiences in this group than he could possibly get in any other. Yet the report of his standing leaves the impression that he is doing poor work and is unsuccessful in school. Further, marks based on class standing promote competitiveness instead of cooperative learning. The comparative-standing method of marking forces each child to use every stratagem at his command in his efforts to excel his friends. He may even resort to cheating when approved procedures fail. An improvement in standing may mean only the development of more effective techniques of cheating.

In the past, reports have often consisted of comparative ratings for work already finished. They have told parents nothing about what they can do to help their child succeed in what he is currently doing. Parents have not been recognized as partners in education. Rather, they have been regarded as stockholders to whom dividend declarations must be sent at regular intervals.

Although many observers have recognized these shortcomings in the reporting system for some time, few steps have been taken to improve the procedure. Most school systems have felt that parents were so accustomed to the present marks that any change in the system would be resented.

However, a study at mid-century offers opposing evidence. In a survey of a carefully selected sampling of 387 parents of secondary school pupils conducted by a committee of the Portland Council of the Oregon Parents and Teachers, it was found that the majority of parents would like the report card to include the following information about their children: (1) Social habits (adjustment to other children, pride in class, accomplishments, and school activities, desire to improve self) (60 per cent). (2) Intellectual habits (pride in work, accuracy, completed work, ready to work at right time) (62 per cent). (3) Special interests, abilities, and extracurricular activities (69 per cent). (4) Child's rating on standard achievement tests in various fields (92 per cent). (5) General achievement to be expected of a child of his age level (79 per cent). (6) General achievement to be expected of a child of his grade level (88 per cent). Parents desired that the report contain space for teacher comments (84 per cent), parent comments (61 per cent), and pupil comments (53 per cent). These figures indicate that parents are willing and ready to take a larger part in the judgment-making.

Parents who want to take an active part in the judgment-making seek to know more about the strengths and weaknesses of their children, the skills their children are developing, the progress they are making, and the ways in which they, as parents, can help. They want *more* information, not less. Information of this sort is of real interest to parents, and they have a legitimate right to it. The fact that they do want to be informed presents teachers with a real challenge, and many ingenious methods for better reporting are being developed.

For instance, teachers can give parents more information by substituting descriptive paragraphs for ambiguous symbols. The following report on the work of a third-grade boy during his third month in a new school is an example:

> Sam has a fine quality of honesty in dealing with himself and with others. It helps him meet problems squarely. He is coming to find his place in the group. He is showing some willingness to allow others their turns and to act, himself, as follower at times as well as to take leadership.
>
> He seems to be happy, and he is much more willing to accept suggestions.
>
> Sam can work quite independently. He can stick to a piece of work until it is finished. He plans, and he can work by these plans.
>
> He is not particularly thrifty, nor does he show much concern about caring for materials. However, he will join a group which is caring for materials and do a moderate share of it willingly, if asked.
>
> He has high standards for most types of work. He holds himself to these standards.
>
> He is doing quite mature work in all subject matter. He reads well and avidly. He has wide interests.
>
> There are days when arithmetic seems uninteresting to him until we get well into it; then he seems to forget he preferred something else and loses himself in trying out his skill.
>
> He has a fine speaking vocabulary, expresses himself well, and enjoys sharing his experiences.
>
> He has a fine sense of drama and contributes richly to group situations of this nature.
>
> He enjoys music as a usual thing. He is interested in sound production as well as in the music itself.
>
> Sam has a very fine curiosity. He is alert and asks many highly intelligent questions. He is learning to use the library.

This report was one of two sent to the parents during the year. The reports were supplemented by individual interviews, as desired, and by meetings of all the parents with the teacher to discuss the class activities. Thus, reports to parents included a description of the program as well as of pupil growth and served as the basis for parent discussions with the pupil about his plans and procedures.

The second report, sent home in the eighth month, stated:

> Sam has continued his growth in reading ability. He knows all the addition facts, most of the subtraction facts, and several multiplication facts. He has a beginning understanding of multiplication. He is

showing more interest and more carefulness in penmanship. Spelling seems to him quite unimportant and hardly worth the bother, since one can express ideas through other means. However, he works on spelling with his small group of closest friends when they try themselves out on it. He has written some good letters, one brief story, and directions for puppet plays.

He has grown in consideration of others. He is more willing to allow others their turns with tools, privileges, and play things.

Sam is deeply concerned about the war situation to the point of worrying about whether it is going "to get me when I get big." This has shown up in puppet plays, dramatizations, and paintings.

In a few high schools, pupils write the major portion of the report. In an Alabama school, the student writes a letter to his parents each month telling the things he has been doing in school, the progress he feels he has made, and his plans for his next month's work. Each letter is used as the basis of a conference between pupil and teacher. If necessary, the teacher adds additional comments to the letter. In this procedure, the student and the teacher evaluate the work together, and each has an opportunity to call to the attention of the other any factors in the situation they feel are being overlooked.

Parents are also given an opportunity to express their judgment of the child's performance. A space is provided on the report forms in which they can list changes they would like to see made, reports on the child's home behavior, and suggestions about ways in which they feel they can be of help.

A few schools, mostly elementary, have dispensed completely with written reports to parents by substituting scheduled interviews at certain designated intervals. In the interview, the parents are told of their child's academic progress, citizenship, aptitudes, and other activities. In turn, the parents raise questions about the teacher's analysis and procedures and discuss ways in which the teacher and parents can work together to do a better job of educating the child. Such interviews provide real opportunity for interaction and joint planning. *Reporting and judgment-making are conducted together under such a plan.*

Many teachers and parents are fully aware of the frustration caused by ratings, but they have accepted the system as a necessary evil. Leadership is needed in helping all concerned to face the fact that marks as a method of reporting are a device that can be altered.

Creative effort in formulating a better system of reporting will make possible wider participation in judgment-making and increase the efficiency of learning situations.

The Product Sought

The judgment-making process can be applied successfully when: the teacher, parents, and students have agreed on goals sought; all persons involved understand and accept the criteria used; behavior about which judgments are made is adequately sampled and recorded. When these conditions exist, judgment-making has reached the level which produces self-directing students able to continue their education intelligently beyond formal education.

SELF-EVALUATION CHECKLIST
Developing Self-Direction

Do I:

1. Consider the teaching of values one of my major responsibilities?
2. Have the ability to state clearly the values by which I live?
3. Re-examine my basic beliefs frequently?
4. Live consistently by the values I hold?
5. Incorporate the values held in common in our society into the way of living in the classroom?
6. Verbalize with the class the values inherent in the way of life in the classroom?
7. Recognize with pupils that various groups in the community hold different values?
8. Aid pupils to discover the values held throughout the nation and world?
9. Establish a permissive relationship where pupils can be frank with me?
10. Assist pupils in determining the values they hold?
11. Make the classroom a place where different values can be examined?
12. Emphasize that pupils may hold and express values which conflict with my own?
13. Encourage pupils to share without anger or disparagement of others beliefs and opinions held?
14. Give guidance in identifying the issues involved in disputes?
15. Analyze with the class the experiences the class has had to determine the desirable and undesirable aspects of them?
16. Take time to discuss personal problems when they arise if they are important to the total class?

Promotion of Ability to Make Intelligent Decisions

17. Counsel with individuals about personal problems when they request opportunity to talk?
18. Interrupt classwork to discuss conflicts that arise?
19. Help the class recognize that more than two points of view may be held concerning the solution of any problem?
20. Listen carefully to people who express values in opposition to my own?
21. Build mutual respect before introducing the evaluative process?
22. Utilize pupil-teacher planning as the first step in evaluation?
23. Seek agreement with pupils on desired goals for class activity?
24. Use the goals established as criteria for judging progress?
25. Discover a pupil's status as soon as possible after starting to work with him? Establish a baseline from which amount of change can be determined?
26. Help pupils discover and record the skills, knowledge, attitudes, and interests they possess as they begin work with me?
27. Take time to discuss with pupils the type of behavior which represents attainment of desired goals?
28. Collect and record samples of both individual and group change?
29. Secure evidence of pupil growth, where possible, in actual problem-solving situations?
30. Bring pupils and parents into the process of collecting, recording, and interpreting evidence?
31. Recognize that paper-and-pencil tests are only one way of collecting evidence, useful only when they measure the kind of growth sought?
32. Use many ways of sampling pupil growth—plans, products, diaries, and other records kept?
33. Provide space for pupils to file evidence of growth?
34. Make a pupil's records available to him?
35. Keep records of group progress and achievement—plans, minutes, and products?
36. Consider past progress and conditioning factors in the environment in making judgments concerning the quality of a pupil's growth?
37. Bring pupils, parents, and other persons concerned into the judgment making?
38. Enter into an agreement to test judgments against future developments when judgments of parent or pupil disagree with my own?
39. Make judgments in such a way as to make possible continued evaluation?
40. Strive constantly to increase the amount of information shared with parents?

41. Invite parents to plan the reporting procedure with me?
42. Provide an opportunity for parents to join in making judgments about the changes reported?
43. Use evidence collected concerning pupil growth as evidence in judging the quality of the learning experience?

BIBLIOGRAPHY

Developing Self-Direction

Association for Supervision and Curriculum Development, *Toward Better Teaching*. Washington, D.C.: N.E.A., 1949.

Baruch, Dorothy, *New Ways in Discipline*. New York: McGraw-Hill Book Co., 1949.

Baysinger, G. B., "Teacher-Student Relationships: Two Patterns of Operation," *Industrial Arts and Vocational Education*, 42 (October, 1953), pp. 245–49.

Benne, K. D., *et al.*, "Group Membership and the Learning of Responsibility," *Childhood Education*, 27 (April, 1951), pp. 352–58.

Berger, Donald, "When a Class Evaluates," *Educational Leadership*, 6 (March, 1949), pp. 395–99.

Bode, Boyd, *Democracy As a Way of Life*. New York: The Macmillan Co., 1937.

Ciernick, Sylvia, "What Can We Do About Cheating?" *N.E.A. Journal*, 39 (January, 1950), p. 57.

Cleary, Florence, *et al.*, "Project in Problem Solving," *Clearing House*, 23 (October, 1948), pp. 67–70; Erickson, Edith, "The Study of a Problem," *Clearing House*, 26 (October, 1951), pp. 82–6; and Hanson, J. W., "A High School Experiment," *Educational Leadership*, (January, 1949), pp. 220–27.

Collier, C. C., "We Believe in Teacher-Pupil Planning," *National Education Association Journal*, 43 (May, 1954), p. 315.

Educational Policies Commission, *Learning the Ways of Democracy*. Washington, D.C.: N.E.A., 1940.

Foshay, Arthur W., "Evaluating Social Learnings," *Childhood Education*, 26 (October, 1949), pp. 65–69.

Frymier, J. R., "Dare They Differ?" *Educational Forum*, 18 (January, 1954), pp. 231–33.

Giles, H. H., *Teacher-Pupil Planning*. New York: Harper and Brothers, 1941.

Heffernan, Helen, "Each Child is a Custom Job," *Childhood Education*, 30 (November, 1953), pp. 109–12.

——— "Teacher Helps Children to Build Values," *California Journal of Elementary Education*, 23 (May, 1955), pp. 243–53.

Hoppe, A., "Don't Forget the Student," *Educational Digest,* 19 (May, 1954), pp. 44–45.

Horace Mann Institute of School Experimentation, *The Teacher's Role in Teacher-Pupil Planning.* New York: Bureau of Publications, Teachers College, Columbia University, 1947.

Hymes, James L., *Discipline.* New York: Bureau of Publications, Teachers College, Columbia University, 1949.

Johnson, D. M., "A Modern Account of Problem Solving," *Psychological Bulletin,* 41 (April, 1944), pp. 201–29.

McCowen, E. J., "Rich Learning Experiences in the Third Grade," *Elementary English,* 30 (October, 1953), pp. 343–51.

McKeachie, W. J., "Student-Centered vs Instructor-Centered Instruction," *Journal of Educational Psychology,* 45 (March, 1954), pp. 143–50.

Miller, Jemina, and Grace Weston, "Slow Learners Improve in Critical Thinking," *Social Education,* 13 (November, 1949), pp. 315–16.

Mudd, Dorothy, "A Core Program Uses Evaluation," *Educational Leadership,* 8 (November, 1950), pp. 82–86.

Noar, Gertrude, *Freedom to Live and Learn.* Philadelphia: Franklin Publishing Company, 1948.

Obourn, E., and G. Montgomery, "Classroom Procedures for Developing the Elements of Problem Solving," *Science Education* (February, 1941), pp. 72–80.

Petrat, R. K., "Want to Try It? The Carl Steele School Did and It Works," *The Instructor,* 67 (February, 1958), p. 113.

Pflieger, Elmer, and Grace L. Weston, "Learning Discipline in a Democracy," *N.E.A. Journal,* 38 (April, 1949), pp. 256–57.

Redl, Fritz, and George Sheviakov, *Discipline for Today's Children and Youth* (rev. ed.). Washington, D.C.: N.E.A., 1956.

Rothstein, Edward, "The Techniques of Teaching Controversial Issues," *Social Education,* 13 (February, 1949), p. 82.

Rinker, F., "Subject Matter, Students, Teachers, Methods of Teaching and Space are Redeployed in the Newton, Massachusetts High School," *National Association of Secondary School Principals Bulletin,* 42 (January, 1958), pp. 69–80.

Sears, E. L., "By What Methods Do Pupils Think They Learn More," *Ohio Schools,* 30 (December, 1952), p. 418.

Scobey, M. M., "Sharing Responsibility in Instruction," *Educational Leadership,* 13 (December, 1955), pp. 157–61.

Simpson, Ray, "Students Help Set Up Criteria To Aid in Deciding What To Study," *Journal of Educational Research,* 36 (November, 1942), pp. 192–99.

Smith, Eugene R., and R. W. Tyler, *Appraising and Recording Student Progress.* New York: Harper and Brothers, 1942.

Stapleton, P. L., "School Problems and the Student Council," *Childhood Education,* 31 (April, 1955), pp. 375–76.

Thompson, Eleanor W., "Toward the Open Mind," *Educational Leadership,* 8 (December, 1950), pp. 158–63.

Woody, C., "Nature of Evaluation," *Journal of Educational Research,* 35 (March, 1942), pp. 481–91.

••• Exerting Leadership in School and Community

Each teacher is affected by the type of faculty and community in which he teaches. No matter how sure he is of his convictions or how independent he is in his thinking, he will feel the pressure of group norms and the opinion of his fellows.

To insure that he will have the type of relationships which enable him to do his most creative work, he needs to exert effort that will make the faculty and the community more cooperative, more thoughtful, more permissive and more willing to base decisions on evidence. Research evidence indicates that leadership is widespread and diffused throughout any group. No individual can deny his responsibility. Each faculty member is a part of the leadership of the school and the community and takes an active part in seeking program improvement if he is a positive force.

UNSATISFACTORY TEACHER

He gets to the building as late as he can and leaves as early as he can. He avoids faculty meetings if it is possible and sits quietly at all he is forced to attend. Because he shirked his responsibilities on all committees to which he was appointed and the other members had to do his work, the principal no longer appoints him. At the present time his primary interests are fishing and bridge, and he enjoys these pursuits with people who are not in education. After all, teachers are so boring!

He lives in another community and makes no attempt to learn about the one in which the school is located. If the truth were known, he feels the patrons of the school are beneath him socially and intellectually. He tells his colleagues frequently, and with emotion, that the curriculum should be the same in all communities, that any emphasis on adapting the curriculum to the community needs is an excuse for lowering academic standards. Although he does not want the principal to know, he has an application pending in a school in a higher-class community.

MINIMUM SATISFACTORY TEACHER

"Faculty meetings are not much fun. It is hard to sit and listen to all the people who feel compelled to talk, but it is the only way to reach a decision. Committee work is deadly—but somebody has to do it." He is not enthusiastic about participation in faculty work, but he is willing to do his share.

Although he prides himself on not being a "joiner," he knows many members of the community. He has made an attempt to become acquainted with the economic and social structure of the locality and is aware of the current political issues. He makes some references to ways application of the content of his class can be applied to improvement of living in the community. And he meets at least once, in an interview or in a group situation, with the parents of the children in his homeroom.

13 · *Exerting Leadership in the Faculty*

A class does not exist on an island. The way the administration operates, the opinions other faculty members hold, the policies that govern the school, all affect the work of the teacher. To create a more desirable teaching-learning situation, the teacher must exert leadership in the faculty.

Becomes Acquainted with the School

A teacher who wishes to exert leadership in a faculty seeks to become acquainted with present policy and teaching practice in the school.

The pattern of teaching in other classes affects the way a teacher can work with his own class. In all schools, the prevailing faculty point of view toward discipline, homework, trips, and seating arrangements, for example, necessarily influences the teaching procedures of each member.

> A teacher in a New York City elementary school believed in democratic living in the classroom. As she began to work with third-graders she brought them into the planning, had them assist in making decisions concerning discipline and what they were going to study, had them evaluate with her their experiences, and had them use their own judgments as a basis for improvements. When this third grade moved on to the fourth grade the next year, they were confronted with a teacher who believed that she should make all the decisions and that youngsters should do only what they were told, without asking questions. She found that the new class objected to teacher-domination and rebelled against imposed authority. Consequently, she complained to the principal against the type of teaching that the third-grade teacher had been doing. The principal, in turn, called the third-grade teacher to his office and told her that she would have to conform to the pattern of discipline that existed in the school. The third-grade teacher resigned.

Even in the elementary school, where teachers spend most of the day with the same pupils, the opinions of colleagues must influence their decisions to some degree.

In the secondary school, the problem of varying standards of acceptable behavior is accentuated by the fact that boys and girls usually change teachers every period. If one teacher is a strict disciplinarian, and the teacher in the succeeding period encourages self-direction, students will naturally become confused. They may decide that the teacher who tries to help them become more self-directing is "easy" and begin to take advantage of him. If the total discipline pattern of the school, with only a few exceptions, is largely authoritarian, students may regard the classrooms where they are encouraged to make their own decisions as places where they can do as they please. Or, once they begin to make real progress in self-direction, they may begin to question the other teachers and rebel in classes in which they are not given a chance to participate.

If a teacher operates a freer type of class, he may run into difficulty with the adjoining classes. Boys and girls working together in groups are noisier than classes conducted according to a question-and-answer pattern. As pupils talk and think together and become enthusiastic about their work, their excitement leads to higher voices and a greater volume of noise. Teachers in adjoining rooms may feel that such behavior is disrupting their class procedures.

Even the way pupils pass from one class to another may become an issue. For example, if the school has a regulation that boys and girls must walk from one class to another two-by-two on the right side of the hall, a teacher cannot decide to promote self-direction by allowing his class to work out their own method for going through the halls. If he does, he will encounter opposition from the rest of the faculty, and the administration will probably rule with the majority against him and his attempt to help pupils achieve self-discipline.

Homework is another area in which agreement among teachers concerning policy is desirable. In the high school, particularly, the type of homework given by one teacher affects the total program. If students are accustomed to having specific, day-by-day assignments, with daily or weekly tests to check on whether or not they have done them, they will find it hard to adjust to a situation in which they have a voice in setting up assignments which are to be worked on over a relatively long period of time. They lose a sense of security as they move from a very specific kind of assignment to the study of long-term problems, with no specific detail for each individual to carry out. If a teacher does not make specific assignments, he will find that some children will concentrate on the work required of them by other teachers. The pressure of the other teachers' assignments causes the youngsters to let assignments of a more general, long-term nature "ride."

A teacher who goes into a new school should first determine the pattern to which the youngsters are accustomed, and then move slowly toward a type of assignment that seems more satisfactory. Too sudden a change may confuse students, or lead them to become dissatisfied with classes in which the pattern is different. It may be necessary to give teacher-made assignments at the beginning. But gradually the youngsters' suggestions for improvement can be permitted to exercise more and more influence. Once the pupils have a part in planning a more satisfactory type of assignment, they will assume responsibility for carrying through on the agreements they have reached.

Even though a teacher may be convinced of the value of taking field trips into the community, he may find it difficult in secondary schools to have the boys and girls leave the building for two or three hours during the school day. Such an absence would mean that they would have to miss other classes.

Unorthodox seating arrangements may be another source of disagreement. In the secondary school, where from three to five teachers may occupy the same room during a given day, the furniture arrangement in one period affects the work of the teacher who occupies that room in the next period. If a teacher has his class move into small circles for group work, he may receive complaints from teachers who wish to have the chairs all in straight rows. It helps if he plans with the students to have chairs returned to their original position at the end of the sessions.

These are only a few of the misunderstandings that can arise among fellow faculty members unless precautions are taken to avoid them.

To be an effective leader in any group, it is necessary for the individual to discover the goals, sentiments, norms, and procedures of the group. If he attempts to act without gaining an understanding of present practice, his contributions will be rejected and perhaps resented. A faculty has this common group characteristic. Leadership is exerted from within, not by prodding or criticism from an outsider. Talking with other teachers, listening in faculty meetings, and reading the teacher's handbook and any study guides provided are important first steps.

Takes Action in the Faculty

A teacher takes leadership as he encourages the administrators to do cooperative planning with the staff. People grow as they think with each other. Ideas are shared and new ones generated through the interaction which occurs during planning. Administrators need to know that teachers want to participate in planning and are willing to take time for it. Unless teachers, who know that growth for them occurs as they think with other staff members, tell the administrator they value it, he may feel alone and fear that asking teachers to plan with him is an imposition.

Time spent in pre-school planning conferences, in week-end conferences at camp, in faculty meetings, or around the coffee pot or coke machine at the end of the school day is helpful in uniting the thinking of a school staff. A teacher can assist in the development of mutual understanding and cooperation by letting the administration know that he wants such experiences and by helping the staff tackle problems and work out agreements.

A teacher exerts faculty leadership as he seeks to develop agreement on policies affecting instruction practices. A first step is suggesting items for the agenda of faculty meetings that are instructional problems for the teachers such as: reading material all at the same reading level; not being able to take the class on field trips because of insufficient time without interfering with the classes of other teachers; not having an opportunity to preview films before showing them in class. Merely listing the problem is not enough. Undoubtedly the faculty, after brief analysis of the item, and determination that the problem is of concern to a number in the faculty, will appoint a committee to collect information and make a proposal. The teacher who is exerting leadership will volunteer to work on committees studying instruction problems important to him. He will see it as an opportunity to grow and the way to secure a better program for the school.

Faculties need to take the time to talk together about what they are trying to do with boys and girls, arrive at some common agreements that will guide their work, and define areas of disagreements so that they will study them together. Faculty members need to achieve some degree of consistency in their way of working with boys and girls to insure that they are not trying to develop conflicting values. Otherwise, the youngsters are caught in the conflict between the different philosophies and may become cynical about all of them.

Many faculties work on policy and instructional problems. In some schools, student-faculty committees have formulated policies on conduct and homework, and individual classes are permitted to work out a pattern that is consistent with the school policy. If any teacher is dissatisfied with an existing policy, he is free to try to influence the schoolwide committee to change it.

As the teacher who exerts faculty leadership works on instructional problems as an individual and as a member of a committee, he seeks new ideas through reading, through attending conventions, through visits to other schools. He recognizes that leadership is exerted by bringing ideas to the faculty. If he has discovered some new techniques of pupil-teacher planning, counseling, evaluation, reporting to parents, or study materials which have proved helpful to him, he shares them.

Being willing to share materials as well as ideas is important. When two or more teachers read the same books or magazines, the ideas covered provide a basis for discussion. It is easier to criticize honestly the ideas a writer has presented than to analyze and make judgments about the proposals of someone present. Further, as a teacher shares his professional materials, he makes clear his interest in the growth of the person with whom he has shared the material. Such a demonstration of concern provides the basis for leadership.

A teacher leads as he shares teaching resources with his fellows. He may find that his faculty does not share. Some do not. When a teacher develops a teaching aid, he keeps it to himself so he will have an advantage and look better to the students. Instead of seeing that all become stronger as they share, teachers in these selfish faculties each seek to be superior to the others. If a teacher, who believes that he gains in ability by being a part of a staff whose members help each other, shares his resources, he affects the others. Teachers find it hard to withhold their teaching aids from another teacher who shares his. A teacher who experiments and is willing to make the products of his efforts available to the total staff can be instrumental in raising the teaching level of his colleagues as well as the morale. Not all associations with other teachers are restrictive, however. Actually, other teachers provide a rich resource for stimulation and professional growth. Through conversation and visits, a teacher can gain many new ideas about ways to help boys and girls. If sharing of materials can be promoted, teaching aids can be multiplied. Teaching teams can be formed whose members supplement each other. For example, in a Colorado school, teams of science, English, and social studies teachers exchange class groups whenever one class is undertaking a project in which the competency of another specialist is needed.

> In a Tulsa Junior high school, specific groups of teachers are organized. As far as possible, they teach the same pupils and have the same period free for planning. Three days a week they meet together to discuss individual pupils and what each teacher can do to help. The other two weekly planning periods are used for counseling with students.

Any school can devise ways in which staff members can work together to help pupils and one another. It's up to each staff member to take the leadership in encouraging joint planning and thinking in the staff.

Experiments and Supports Experimentation

A teacher who experiments in his teaching and encourages the development of experimental programs leads in a faculty. Although all may appear calm on the surface, no teacher is satisfied with his work or a faculty with its program. Some dissatisfaction exists with current procedures or results. Leadership is provided by the individual who can help identify the difficulty and formulate a hypothesis about a better way to work. A teacher contributes even more when he tries out a new idea and shares his results with the faculty. Leadership in the emerging program comes from people who say why not, rather than why. Progress comes from the persons who are seeking better procedures rather than from those who are attempting to preserve the old.

If a teacher wants support for the innovations and improvements he initiates, doing new things himself is not enough. He will need to give encouragement and assistance to other teachers who experiment. To try new procedures calls for going into the unknown, away from the security of the tried and proven. To venture requires courage, and people are braver and more willing to go beyond the known when they know that others approve experimentation and are willing to help. Through many years of experience with various types of workshops, it has been found to be more effective in securing change if more than one member from a staff attends a workshop. After the teachers return to their schools from workshops and attempt to institute change, the two or more who have attended in a group give support to each other and withstand disappointments, rebuffs, and trials that the one who attended alone cannot endure. Each faculty needs a nucleus of teachers who believe in experimentation and support all experimental efforts in the school.

A teacher promotes better teaching-learning situations if, in faculty planning, he encourages the administration to adopt a permissive attitude toward experimentation. An atmosphere in which each teacher is encouraged to improve his instructional practices promotes more effective application of the evaluative process and stimulates the sharing of results.

To insure that the change is for the better, the teacher who leads will support and contribute to evaluation. Most administrators welcome and need the help of the staff in making the judgments about instructional and curricular innovations. A leader in the faculty accepts responsibility for collecting evidence and deciding upon the incorporation or revision or abandonment of new practices and provides leadership through a contribution of evaluative know-how.

To lead, a teacher participates in professional organizations. If leadership is a product of interaction—and research evidence supports this viewpoint—the teacher who wants to promote improvement hunts opportunities to work and study with other staff members. Professional organizations bring him into contact with the more active, more interested, and more able teachers. As they get to know and to trust him, they are willing to give consideration to his ideas and suggestions. Through participation in the professional organizations the teacher gains new ideas, grows, and has more to contribute to the staff.

Works Through Students

Each class group should feel that it is contributing to the welfare of the student body of the entire school. Through such a feeling, boys and girls achieve a sense of belonging and pride in the school that they attend. A teacher needs to think through with his class the contributions they can make to the school.

One specific contribution that a group can make is to perform some service for the school. Boys and girls may examine the daily program to see where there is need of assistance. Does the library have enough assistants to keep all the books in place? Are there enough workers to prepare newspaper clippings for the vertical file? Are there ushers to help people find seats and get programs at school affairs? Are there hospitality committees to welcome guests at school? Are there safety committees to safeguard the students who attend the school? Is there a school newspaper? Is help needed in beautifying the school grounds? Would it be helpful to have a clean-up squad? Could the class be of assistance in making the cafeteria more attractive? Could the cafeteria operators use more help in serving? Should studies be made of traffic patterns or of behavior in assemblies?

A group that really accepts school improvement as one of its responsibilities can find many ways to make the school a better place in which to live. Some classes have assumed responsibility for the preparation and distribution of mimeographed materials, or have accepted the job of keeping certain portions of the playground clear. Others have volunteered to serve as safety monitors. And still others have spent their time preparing murals for the school walls. It doesn't matter what type of service the group decides to perform. The important element lies in knowing that their being in the school makes a difference, that they are making a real contribution in the life of the total school group.

Or, on another level, a class may decide to share its learning with other groups. Some fifth-grade classes, for example, develop plays which they present to first- and second-grade classes. One ninth-grade English class writes and stages a play for presentation to other ninth-grade classes. This type of sharing is a stimulating experience, both to the students who perform the activity and to those who are given a chance to see what other classes in the school are doing. It often leads directly to more rewarding activities in both groups.

Inviting other classes to visit the class and to inspect work increases friendliness in the school and gives a class an opportunity to get better acquainted with a greater number of boys and girls. It also leads to the development of certain specific skills: how to prepare an invitation; how to welcome guests; how to share experiences in a modest and unassuming manner; how to converse with guests in a way that will put them at their ease; how to serve refreshments and conduct a social period; how to bid guests farewell with a gracious invitation to come again.

Sometimes joint projects can be devised that will permit students from different classes to work together. One teacher describes her experience as follows:

> I thought that the children in my class needed practice in working more closely with other grades in the school, so just before Easter I asked the class if they would be interested in working on a project with the other fifth-grade group. We decided that a library exhibit would be a good project to undertake. Since all six grades in our school use this library, I knew that we would have to include some material in our project that would be of interest to the younger children. (We speak of teaching children to be "world-minded" but we sometimes miss a good teaching technique when we fail to train children to think not only of their own class but to go beyond that and to think of other classes; of their school and of their community.)
>
> When the various committees from the two rooms met to confer with each other, the "fur flew" at first. Each room seemed to think that it was a sort of competition that they had entered and each wanted to outdo the other in thinking of things that they could do that would be better than what the other fellow was doing. After they had worked together for several days, they found that they could produce better results if they worked more cooperatively—for example, John, from the other room, had a story on training certain wild animals and when he found that Sam, from my room, had received pictures of these animals from Barnum, Bailey and Ringling Brothers, they found that by combining the pictures and the book they had an interesting and stimulating exhibit as their contribution to the group enterprise. An interesting thing about this experience was that both of these classes had been doing group work fairly successfully in their own rooms but when they got together there didn't seem to be much carry-over. However, they finally found that the same principles of group work that they followed in their own rooms applied when they did interclass work and I think that this was one of the most valuable learnings from this experiment—principles of group work learned in the classroom apply to all group situations.
>
> During our planning sessions we appointed children to visit each of the lower grades to explain what we were trying to do and to invite them to visit the library to see what had been done. We appointed guides for these visits. The fifth-graders who participated in this part of the project were so enthusiastic about their work with the younger children that they suggested reading stories to these children.

Classes may also share resources and materials. Even if teachers, together with the class members, bring in all the materials that they can collect, there will still not be an adequate supply for dealing with all the topics that students will want to investigate. This shortage can be reduced by having all the classes share their materials with one another. Two seventh-grade English classes, for example, may not deal with the same topic at the same time. The materials assembled in one room can be used by the other class when it studies the unit at a later date. Or, if the pupils in one class invite a resource person with experiences that would be interesting and valuable to other classes, they may offer their fellow students an opportunity to join with them in listening to the speaker.

Some schools have set up joint planning committees composed of students from various classes that are working in the same subject-matter field. These committees meet on a weekly or semi-weekly basis. At their joint planning sessions, they discuss the various activities that they are going to engage in. Where possible, they plan ways of sharing experiences as well as materials. These inter-class planning groups have three benefits: (1) They permit greater coordination of the program. (2) They stimulate new ideas. Students get suggestions for projects that they would never have thought of otherwise. (3) They provide more students an opportunity to serve in a representative capacity and to have experiences in planning.

Some schools arrange for both small and large assemblies. In the large assemblies, various clubs or classes prepare and present programs that they feel will be important and of interest to the total student body. In the small assemblies, various groups with homogeneity of interests come together to share the results of various activities carried on within the classes. In secondary schools where this sharing is not an established pattern, a teacher may introduce it by inviting other classes that meet at the same period to join with his class and share the results of their learning experiences. This can be done within the normal schedule.

An important relationship of the class, sometimes neglected, is that with younger children. In some communities children work out their antagonisms and frustrations on those younger than themselves. Teachers can help combat this tendency, if it exists in their classes, by creating classroom environments in which children do not experience violent frustrations and by undertaking projects where pupils can assist less mature schoolmates.

> In one rural high school, one-fourth of the juniors and seniors belong to a leadership organization that serves the school. During periods when they are not in classes, they serve as assistants to teachers in the industrial arts shop, on the playground, on the school farm, or wherever they can provide needed leadership. They do anything that will make possible a richer program for the elementary and junior-high-school

pupils. Through these experiences, they gain a greater understanding of human growth and development, and progress in their sense of responsibility for younger children.

Friendliness in the school can be directly promoted through interroom social activities. The group may want to hold parties for students from other rooms or to entertain groups from the community. Pupils who are in school for their first year need special help. Can the pupils in our class be of service to them? Is there a big sister or a big brother program in the school? Would it be desirable to develop one?

Pupils can perform a real service to their school by providing more effective ways of spreading information. They might volunteer to initiate a school paper, for example. Or they might offer suggestions for improving the one that is already being published, undertaking to provide new columns and features.

No group can exist by itself. What happens anywhere in the school affects every class. If one class paints a mural in the hallway and makes the school a more attractive place, others will want to do something to make the school more beautiful too. A class cannot expect the school to improve unless it takes some initiative for bringing about improvement.

The student council is the means by which student opinion can be formulated and utilized. It is the organization through which any class group may make its contribution to the development of school policy.

A teacher concerned with school unity will want all members of the class with whom he works to have access to information from the student council. When the council is made up of representatives from each homeroom, the problem is easy. Each representative brings back to his class a report on the actions and procedures of the student council. But if representation is based on some other plan, the teacher will want to devise with pupils procedures by which they can get up-to-date reports of the activities of the council and keep fully informed on new developments in the school program.

Information will have to flow in the other direction as well—from each small group to the student council. So the members of the class will also want to devise an effective means of drawing the council's attention to ideas that they think are valuable. One way is to have a class secretary keep a record of the decisions made within the class that the group feels should be referred to the total student body. These can either be carried to the student council by the class representative or sent directly to the president of the student council.

One of the procedures that make student government effective is a referral back to the student body of issues and problems that are before the council. A class can encourage this democratic procedure by instructing its representative constantly to call to the attention of the other council members the desirability of taking samplings of total student opinion before making decisions. The class representative can advocate: (1) presentation and exploration of new issues in council meeting; (2) discussion of issues by each class group, under the guidance of its own representative; and (3) final action by the council, on the basis of the reactions of the total student body.

Once the student council has set up a policy, every class has the responsibility for carrying it out. Even though the class members disagree with it, they must respect the policy until such time as they, working through their representatives, can get the total student council to change it. When the class disagrees with the council, they may organize a campaign to change the opinion of the total student body so that when the representatives go to the next council meeting, the majority will vote in favor of the change.

The administration is a part of the classroom learning situation. Unless channels of communication are open between the pupils and the administration, the full potential of the administrators will not be used in improving the learning situation, and school policy will not receive the benefit of pupil thought during its formation.

Unless a teacher has close communication with the administration, he cannot expect the pupils in his class to have it.

A teacher can do a great deal to help pupils establish friendly relations with the administration if he refrains from using the administration as a threat, or picturing it as a restrictive force that keeps him from doing a good job. Such an attitude prevents administrators from contributing to the class and limits the pupil's freedom to use the total facilities of the school in securing the most educative experiences.

He helps pupils by regarding administrators as resource persons who are available when assistance is needed and by encouraging the class to do the same. He may invite the principal to sit in as a member of the group during a planning session, for example. As the principal contributes suggestions on ways in which students can use the school facilities more effectively in carrying out their activities, they begin to understand and appreciate his function.

Once the students have recognized the value of an administrator's potential contribution, they will want to invite him back frequently.

They will have special times when they want the counsel of the administrator. Moreover, when he is considered a friend, they will want him to see the results of their efforts. For example—

> In a Kentucky high school the principal and supervisor were asked to assist in photographing and recording a class project. The cooperation essential in the activity improved the working relationship between the teacher and the administration and deepened the appreciation of the pupils for the principal and supervisor to the point where these men were continually besieged by pupil requests to return for a visit.

A staff member can exert leadership in the faculty by aiding his class to find ways of planning and working with other classes.

In the process of change, pressures and conflicts arise. Persons who understand and respect the feelings of others are needed; persons who have skill in promoting the reaching of agreements are essential. A teacher exerts leadership in the faculty as he helps others to communicate, to increase in understanding of each other, and to operate more skillfully and with greater maturity in reaching decisions.

14 · *Exerting Leadership in the Community*

To be most effective in the education of children and youth, the school must work cooperatively with the other educational institutions in the community, the family, the church, the governmental agencies, the associations, and the mass media of communication. Cooperation is not developed in the abstract. It is comprised of the actions of individual teachers and administrators. Teachers who are leaders in this process exercise initiative in learning about the community, in planning with parents, in participation in community activities, in bringing community members into the school, and in serving as liaison persons between school and other community groups.

Education is a total community process. Youngsters learn from their parents, from adults outside their parental group, from other youngsters, from community social activities, from community institutions, and from mass media of communication. They live in a community; they absorb its beliefs and patterns of behavior. If the classroom is to be an effective learning situation, teachers are forced to work with all the educative forces in the community. Their role includes establishing working relationships with the out-of-school forces that influence the child's development.

The teacher who hopes to exert leadership in community-wide educational activities seeks to gain an understanding of the community. What type of people live there? What are their living conditions, their hopes and their goals? What groups have organized educational programs? What activities educate boys and girls incidentally? A new teacher will need to make a systematic study if he is to gain the needed information. Many teachers who have worked in the community a number of years do not know the educational forces that play on the children they teach. They, too, become more effective as they become acquainted with these forces.

Learns About the Community

Radio is one of the educational agencies. Youngsters hear singing commercials; they learn trade names; they develop an understanding of comedy; they learn the news of the day and come to depend upon radio newscasts as an authoritative source of information about happenings in the world; they learn about sport events; and to a lesser extent they hear the important speeches made by statesmen and politicians. For some pupils, radio is also a source of information about religion.

The impact of television, if we can judge by the few studies that have been made, is even stronger than that of radio. Boys and girls are spending more time in front of the television set than they did listening to the radio. Through television, today's children see and hear ideas, events, and foreign lands that youngsters of previous generations never had the opportunity to know. No teacher who makes adequate use of resources ignores the learning that children are getting from television, and he seeks to keep informed himself.

Movies play an important role in providing stereotypes and generalizations. Boys and girls gain many of their understandings about Indians, Mexicans, Chinese, and other racial and national groups from the movies. They acquire many of the social cues by which they judge community situations from the same source. They gain some impression of what constitutes false and real values in adult situations. If teachers pretend that this influence does not affect the child, they are ignoring one of the most potent sources of education.

Newspapers educate boys and girls. If the newspapers are biased, if they present distorted facts, the attitudes that boys and girls develop are also biased and distorted. In some communities in America there is only one newspaper or one radio station, which in some cases does not always attempt to give an objective analysis of the news. Consequently, whole generations may grow up with little opportunity to contrast various viewpoints and to draw their own conclusions on major social issues. Most of the boys and girls in such communities are handicapped by this limited treatment of significant trends outside the community.

In any community, teachers need to be aware of how limited or how rich the facilities of mass communication are in bringing to the people of the community an honest, objective analysis of the problems being decided in our society.

The civic groups of the community, through the type of activity they choose to promote, exert a strong influence on boys' and girls' out-of-school learning. In some communities, major emphasis is placed on sports activities. In others, civic groups promote dramatic organizations, music societies, libraries, and other activities which stress the more cultural aspects of living. The adult concerns are reflected in the learning of the children. If boys and girls see adults concerned about the improvement of living for all, they draw certain conclusions on what values are important. If, on the other hand, the adults of the community are concerned about a very restricted phase of living, the children draw altogether different conclusions.

The economic forces of the community also provide a part of the background which boys and girls bring to their school experiences. In some communities there is a strong labor bias. In others, boys and girls have no opportunity to come in contact with labor leaders or with persons who represent the labor viewpoint. In either case, they bring to school attitudes and interpretations which the teachers need to help them examine if they are to attain proper perspective.

The churches are a major educative force in many communities. In some, the church actually dictates the type of recreation that will be carried on. Where there are many churches, reflecting a wide range of denominational beliefs, a divergence in viewpoint may develop among the boys and girls as to what constitutes the most acceptable type of religion. This divergence may, in some cases, lead to violent prejudices or even to actual conflict.

Housing, law enforcement, local politics, sanitation, morals, recreation, natural resources, and economic structure are all potent in determining what children of the community will be like. If the quality of community living is low, the school's task will be much more difficult but much more essential. Even though they work in communities with narrow points of view or limited resources, teachers can feel confident if they remember that each community exists within larger communities and rich educational experiences are possible in contrasting the standards of overlapping communities. For example, a teacher in a community with strong anti-Mexican prejudice can contrast its attitude with our national emphasis on inter-American understanding.

All these community forces are a part of the educational environment. They all have a share in creating the attitudes that boys and girls bring to the classroom. And they continue to exercise their influence all the time the children are in school. One of the teacher's jobs is to work with boys and girls so that they will develop a critical awareness of these community resources, and will use them to the best advantage in increasing their insight and understanding, and their skill in working within the community.

Effective teachers bring into the classroom as much of community living as they can. They have boys and girls discuss the experiences they have in the community: the programs going on in their churches; the Community Chest Drive; the American Legion parade, the new real estate development; garbage collection and sanitation; the fire department; and police operation. The list is endless. Boys and girls have many rich experiences every day which they can share with one another. Studying and analyzing community papers, pictures of the town, and publications of the local Chamber of Commerce or of other local organizations can also be tried. The only way a teacher can really prevent pupils from bringing their community life into the classroom is to insist that they stick to the printed word rather than use the real experiences that they have every day as the basis of educational activity in the classroom.

One of the types of important information for those who wish to exert educational leadership in the community is to know what community leaders believe about education. What types of growth do they want children to make? What is the school's responsibility? What support are they willing to give the schools? What cooperation between the schools and other educational forces do they deem desirable?

Community leaders assist or block the development of a desirable education for youngsters. To work skillfully with community groups, teachers need to be aware of the values and perceptions of the powerful members.

To gain an understanding of beliefs of leaders, it is necessary to identify the power structure of the community. The people who speak the loudest and most frequently or who are in the status positions may not be the power figures. Unless teachers know which people control and influence, they may find themselves wondering why their efforts are relatively fruitless in securing more cooperation and agreement. A few quiet words spoken by the unidentified power figures may completely undermine months of effort if teachers are naive in their approach to understanding community structure and operation.

Oftentimes, it is hard to ascertain the power persons in a community. Money and status are not the chief criteria. To whom do people feel obligated? Who is trusted as fair and honest? Who is at the center of the lines of communication? These questions offer cues, but it will take time and listening and watching to determine the power structure and the ways teachers can best relate to it.

Works with Parents

The school and the home must work together if the student is to derive the maximum benefit from his educational experience. If learning is to be efficient, channels of communication must be maintained through which teachers and parents can plan together. That means that teachers will want the parents to visit the classroom, to have first-hand experience with the atmosphere in which their children live day by day, and to have a part in planning the program.

Many children are embarrassed when their parents come to school. After they reach the third or fourth grade they begin to feel that such visits degrade them in the eyes of their classmates. They feel that parental visits take away from their sense of independence and extend their babyhood unnecessarily. In many neighborhoods, a visit by a parent means that the child is in trouble and that the parent has been called on the carpet or has been asked to help out in disciplining the child. Naturally, such attitudes militate against efforts to include parents in program planning.

Teachers can help pupils to regard parental participation more favorably by encouraging them to arrange social activities for their parents —parties or receptions, or programs followed by refreshments. Pupils can feel that they are entertaining their parents on a social level. They need not feel that the parents are coming to the school to check on them. Rather, they can be helped to welcome a situation in which they play hosts to their parents.

Teachers can set aside portions of the class time to discuss with students their relationship with their parents. As soon as high school pupils feel that they can trust a teacher, they will begin to bring out into the open some of the problems that they are facing in their relationships at home. If the questions are considered sincerely, honestly, and with complete frankness, teachers can discuss with students ways of living and working with their parents to the mutual benefit of all.

Some teachers of youth have found it helpful to invite certain parents who speak fluently and who feel at ease to come to the class to discuss their problems as parents. If youth can see the parents of some of their peers sitting down and talking with them frankly and openly about problems that arise in the home, they will feel freer to invite other parents, who may be less articulate or less at ease with their children, to become a part of the discussion group.

One of the easiest ways of bringing parents into the classroom situation is to have them work with the class in the improvement of the room and equipment. Most classrooms lack certain pieces of equipment that would greatly facilitate the work of the group. If parents can be brought in to work jointly with youngsters in preparing such materials and equipment, a natural, cooperative work situation develops between children and parents which leads directly to the joint planning of more and more class activities. In the lower grades, particularly, parents are helpful in the planning and carrying out of trips and parties. Once the children begin to find that parents can be a natural part of the school environment, even the more reticent pupils will feel less hesitancy in having their parents come to the school.

In some schools, where there is no full-time librarian, parents organize voluntarily to supply library service. As various parents take their turn in serving as librarian or in working with teachers who are coordinating the library service, the children become accustomed to having their parents in the school situation. The same results occur when parents help with the cafeteria or with traffic problems. Pupils begin to regard their parents as natural members of the work group whose presence in the school is normal, and in no way extraordinary.

During every school year, many opportunities arise for inviting resource people from the community to share their experiences with the boys and girls in the school.

In some school systems, a card file of resource people in the community has been developed. Sometimes this file is prepared by the local PTA or other parent groups. Or teachers and students, working together, may develop their own file. Undoubtedly, a given teacher's list of resource people will begin with the parents of the boys and girls in the classroom. Since they have a vested interest in their children's education, a teacher should not hesitate to call upon them to share their knowledge and experiences with the group.

Having many different adults in the school contributes to the richness of the learning situation. Since each pupil interacts with different stimuli, teachers can insure a significant experience for more students by increasing the number of contacts with persons of different ages, interests, talents, and responsibilities.

Planning together effectively necessitates parent-teacher conferences —either group conferences or person-to-person talks.

Some schools have initiated programs in which the teacher meets with the parents of his homeroom group once a month. These meetings occur either in the school or in the home of one of the parents, and the time is devoted to discussing the class program, the actual work, and any questions the parents may have about it. Usually the first meetings are devoted to outlining the plan of work, the purposes behind the plan, and the status of the class as it begins the program. Later sessions deal with progress reports of steps that have been taken, successes and failures that have occurred, and any changes that have been made. As the year continues, the sessions are more frequently devoted to questions asked by the parents or to topics that are of major interest to a particular group of parents.

Ideally, these meetings should be held on different nights of the week. So many of the parents have social responsibilities or work on certain nights of the week that some will not be able to attend during the year unless the night for the meeting is varied. Better attendance and more effective meetings result if refreshments are available and if parents are able to smoke. Some teachers have found that the meetings are more successful if one parent serves as chairman while the teacher serves only as a resource person and consultant.

When parents and teachers meet together frequently to discuss the work of the class, it is very easy to bring into the sessions class committees or even the total class group to talk with their parents about the various activities in which they are engaging or the various projects that they have completed. Then, as the work is discussed and evaluated, the teacher plans with parents and pupils the steps the class will take next.

Just as important as group conferences are person-to-person conferences with parents.

> Soon after he had arrived at a new school, one teacher found that there were two brothers in his class who had been major discipline problems in the school. When he went to visit their home, he was met at the door by a hostile mother who demanded that he tell her what he wanted her to do and get it over quickly because she was busy. The teacher countered with, "I'm not here to tell you anything. I want advice. You know your boys better than anyone else. Won't you tell me how I can be of most help to them?" The mother's attitude changed instantly. She said, "You are the first teacher who has come to see me in the five years my boys have been in school who has not told me what to do." And then she began to discuss her concern for the boys and the kind of help she needed. After that conference the parents worked with the teacher throughout the year and the boys' behavior in school improved.

Naturally, every parent regards his child as a very special and very wonderful person. He should! Any teacher remark that belittles or disparages the child insults the parent. Any advice that is not requested discredits the parents' best efforts in rearing their child.

Too frequently, the teacher-parent conferences have been limited to a discussion of the youngsters' difficulties in school. As a result, many parents come to a conference fully expecting their youngster to be criticized or expecting to be asked to improve the behavior of the child in school. Such an attitude obviously calls for careful procedure on the teacher's part.

At the beginning of the conference, the teacher tries to put the parent at ease. It helps if he remembers that many parents have had unpleasant experiences with teachers all their lives. He avoids formality. He does not keep the parent sitting on a hard chair in front of the desk while he sits on a comfortable swivel chair. He does not talk in technical language, attempting to impress the parent with his learning. He does not talk down. He does not rush the conference. It cannot be hurried. Neither should other parents be able to listen while they sit and wait their turn. In fact, any appearance of a routine, assembly-line type of interview will impair the possibilities of success.

It is better if the first conference is held early in the year, before any student has run into trouble. By this procedure, it is made evident that cooperative planning, not help with discipline, is desired by the teacher.

At the first conference the focus may be on the progress the teacher and the parent hopes the pupil will make during the year and the sharing of experiences that will help both to understand the child. Plans are made of ways in which both, working together, can help the child in his total growth, attitudes, self-direction, and social skills, as well as in his academic achievement. At later conferences, it may be well to let the parent take the initiative in the discussion, particularly if the parent has any dissatisfaction with the youngster's progress. Opportunity should be provided for the parent to make suggestions for improvement. The teacher's contribution can be in answering questions, sharing his concerns, and getting the parent's reaction to plans that seem to offer hope for success.

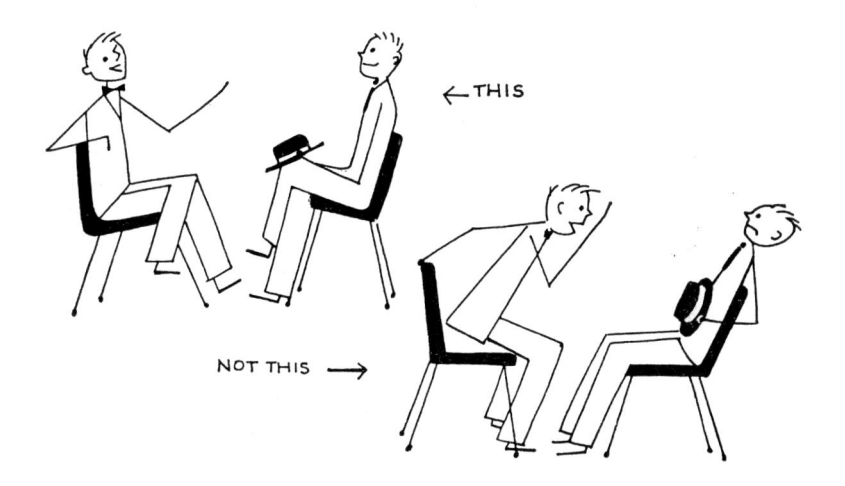

The emphasis during an interview should be on thinking with the parent rather than on attempting to sell him on any given procedure. If the teacher is willing to think with the parent, no feeling that pressure is being exerted results. If, on the other hand, the parent feels that the interview is to get him to do what the teacher wants done, without consideration for home conditions, the interview will be doomed to failure. And it will become increasingly difficult even to schedule interviews as the year progresses.

The teacher may choose to hold interviews in the home, rather than at the school. But in no sense should home visits be inspections. If the parent feels that the teacher is coming in a critical, inspectorial frame of mind, the home visit will be defeated before it starts. The parent will resent the visit and the teacher will gain little helpful insight into the personality of the boy or girl involved. The first few minutes of a home visit, as in any interview, are used to develop an acquaintanceship which will serve as a foundation for parent-teacher planning. It is a time for getting to know each other as people. As the home visit progresses, the center of emphasis usually shifts to a discussion of the child, who is, after all, the major concern of both the parent and teachers.

Home visits are easier in the elementary school, because the child is usually under the care of only one teacher. In the high school where each child has daily contacts with four or five teachers, it is not easy to assign major responsibility for the pupils to any one teacher. It is impossible for each high-school teacher to visit the homes of all of the 200 youngsters whom he teaches in a given year. If it were, parents would resent having five or six teachers for each of their children coming for home visits. But some high schools have faced the problem by assigning responsibility for home visits for a given pupil to a teacher, usually the home-room teacher, who shares whatever information, ideas, and suggestions that he gains with the other teachers who work with the child.

Close association with parents is rewarding if teachers look upon parents as partners in planning; it is a bore if the teacher regards himself as a superior intellect trying to enlighten the uneducated.

Participates in Community Activities

A teacher demonstrates to the community that he has concern for young people when he supports and participates in organizations working for the welfare of children and youth. The groups may have no official connection with the school, but the teacher serves as an informal liaison person. His participation influences group policy and he, in turn, brings back to the school ideas that affect school policy. Through the interaction of the teacher in the community group and the school faculty the programs of both are brought closer together without any formal community planning.

> Jack Jones is a second year teacher. In college he was active in sports and enjoyed recreational activities even though he majored in

science. His personality and enthusiasm soon won him friends among the parents of his pupils and the young adults of the community.

The social and civic life of the small community centered around the Community Club. It was open to all and included members from all segments of the population. Jack joined. At the end of his first year in the community he was asked by the nominating committee to accept the office of Recreation Director in the club. He accepted because he felt that in this role which he knew he could perform well, he would learn about the community, and be able to influence those with whom he came into contact.

In planning the use of his time, the teacher who expects to contribute to community leadership will allocate a portion of this week for community activities. Unless he plans to contribute a portion of his time to community activities, the teacher will not find the day long enough for nonschool activities; school responsibilities and family and recreation will consume all waking hours.

Maxine Thomas, a high-school social studies teacher, is a member of the executive board of the local unit of the League of Women Voters. Her role during the current year is Program Chairman, and she finds that her effectiveness is increased two ways. She is able to have a greater influence on the social issues the adults of the community examine and discuss at dinner with their children and she secures up-to-date information about the political activity of the state. Although the League work takes time, she is happy about her participation. She feels she has a more accurate picture of adult thinking in the community in which she works than she would have without the League contact, and she believes she has a better opportunity to practice and test what she teaches about citizenship.

The time that is set aside for community participation is too precious to waste. If the results are to be satisfying, the hours must be spent carefully, devoted to the organizations which support and enhance the values of the teacher. Becoming involved in a group whose purposes cannot be supported wholeheartedly is reckless. Not only does it waste important time, it also gives strength to the type of educational influence the teacher in his classroom is trying to combat.

Since teachers constitute one of the most educated elements of the community, many community groups turn to teachers as resource people. Some are asked to speak. Others are invited to serve as consultants or to provide some special competency. Viewed from one angle these requests are a nuisance and to accept them calls for hours of labor beyond the requirements of the job. From the point of view of the teacher seeking to affect community thinking with regard to education, each call to participate is an opportunity. As the teacher interacts with adults in community organizations, his presence, his behavior, and his thoughts change what people do with regard to education in the home, school, and community. Even if no word is spoken about education, the teacher's actions cause laymen to rethink the educative process and the teacher's role.

Students Participate in Community Projects

Cooperation on community projects is another way of combining school and community learning. Many boys and girls have gained valuable educational experiences by participating in community drives, by sitting in on the planning of community projects, or by joining with other child or youth groups in planning and carrying on some program or celebration.

A still higher level of community participation, which enables boys and girls to develop valuable democratic skills, is that of community improvement projects. In a New York school, students undertook a "block beautiful" campaign. In a Colorado school, youngsters studied the garbage collection service and carried through a petition for improvement. In an Alabama school, classes undertook landscaping and beautification for their entire community. Another class in an Alabama school undertook a terracing project for the farmlands of the community. Such activities give boys and girls a sense of contributing to the improvement of the community in which they live, a feeling that they have an important contribution to make.

Every citizen in the community, including students, has a responsibility for improving living in the community. The things that students should do are determined by the needs they feel to be vital in their community. The same activities are not appropriate in all communities. A class must determine for itself what the community needs to make it a better place in which to live.

Working with a class on such a project involves a willingness to help and an awareness of the educational implications and possibilities of the situation. It also requires a knowledge of community organization and skill in working with the adults of the community. A public relations or a publicity program may have to be set up to inform the parents and community about the educational values involved.

The class members themselves will need to have criteria by which they can judge the relative importance of such activities, so that they can determine which projects fall within the province of the educational program conducted by the school. Certainly they will not want to repeat the same project over and over. For example, one clean-up campaign might be a valuable educational experience. But if the students were to engage in a series of drives over a period of time, they would probably cease to derive much educational value from the successive experiences.

Of course, boys and girls should not be exploited by the community to carry on routine functions as a part of the school program. Basically, any activity in which boys and girls engage should be judged in terms of the contribution that it is making to their immediate growth, rather than in terms of the continuing advantages it contributes to the community living of adults.

The community does not stop a few miles from the school building. Increased speed in transportation and communication is making the world smaller and smaller, and it is becoming increasingly apparent that the world is really one community. What affects one group affects the others as well. Many classroom activities enable boys and girls to contribute directly to the improvement of the world community. Some classes correspond with classes in Europe. Others send food and clothes to needy boys and girls in other parts of the world. Still others undertake projects to help their communities gain a clearer understanding of their place in the world and to improve their relationships with the communities of other countries.

Many classes are asking themselves these questions: Are we completely informed about the United Nations? Are the members of our community doing as much as they can to help the United Nations? Would it be helpful for us to get more information about the United Nations and make it available to our class, our school, and our community? Are we doing enough to help other people become informed of democracy and its importance in America? Are we doing our part in improving human relations in our own community and in other parts of the world as well?

Reports to the Community

An understanding that education is a total community operation, requiring the full use of community resources, brings the realization that pupils must learn to live not only with the other members of the school but with the adult members of the community as well. Certain relationships must be established between the school group and community groups to insure cooperative planning and to guarantee full flow of information in both directions.

Some schools have formed community advisory committees composed of representatives of important groups in the community. Other schools are represented on community coordinating councils. Faculties can encourage members to join community organizations or to take the leadership in initiating them if they do not already exist. Even if a teacher must work alone, he can develop adult advisory groups for projects undertaken by his class. At the very least he can take steps to inform the community of the program.

Under any procedure adopted, the purpose is to improve community living for pupils of the age group with which the school is concerned by securing greater cooperation.

A school's best representatives in the community are the students themselves. If they are happy, if they know what they are doing and why they are doing it, if they are convinced of the importance of their work because they have had a part in planning it, they are evidence to the community of the quality of the educational program.

The culminating activities of class projects are another way of reporting to the community.

> In a Long Island elementary school, a fourth-grade class centered its attention for two months on a Gilbert and Sullivan operetta. Their art experience was preparation of backdrops, scenery, and costumes. Their English, oral and written, was the revision of the operetta to make it suitable for fourth-graders. Their musical experience was in learning the Gilbert and Sullivan songs and selecting the persons to sing the various roles. This two-month project was climaxed by a presentation of the operetta for the parents of the class members, followed by a performance for everyone from the community who wished to come. It was a learning experience—not a show. In addition to being a highlight of their elementary school career for the youngsters, it was a selling point for the school. It gave many adults in the community who did not understand the type of program that was being developed an opportunity to see what the boys and girls did.

The columns of the local newspaper constitute another channel of communication in smaller communities. Many times items in such columns are limited to the social activities of the school or to sports and intramural programs. One reason for this restricted coverage is that teachers and classes do not supply the columnists with information about new and different things that are occurring in the classes. If a teacher takes the time to work out with youngsters reports of class activities, he enables the local newspaper to be much more effective in keeping the members of the community informed on the total program of the school.

A fairly common method of reporting to the community is through the use of the radio programs over the local stations. With the development of the tape recorder and the techniques of recording programs, it is now possible for classes to develop scripts of their own activities, to produce them, and to revise the productions until they get a finished product that they want to share with members of the community.

A still more common way of letting the community know what is going on in the school is to invite parents and taxpayers to an "open house" program. Each class group arranges exhibits of the type of work that it is carrying on. These exhibits, if conceived of as opportunities for really sharing what is going on in the classroom, can be used to summarize the progress that has been made and to serve as a basis for further planning. If plans of work and projects in various stages of development are included, the community can see how work is done and how self-direction is developed. Class preparation for such events should be a summarizing, evaluating phase of the regular school work rather than time out of the program.

Any relationship with the community is a part of a continuing process. If a teacher judges his participation in each situation by whether or not it increases the chances that the next contacts will be even more beneficial in assisting pupils to assume a more mature role in the community, he is making possible richer educational experiences for pupils. One type of quality teaching is providing leadership in the development of coordination in the community's educational activities.

SELF-EVALUATION CHECKLIST
Exerting Leadership in School and Community

Do I:

1. Become acquainted with present policy and teaching practice in the school?
2. Encourage the administrator to foster cooperative planning in the staff?
3. Seek agreement in the staff on policies which affect our instructional practice?
4. Suggest items for the agenda of the faculty meeting?

5. Volunteer to work on committees studying instructional problems that are important to me?
6. Share my professional materials with fellow teachers?
7. Share resource materials and persons with other teachers?
8. Experiment in my teaching?
9. Seek new ideas for improvement of the school?
10. Support other teachers who experiment?
11. Help in evaluating the new ideas being tried?
12. Participate in teacher's organizations?
13. Investigate with my pupils various services they might render to the school?
14. Encourage students to share their projects with other classes?
15. Help the class establish channels of communication with the student council?
16. Encourage the class to make recommendations to student government?
17. Help pupils establish friendly relations with the administration?
18. Seek to learn about the community?
19. Know what the community leaders believe about education?
20. Attempt to identify the power structure of the community?
21. Encourage pupils to hold meetings with parents?
22. Invite parents to help with the work of the class, serve as resource persons, or aid in improving class equipment?
23. Use community members as resource people in class?
24. Use meetings with parents to reach agreement concerning the type of pupil growth desired?
25. Hold parent conferences before difficulties with pupils arise?
26. Think with parents instead of trying to sell them on my answer?
27. Bring information about the community into the class?
28. Support community organizations working for the welfare of children and youth?
29. Become a member of community organizations which promote the values I hold?
30. Allocate a portion of my time to work in community groups?
31. Serve as a speaker or consultant for community groups when they request my services?
32. Supply information to the community about the work of the class?

33. Seek projects through which pupils can work for community improvement?
34. Participate in community groups that are working for improved programs for children and youth?

BIBLIOGRAPHY

Exerting Leadership in School and Community

Community Cooperation

Afralmson, M. W., "Togetherness Can Be Built," *National Elementary Principal*, 37 (September, 1957), pp. 46–51.

Department of Elementary School Principals, *How To Know and Use Your Community*. Washington, D.C.: N.E.A., 1942.

Department of Supervisors and Directors of Instruction, *Leadership at Work*, Fifteenth Yearbook. Washington, D.C.: N.E.A., 1943.

Gabbard, Hazel F., *Working With Parents*, A Handbook, Bulletin No. 7. Washington, D.C.: U. S. Office of Education, 1949.

Keliher, A. V., "You Are A Good Teacher If . . . You Are A Good Team Member," *Grade Teacher* (April, 1955), p. 117.

———, "You Are a Good Teacher If . . . You Can Build Partnership With Parents," *Grade Teacher* (March, 1955), p. 113.

Menoher, O. C., "Taking Part in Community Activities," *Agricultural Education Magazine*, 30 (December, 1957), p. 135.

McKibbin, M. A., "School-Community Interaction," *Education*, 77 (November, 1956), pp. 177–82.

Olson, Edward G., *et al.*, *School and Community* (2nd ed.). Englewood Cliffs, N. J.: Prentice-Hall, Inc., 1954.

Strauss, Bert, and Frances Strauss, *New Ways To Better Meetings*. New York: The Viking Press, 1951.

III · *The Source of Quality Teaching*

The quality teachers of tomorrow are to be found within the teaching force today. Although pre-service teacher training institutions can help students gain a picture of human growth and development, the role of the school and the teacher, and develop a degree of competency in working with pupils, they supply only the beginning steps. Whether their graduates and the persons now in the profession become quality teachers depends upon the extent to which they continue to grow as they work. Quality teaching is the result of continued search for greater insight and constant effort to improve skills and procedures. It is achieved, if ever, by study, by evaluation, by experimentation, and by revision of goals, theory, and techniques in light of new data.

15 · *The Process of Becoming a Quality Teacher*

A teacher becomes a quality teacher by his own efforts. Although some school systems provide more assistance and more financial incentive than others, the deciding factors in the achievement of quality teaching lie in the individual's determination and action. Each teacher must become the implementer of his dreams.

To become a quality teacher, the individual must: want to grow and become more mature; decide what he believes and the special contribution he feels he can make; evaluate his present procedures; secure new ideas which hold promise for improvement; and experiment to determine the value of the new ideas.

Increase in Maturity

To become a quality teacher, a teacher must seek greater maturity as an individual. No one can hope to increase in skill in working with young people unless he develops the qualities of maturity which enable him to understand pupils and to relate to them more effectively.

But how does a person become more mature? What does he do?

He seeks to develop sufficient social skills to give himself a greater feeling of adequacy in social situations. Much of the shyness and embarrassment felt by some teachers comes from a lack of sufficient practice in basic social skills which would enable them to enjoy living and thinking with others. An unskilled dancer often fails to enjoy the rhythm of the dance because of his need to concentrate on steps. A girl attending her first tea may worry so much about social etiquette that she cannot enjoy the conversation. A teacher with a strong background of information but with so little social poise that he is unable to go to the home of one of his pupils for dinner or to other social affairs is not able to help young people mature socially. Such a teacher will be completely at a loss at a school dance or banquet. Without essential social skills, a teacher lacks the poise commonly associated with maturity.

He is more willing to accept himself as having worth. As a person begins to respect his own personality, he ceases imitating other people. If he copies what the "superior" teacher in the next room is doing, he denies the worth of his own judgment and teaching procedures. When, on the other hand, he begins to make judgments concerning his teaching in terms of the evidence of pupil growth toward desired objectives and then revises his procedures on the basis of the evidence, he is behaving as a mature person.

He seeks to become more self-directing. A mature person does not always want to be told what to do. He wants to work out for himself the best solution. An immature person is likely to be dependent, leaning on someone else for specific directions and information concerning steps to be taken. Achievement of a sense of self-direction gives purpose and meaning to life for the individual.

He seeks to improve his problem-solving technique. To have self-direction a person must be willing to work out solutions to his own problems. Unless he has learned to make intelligent decisions, he cannot be a mature participant in a democratic society or school.

He uses supervisors, principals, and college personnel for suggestions rather than asking someone in authority to tell him the exact steps which he must take. An immature person wants someone to whom he can turn to find relief from his problems. Children turn to their mothers or fathers when they get into difficulty and expect them to work out the problem. As a person becomes more mature, he accepts greater responsibility for solving the difficulties which confront him. A teacher who always wants the principal to make his decision for him or who depends on his supervisor for judgments concerning the quality of his teaching is displaying qualities of an immature person.

He seeks to become more willing to accept reality. As children some individuals live much of their time in a dream world made up of the companions they would like to have and an environmental setting in which they would most like to find themselves. Less mature individuals continue to insist on looking at the world through rose-colored glasses and on believing that things are the way they want them to be, whether they actually are that way or not.

A teacher must accept reality. He must recognize that he cannot have all the equipment or materials he wants. Only then can he begin to make the most effective use of the materials that are available. An immature teacher is always inclined to place the blame for lack of supplies on the administration or community, while making little or no constructive effort himself to improve the situation. Maturity involves facing the realities of the existing environment—personal shortcomings, weaknesses, and strengths—and working with full energy to achieve the kinds of reality desired.

He recognizes his needs and shortcomings and by volunteering special skills which he possesses, makes up for his lack of ability in other areas. At the same time, he seeks training which will help him overcome his handicaps.

He attempts to face his frustrations. This does not mean that he must accept complacently the unsatisfactory qualities of his situation, but it does mean that he should be willing to take a long-term view and to engage in a lengthy, constructive process. Youth is inclined to be impatient. Youth wants to move into the high-salaried bracket very quickly or to bring about a complete social change overnight. As a person achieves maturity, however, he recognizes that things are likely not to happen that fast, and he begins to see the importance of small gains and to use them as ways of achieving the long-term values for which he strives.

He tries to take disappointments without becoming completely discouraged. Here the old quotation, "The man worthwhile is the man who can smile when everything goes dead wrong," applies. Any child or youth can be happy in a situation in which his slightest wish is fulfilled. A mature person is one who can face disappointment, upset, and heartache and still build a world out of the satisfactory features of the situation.

He tries to become less egocentric. A baby sees and feels only the things that come into immediate contact with him. A child judges everything by whether or not it satisfies his immediate desires. Many people remain largely egocentric through a major portion of their lives. A mature person recognizes that the world is not centered around him. He begins to see himself as making a contribution to the group and to the on-going process of civilization. He recognizes that he has a part to play, that he has value as a unique individual, but he also sees the center of emphasis on the social group of which he is a part. As he develops this concept, he begins to put himself into proper reference to life.

A pre-service teacher, commenting on a teachers' meeting she had attended said, "The best part of all was the feeling that in my own small way I was able to contribute and to know that people were listening to my questions and comments with sincere interest."

Some teachers are inclined to be prima donnas. They are able to do creative work only so long as everything is going their way and everyone praises their efforts. It takes a much more mature person to be able to work cooperatively with the rest of the faculty and to share with others the credit for the program. The immature person usually wants assurance that others always identify him as being the one who has made the greatest contribution and who is the most creative person.

He seeks to control himself and to adjust his behavior to the situation. A child may lose his temper and engage in extremely antisocial behavior in almost any situation. As a person matures, he learns to distinguish among kinds of situations and to recognize that some types of behavior are appropriate on one occasion and not on another. Maturing involves learning enough of the social cues to be able to get the insight that makes possible interpretation of various situations and the development of sufficient self-control to abide by the insight possessed.

He works to achieve the type of social relationships that makes it possible for everyone involved in a situation to attain the greatest possible degree of satisfaction of his needs. Insight in a social situation depends largely upon understanding one's own needs and the needs of others. Viewed in this light, maturity includes understanding of others and ability to get along with others.

Maturity involves working out satisfactory relationships with persons who may have different viewpoints, different religions, different colors. If a person is immature, he tends to be afraid of difference and to insist on staying with persons whose beliefs or backgrounds are similar to his. He tends also to fear the unknown, and he attempts to take steps to insure that he will not come in contact with persons unlike himself. These steps may even involve aggression against persons who are different, or the calling of these persons by derogatory names. If he is immature, he may cause social restrictions to be established which prevent development of better understanding. Maturity involves willingness to accept the worth of other points of view and of other ways of life, and willingness to analyze objectively the extent to which different groups can contribute to the attainment of the satisfaction of all.

He seeks to develop, through objective analysis of his experiences and of the different points of view with which he has come in contact, *conscious values which give purpose, direction, and meaning to his living*. An immature person accepts the joys or the sorrows of the moment in terms of whether or not they contribute to his immediate satisfaction. A mature person has a life-purpose and uses the experiences of the moment for the fulfillment of that purpose as well as for the satisfactions that come out of the immediate occasion.

If a person does not have a consistent set of values, he can make decisions based only on expediency. For this reason, other staff members can seldom depend upon him.

> Recently, a principal was confronted with a problem concerning the type of poster to be used for getting books returned to the library. One teacher objected to the snooping, finger-pointing, accusing, guilt-fixing, teacher vs. pupil implications of the posters being used. The principal's reaction was, "I don't see anything wrong with the posters. They get the books back, don't they?" His decision was made entirely in terms of how well the posters accomplished his desire, not in terms of the learnings the pupils might derive from the experience. Either he had not thought through the values he held or he was not using the values to which he gave verbal allegiance as the basis for his decisions in other situations.

He recognizes that maturity is never attained, that through new experiences and new insights he will develop a new picture of what maturity can mean. Although at the age of twenty-five he may have felt relatively mature, at thirty-five he may see new possibilities of growth which cause him to look back at his maturation attained at the age of twenty-five and feel that it represented a very immature stage in his life-pattern.

A person grows more mature as long as he continues to recognize that he does not have the final answers about the best methods of teaching or about solutions to world problems. He becomes increasingly mature through humble and intelligent application of the scientific method.

Decides on Major Contribution

Unless a teacher knows what he believes, his work will lack a sense of direction, and he will experience difficulty in making the minute-by-minute decisions a teacher must make. He will be forced to hesitate before he can decide on the next step and can never have any basis for deciding whether he has done the right thing or not.

No teacher wants to be a failure. Each one expects to be at least satisfactory in all aspects of teaching. But this level is not enough for most persons. Most want to be good teachers, quality teachers.

This desire to be excellent has caused deep frustration, and thus cynicism for many in the profession. They have listened to descriptions of excellent teaching which were a composite of the best features of a number of teachers and have gone back to their classrooms and tried to emulate the descriptions. Out of the disappointment that came from being unable to be equal to the composite of the best of many good teachers, came a loss of a sense of worth and a resentment manifest in the assertion, "Oh, this stuff is a lot of theory. It won't work in practice."

Not enough recognition has been given to the uniqueness of the personality of teachers. No teacher can be all things to all people. No teacher can do all things well. Each has a unique contribution to make. In terms of his beliefs, his personality, his skills, his perception of himself, others, and the world, he can work with pupils in a way that is all his own. Great teachers have studied themselves and decided how they can be of most help, or they have found themselves in the type of situation where they can contribute exactly what is needed.

To become a quality teacher, a person must decide which types of pupil growth he deems most important and the competencies he has which can best promote them. He must decide what his fundamental contribution will be—improving human relations, promoting group development, providing for individual difference, stimulating intellectual growth, developing self-direction or exerting the leadership with adults that improves the learning situation for children. The choice could not be, and should not be, an exclusive one. All teachers contribute to all of these activities. And they must! But each person should decide which one or two or three of these areas are the places where the use of his energies will be most effective and rewarding and which are the areas in which he will be a quality teacher.

Evaluates Present Procedures

No one teaches as well as he would like. In varying degrees, all fail to achieve the dream of successful teaching because of ineffective procedures, poverty of ideas, lack of maturity, or limited understanding of the process of change.

Evaluation, a process of defining goals, collecting evidence, recording the evidence, making judgments, revising procedures, is helpful in promoting self-improvement.

As a result of study of human growth, democracy, and the community in which they teach, most teachers are fairly clear about the goals they are trying to achieve through the experiences they help pupils have in those areas in which they are competent guides. Moreover, through effective use of pupil-teacher planning, they can also secure a definition of the purposes of pupils, and through parent-teacher conferences, they can determine the results that parents desire.

These additional sources supplement and condition their own purposes as they form the criteria by which they evaluate their teaching.

The next step in evaluating themselves is collecting evidence that indicates how closely they have been able to approach their goals. They find such evidence in the records of pupil progress, pupil-teacher planning sessions, anonymous judgments by pupils as they leave classes, parent reactions, and their own records.

An important element in this evidence is the actual degree of pupil progress. What was the status of pupils as they began to work in the class? To what point have they progressed? Test scores and samples of pupil work provide evidence of a teacher's success in stimulating pupil growth. Marks, as customarily given, and final scores do not. *Evidence of successful teaching lies in the amount of progress pupils make, not in their final achievement.*

Even progress must be considered in terms of the limitations of the pupils and the situation. A highly intelligent class may make much progress in spite of poor teaching; a class with less intelligence may make little progress with the most effective teaching.

In any case, the evidence about pupil progress is basic. Unless pupils are growing in the desired directions, the ways of working with them are ineffective.

Pupil-teacher planning provides one of the best means of collecting evidence on how to improve a teacher's methods. As students plan with him, they indicate their approval of certain work procedures and suggest improvements in others. The teacher's main concern in a pupil-teacher planning session should be whether or not his actions promote the free exchange of opinions. If his present procedures are the kind that enable students to speak freely, he can be sure that he is obtaining significant evidence in the planning situation. If, however, he finds that students are reticent and hesitant about saying what they think, he needs the help of his principal, or supervisor, or another teacher in analyzing his habits to see how he can eliminate certain of his mannerisms or change his way of participating in a group so that students will feel more free to contribute their opinions and ideas.

A teacher can usually secure a very candid appraisal of his group procedures by asking each member of a departing class to prepare anonymously a list of suggestions on ways in which he might improve. The frequent recurrence of certain items in these lists gives him a clear indication of areas in which he should seek advice and counsel from another teacher or a consultant. Also, the comments made by a single student may be so pertinent that he will want to explore fully the analysis of his procedures.

Parent reactions to the success of their children provide added evidence. If children are satisfied with their experiences, the parents know it and are inclined to believe that the teaching is good. If, in addition, they find their children attaining desirable types of growth, they will be sure of the quality of the teaching. On the other hand, if the parents are disappointed, unhappy, or dissatisfied, the teacher has evidence that either his ways of communicating with them or his teaching methods themselves are in need of improvement.

Observations made by the principal or supervisor provide valuable evidence in the evaluation of teaching. They see the teacher's work from a different angle. They can be more objective and furnish him with comparisons which are really additional data to use in making judgments. From them, he can secure information about the growth of similar pupils in other classes. He can also have them collect evidence by serving as impartial observer to record working sessions of his group. Their help in evaluation is especially important if the total staff has taken the time to agree on the purposes it is striving to attain.

Some teachers help one another collect evidence by devising in faculty groups a self-evaluation checklist which each teacher may use to record evidence about himself from time to time.

It is helpful in such a checklist—or in any self-evaluation device, for that matter—to provide space for recording evidence before judgments are recorded. For example:

Do I accept all pupils?
Evidence

Judgment Yes   No
          1 2 3 4 5

Even if a teacher uses a check list worked out by all the members of the faculty, he will also want to develop an individual check list which includes the values that he deems most important. Frequent comparison of the points on the personal list with his actual performance will provide him with abundant evidence of whether or not he is living up to what he believes.

The evaluation approach described above will prove helpful in improving general method, but in moving toward quality teaching in an area, the data must be more specific. It is necessary to pinpoint the specific actions that represent quality. The self-evaluation checklists at the end of each section of this book, describing a type of quality teaching, are designed to aid a teacher in identifying behavior which represents evidence of success or growth.

A few samples from each checklist will be included to indicate possible data that are significant.

Human Relations

Do I accept each child as I work with the class? Do I find it easy to work with children from underprivileged homes, from homes with moral standards different from my own, from homes of different races or religions, and from homes with opposing political viewpoints? Am I willing to counsel with children who are dirty, who are aggressive, who are below average in intelligence, or who resent me because I am a teacher? Acceptance of each child means that the teacher is willing to spend as much time with the least attractive child in his room and be as helpful to him as he is with the most attractive child.

Do I help all pupils to feel that they belong? A second-grader went into a new school on the first day of the semester. Since he anticipated making new friends, he entered his classroom with a big smile on his face. His teacher, who remained seated at the desk, glanced up and said, "Find a seat." All his enthusiasm gone, Bill, feeling very much alone in a strange school, turned to the nearest desk. Helping each child feel that he belongs means offering a smile, a word of welcome, a demonstration that he is wanted, to each child who enters the class. Of course, this may be hard when there are thirty-five or more pupils, but it is just as important in large groups as it is in small.

Another child entered a first-grade class in which each section had thirty-eight pupils. When the principal took him to the section that had been selected for him, the teacher glanced quickly at the principal with a challenge in her eye which said, "What, another one!" The pupil, a very sensitive youngster, interpreted the glance correctly, and although the teacher held out her hand and gave him a big smile saying, "We are glad to have you, Tom," he began to cry. Helping youngsters feel that they belong is not accomplished just through words. It is shown through manner and actions.

Do I let pupils know that I like them? When a teacher is fearful that pupils will take advantage of his friendliness, he demonstrates a feeling of insecurity about his ability to deal with social situations that may arise. In his work with children, he needs to let them know that he likes them and wants them to succeed. Human beings thrive and grow in an emotional climate of affection and acceptance. Smiles, warm greetings, and expressions of approval and liking are all important qualities of a successful classroom. They do much to enhance the learning situation.

A teacher does not, of course, behave on the same level as youngsters in the class. He is not a chum in the sense that peers are bosom companions. Because of his greater maturity, he must constantly make judgments on whether or not his way of working with pupils can be improved. When he finds that his manifestations of affection and approval lead certain pupils to take advantage of the situation, he withdraws some of them. He evaluates his procedure on the basis of whether or not it is improving the quality of the learning situation for the pupils involved.

Do I help pupils accept one another? A teacher can make a major contribution by helping youngsters understand and accept one another. He can encourage them to look upon their class as a group whose purpose is to help each individual grow. He raises questions such as: What can we do to make Sally feel at home? How can we help Andy become more effective in group discussions? What suggestions do we have for helping Sam improve his study procedures? Helping pupils accept one another also means sitting down with individual students and talking with them about their relationships with other members of the group—how they can become more acceptable to the group.

Do I avoid allowing my feelings to be hurt? As the most mature member of the group, a teacher has the responsibility for helping the others become more mature. He achieves this purpose by constantly keeping in mind the question, "How can I use this situation to help this pupil grow?" Such an attitude prevents him from ever reacting on an angry, emotional basis to children's behavior. Instead, he looks upon all behavior as evidence that will guide him in planning for their continued growth. If his emotions are so near the surface that he interprets the overt behavior of pupils as personal attacks, there will be little prospect of his helping them to grow.

Do I admit a mistake when results show I was wrong? Mistakes cannot be covered up by persons in a position of leadership. Admitting mistakes does not lessen a teacher's prestige. Instead, it permits others to work with him without feeling that he will try to cover up his mistakes by blaming them. In the process of learning, pupils will make mistakes. And in the process of teaching, the teacher will make mistakes too. He can help youngsters understand the learning process by demonstrating to them that he uses his mistakes to improve his procedure.

Group Development

Do I help pupils get acquainted? If a teacher hopes to create a classroom atmosphere in which pupils will exchange experiences and ideas freely, he helps them take the initial steps in getting to know one another. Too many teachers feel that helping students get acquainted is a waste of class time. Actually, it is part of the process by which the class really begins to function. It is the first step in helping a class become a group.

Do I encourage students to work together? Boys and girls are social beings who like to work and play with other people. If a teacher wants to make the classroom environment pleasant, he encourages pupils to work together rather than penalize them for communicating with one another. By encouraging cooperation, he increases the motivation to do work and he stimulates development of the skills necessary for working with other people.

Do I bring all students into the planning? In order to make use of existing motivation, a teacher provides opportunities for students to state their purposes. Unless all students are brought into the planning, the number of people who are really concerned about what happens in the class will be less. Too frequently, a teacher brings the most intelligent students into the thinking and planning and excludes the ones who do not demonstrate leadership. Too frequently, he raises a question about what should be done and then accepts the first suggestion that one of the class leaders makes, without referring it to the total group for a decision. Such a method denies the total class an opportunity to be self-directing just as much as insisting that all students do what he plans them to do.

Do I consult the group about an action before I take it? To encourage students to assume responsibility to the group, the teacher must do the same. If he violates group procedure himself, he cannot teach class members to respect group decisions. When he finds himself faced by a decision on which no group policy has been established, he has an excellent opportunity to help the group grow by referring the decision to the class before he takes action. If he follows this procedure himself, students will be encouraged to do so.

Do I help the group form a code of behavior? Every group has to abide by some rules of behavior. If the teacher does not help the group with which he works to formulate its own code, pupils will lack the security of knowing what is acceptable. He puts himself into the position of having to tell them how they may behave.

Individual Differences

Do I become acquainted with the background of each pupil? A thin, pale seventh-grade boy fell asleep every afternoon in his health class. His teacher, disgusted with his behavior, began to talk seriously with him for the first time. He found that the child worked as an errand boy at a grocery store every evening from 5:00 until 8:00, and that he was up at 3:30 every morning to deliver papers until it was time to come to school. His mother was a widow and the boy's financial contributions were essential. How successful would this teacher have been if he had threatened the boy with failure or punishment?

Do I hold individual conferences with all students? The exceptionally able pupil, the failing pupil, or the behavior problem are those who usually receive most of a teacher's conference time. Unless he keeps a record of the interviews he has with each student, the average, particularly the unattractive, student may be neglected.

Do I help each student state his goals? Class goals are not enough to give a teacher guidance in meeting individual differences. He will be more effective if he assists each pupil to enter in his record of his progress a clear statement of his individual goals. Many pupils need teacher help in identifying the things on which they should work.

Do I encourage pupils to schedule a portion of the class time for individual projects? If the total group works together continually, pupils will have no opportunity to work on individual projects or to drill on areas in which they are weak. Having certain periods devoted to individual work is one way to guarantee an opportunity to follow individualized purposes which do not fall within the area of endeavor established by the total group.

Do I know the work each pupil is doing? Keeping a record book is not enough. Do I look at a sample of each pupil's work each week? Do I have each pupil go over his plan of work with me and show me the progress that he has made and the deadlines he has established for himself? Knowing what each pupil is doing means at least seeing some sample of his work or talking with him about his progress and achievement each week.

Do I expect the same amount of work from all pupils? Whether a teacher expects it or not, he won't get it. The weaker pupils will not be able to produce at the average level and the superior pupils should do much more. If a teacher is working in terms of individual differences, he agrees with each youngster on what he is going to do and holds him to the standards that have been established together.

Do I show likes and dislikes? A teacher cannot like all pupils equally well—he is the product of his experiences, just as students are, and he appreciates and enjoys certain pupils more than he does others. But he is responsible to them all and any overt evidence of preference for some will handicap him with others. If pupils feel that he emphasizes individual learning so that he can spend more time with the persons he prefers, his entire program will be jeopardized.

Do I secure a wide variety of materials for my classes? Pupils learn from different stimuli. The wider the range of stimuli in a room, the more certain a teacher can be that all pupils will learn what he desires them to learn. He knows that he will have pupils with different skills and abilities. Unless he has materials of varying levels of difficulty, some students will never be challenged.

Intellectual Stimulation

Do I vary the organization of the content I teach as I work with different classes? A sixth-grade class was studying various theories of the origin of the earth. As long as the study was limited to reading books and listening to the teacher's explanations, only a few pupils were really enthusiastic. But when the class decided to portray the theories in a "movie" made of a roll of wallpaper, a box, and two broomsticks, all the students became deeply interested. Some prepared the script. Others laid out the rough sketches on the back of the wallpaper. Some painted the pictures. Some measured and cut the box and fitted the broomsticks. All were giving their best to make the project successful. All were involved in some aspect of the group undertaking. All were learning. All evolved some theory of the earth's formation, along with other learnings. No two pupils learned the same things. That would be impossible!

The teacher had never taught this phase of science by this method. He never did again.

Do I encourage pupils to express their interpretations and points of view?

A second-grade class in Kentucky was dictating an account of the day's activities. The teacher wrote their statements on the blackboard. They had agreed upon:

Today is April 3, 1952.
The sun is shining.
It is a beautiful day.
We have been playing store.
Miss Hawkins brought a visitor to our class.

The teacher had had several pupils read what they had stated. Finally, she turned to the total group and asked if there was anything they wanted to add. One little boy raised his hand quickly and, grinning from ear to ear, yelled "School is fun." The entire group chorused, "Yes! Yes!"

Even at the second grade the teacher was teaching pupils to summarize their activities and to express their feelings about them.

Self-Direction

Do I help students determine their status as we begin to work together? Students will not be able to ascertain their progress unless they know the point at which they began to work. If a teacher does not take time at the outset to help youngsters determine their skills, beliefs, and knowledge, they will be unable to make subsequent valid judgments about the effectiveness of the procedures used.

Do I arrange for all persons concerned to help establish the criteria by which a pupil's growth is judged? Much of the concern about the effectiveness of modern education has come about because teachers have not bothered to sit down with parents and talk through with them the kinds of growth they want their children to make. Unless pupils, teachers, and parents come to an understanding on desired results, there exists an incipient cause of misunderstanding and dissatisfaction.

Do I help the pupils devise ways of keeping records? Individualized instruction means helping students to keep records. Knowing what to record and how to record it is a technical process that the teacher cannot expect students to learn without guidance. He needs to take time to discuss various forms and procedures with them, and ways in which their records can be organized in terms of the types of growth they are seeking. He can also help youngsters understand the necessity for recording many and varied samples of their behavior in order to insure valid judgments on the progress they are making.

Do I record pupil behavior that I consider significant? In spite of all a teacher does, pupils will not be able to select and record all the significant evidence themselves. Neither can the teacher for that matter. But, because of his greater maturity and insight, certain types of behavior that are considered unimportant by students will be significant to him. If he keeps a chronological record of a pupil's behavior, certain patterns of development will emerge.

Do I bring pupils and parents into the interpretations of records? By themselves, a teacher's judgments on pupil progress are invalid. He just cannot be as fully conscious of the conditions under which progress has been made, or the goals towards which it was made, as pupils and their parents are. He knows only those experiences that he has actually shared. Consequently, the judgments of all persons involved are necessary in planning the next steps in the education of each student. Since records have different meanings for different people, the only way to insure that everyone will be satisfied with the progress being made is to share with them both the planning and the evaluating.

Do I make myself available when pupils want to see me? If a teacher is going to provide the counsel and guidance that will help individuals grow in solving their personal problems, he takes time to sit down and talk with them when they desire it. If he always appears to be very busy or if he rushes away from school at the close of the day, pupils will sense that he does not want to be bothered with them. And if he continually glances at his watch when he does talk with them, they will know that his attention is not on them and that his concern is not with their problem.

Faculty and Community Leadership

Do I try to develop cooperation among faculty members? A highly respected teacher in a midwestern school was bemoaning the fact that many of the teachers loafed around the coffee urn in the cafeteria each afternoon after school. She said she never had time for such social activities. Even though she was deeply concerned about improving instruction, she thought only of working by herself on improving her course outlines and collecting materials. She was not aware of the leadership she could have supplied in the cafeteria sessions. Nor did she understand why her suggestions never received consideration at faculty meetings.

Do I participate in community organizations? As adults in the community learn to respect a teacher as a person, he will enjoy more security and support. When they find that he can work effectively with adult groups, they will be more willing to trust him with their children. Participation in community organizations permits the coordination of school work with other community activities and provides richer educative experiences for our pupils.

Do I study patterns of community life? A teacher's effectiveness is related to his knowledge of community life. What are the issues confronting the community? What are the assets of the community? Are his courses affected by the problems of the community? Has any change occurred in the community because of his work?

Through questions concerning the areas in which he wishes to improve the quality of his teaching, a teacher may face the data honestly and make judgments concerning his shortcomings, and begin to seek suggestions for eliminating the weaknesses.

Seeks New Ideas

A person seeking to become a quality teacher will study the professional publications to locate new ideas.

Teachers in Pennsylvania put articles in periodicals at the top of their list of helpful sources of suggestions on new teaching procedures. If a teacher glances through the periodicals that come to the school and asks his colleagues to refer him to suggestions they discover, the new publications will bring to him a constant flow of suggestions that he may want to try.

The principal, supervisor, or consultant provides another source of ideas. The primary responsibility of these people is to help teachers improve their performance. When a teacher encounters a problem on which he needs help, he should not hesitate to call on them. Asking for help is not a sign of weakness; instead, it shows the wide-awake supervisor that the teacher is seeking to improve his procedures and is alert to the problems that trouble him. Supervisors recognize that a person who is sincere enough to analyze his work and to seek help is a growing teacher, one who should be given the greatest possible consideration and encouragement.

Visits to teachers in other systems represent still another source of ideas. When opportunity is taken to see how other teachers deal with problems similar to those that confront him, the teacher will get new insights into ways that he can work more effectively. If the school does not provide for such visits, each one can at least spend his planning period in visiting other classes in his own school. However, this procedure should be discussed first in a faculty meeting in order to secure the consent of other teachers. Under no circumstances should a teacher attempt to observe the teaching being done by a teacher who does not want him in the classroom and who resents the observation.

Work on school committees is helpful. As a teacher sits with his colleagues and discusses solutions to school problems, he becomes familiar with their ideas concerning ways to work with boys and girls. He does not need to accept them all, but he can evaluate them in terms of his own purposes and values.

Research in the fields of human growth and development, learning, human relations, and group development provides the teacher with vital information that he can get from no other source. Facts discovered often reveal the need for revising his concept of teaching methods. As new insight is gained into how learning occurs, the teacher has more guidance in determining the part he should play in helping youngsters acquire experiences that bring about desirable growth.

Staff meetings, when they are organized in terms of teachers' problems, are places to acquire new ideas. As teachers exchange experiences that have been successful or have failed, their repertoire of techniques is increased. As outside resource people are brought to the meetings to present the information in their field of specialization, the generalizations teachers have drawn from their experience is supplemented or challenged. One of the biggest services a consultant can offer is to raise questions or make statements which force teachers to rethink their positions. It may result in the decisions that the previous conclusion was correct, but the re-examination process sharpens convictions and strengthens beliefs.

A type of in-service teacher education that has proved to be stimulating is the workshop. It is a program under the sponsorship of a school system, university, or organization to which teachers go to work on their problems or the problems of their school. Work is based on the problems of the enrollees and all participants follow individual programs. Each member has an adviser who helps him plan his work and secure the assistance of the staff members who can contribute to the solution of his problem. Staff members are present to help the workshop participants solve their problems, not to tell students what to do. More and more workshops are being organized for work in special areas such as intercultural education, world understanding, leadership, or economic education. If a teacher chooses a workshop oriented toward the general area in which his problems lie and in terms of the quality of staff available, he will find it one of the most stimulating experiences he has had. Workshops have caused many teachers to rethink their approach to education and teaching.

Any graduate work should be selected in terms of the teacher's problems and purposes. If he chooses courses in terms of his present problems of teaching rather than a vague, long-range hope of being something he is not, such as an administrator, his graduate experience will supply additional ideas.

One of the best ways of growing and increasing his fund of ideas is to participate in experimental studies seeking solutions to problems with which the teacher is concerned. An examination of the history of staffs in schools that have participated in experimental projects leads to the conclusion that such participation produces people who are stronger and more capable than they were before the experimentation started. A teacher grows as he tries something new with consultant service to help him find his solutions. Through participation in an experimental study, he secures additional resource help for himself.

An essential quality for growth is humbleness, an appreciation that there are better answers than present ones, that any person met may contribute the word or fragment of the idea that will open eyes to new possibilities.

No two teachers will gain ideas in the same way. But two elements are essential to anyone's procedure. He must be open-minded and he must seek situations where ideas are shared freely.

Experiments with His Method

If a teacher wants to continue to grow, he engages in a constant process of experimentation. He recognizes that his present teaching method represents the best working hypothesis that he has been able to formulate and that it will change as a result of additional experience as he continues to analyze it critically. Whenever he begins to feel that he has achieved the best possible method, he has begun to decrease in his teaching efficiency. Whenever he starts trying to teach a new class in exactly the way he has taught preceding classes, he loses his creative spark and begins to make teaching hack work and drudgery. If he wants to continue to improve his teaching processes, he needs to look upon his meeting with each new class as a challenge to develop more effective ways of working than he has been able to achieve with any previous class.

A teacher can't change his teaching practices all at once. His present pattern consists of a background of beliefs that he has and an organization of the skills that he has developed. If he tries to change from what he is doing to something totally different, he becomes lost in the process and does not do any of the things he tries to do efficiently.

Before a teacher attempts any change, he needs to be very clear about the type of pupil behavior that he is trying to promote. If he decides that he is going to try something that he has not been doing, he needs to plan how he is going to collect evidence that pupils grow, or fail to grow, in the direction that he hopes they will. He continues to revise his teaching procedures in light of the evaluation of results. When he sees that one method is ineffective in promoting the type of pupil growth that he seeks, he abandons it. When he finds that other techniques that he uses are effective, he increases his use of those techniques.

A teacher alters his pattern of teaching a little bit at a time, undertaking the things he can do without shaking the whole structure of his method. As he tests out a new idea that he has and finds that it works, he incorporates it into his pattern. But if he tries a hunch that doesn't work, he discards it.

The procedure described above is *experimental teaching* and it is the doorway to *quality teaching*.

IV · *Significant Research*

Significant Research

Acceptance

1. Vagharsh, Bedoian H., "Social Acceptability and Social Rejection of the Underage, At-age, and Overage Pupils in the Sixth Grade." *Journal of Educational Research,* 47 (March, 1954), pp. 513–20.

   Seven hundred and forty-three sixth-graders in twenty-two schools were asked to rate their classmates on five indices of acceptance or rejection. The relative acceptance of over-age, average-age, and under-age-pupils was examined. It was found that under-age pupils were more socially acceptable than either at-age or over-age pupils with those who are only slightly under-age being the most acceptable.

   Over-age pupils were least acceptable and more often rejected. When over-age pupils are a minority in a class, they become objects of scorn unless they have some special asset such as outstanding ability in sports.

2. Buswell, Margaret M., "The Relationship Between the Social Structure of the Classroom and the Academic Success of the Pupils." *Journal of Experimental Education,* 22 (Sept., 1953), pp. 37–52.

   An investigation was made of the relationships among academic achievement, socio-economic level, and classroom structure of 286 kindergarten and 321 fifth-grade pupils. Evidence was collected by use of the Iowa Basic Skills Test, the Revised Stanford Binet IQ Test, Sims Score Card for Determining Socio-Economic Status, the Ohio Social Acceptance Scale at the fifth grade, the Detroit Beginning First Grade Intelligence Test, the Gates Reading Readiness Test, and individual interviews at the kindergarten.

   It was found that: (1) pupils who were succeeding in academic work were successful in their social relationships with their peers; (2) the academic achievement of the accepted group was significantly higher than the achievement of the less accepted group; and (3) acceptability at these groups had little relationship to socio-economic status.

3. Forlano, George, "Measuring the Quality of Social Acceptance in Some Ninth Grade Core and Non-Core Classes." *High School Journal*, 38 (October, 1954), pp. 12–16.

Forlano studied two ninth grade core classes and four non-core classes to determine whether or not students in core classes developed better interpersonal relationships than did students in noncore classes.

Thirty-eight core students and seventy-eight noncore students were given the Revised Ohio Social Acceptance Test in January, 1953. The same test was given again in June, 1953. A comparison of the results of the test showed the following results:

The core group showed a significant (.01) reduction in mean rejection score and a correspondingly significant (.02) gain in mean acceptance score.

The noncore group showed a significant (.001) increase in mean rejection score and a significant (.001) decrease in mean acceptance score.

4. McLendon, Ida Ruth, "An Investigation of Factors Associated with the Social Acceptance of Children in the Intermediate Grades of Hamilton, Ohio" (unpublished doctoral dissertation). Columbus, Ohio: Ohio State University, 1947.

Dr. McLendon studied the relationship between social class status and social acceptance and subject-matter achievement among 4,000 fourth-, fifth-, sixth-, and seventh-grade students in a midwestern city of 50,000 population. Under her classification the students were categorized in four social class groups. She found that: (1) social acceptance and academic achievement tended to be in direct proportion to social class status; (2) acceptance for boys and girls decreased proportionately with decline in social status; (3) the mean level of achievement declines as the prestige of the social class decreased but high achievement occurs in each class; and (4) in the two upper classes girls received higher scores on the average than boys, but in the two lower classes boys obtained higher scores than girls.

Anxiety and Social Pressure

5. Alper, Thelma G., "Memory for Completed and Incompleted Tasks as a Function of Personality: An Analysis of Group Data," *Journal of Abnormal and Social Psychology*, 41 (October, 1946), pp. 403–20.

In a study of the effect of self-esteem on intellectual performance and memory, ten college students took difficult tests under two conditions: (1) a relaxed condition, with emphasis on helping to standardize the material, and (2) an "ego involved" condition, in which tasks were presented as an intelligence test and on which the subject knew he was less successful than a contemporary. Under the threatening conditions, the subjects did significantly less well on the tests and also remembered them less well at a later time.

6. Barker, Roger, Tamara Dembo, Kurt Lewin, and Erick Wright, "Experimental Studies of Frustration in Young Children," in *Readings in Social Psychology*. New York: Henry Holt and Company, 1947, pp. 283–90.

   Two groups of children, aged two to six, were studied in a nonfrustrating and a frustrating situation. The nonfrustrating situation was in a standardized playroom under conditions of free play; the frustrating play situation was in the same room with the same toys, but with a number of more attractive, but inaccessible toys present. After the children were allowed to play with the more desirable toys, a wire-net partition was lowered and locked in place, shutting the children from the more desirable toys. Free play activities and barrier and escape activity were observed.

   The experiment was conducted with a group of thirty children and repeated with a group of seventy-eight different children.

   The mean regression in constructiveness of play from the nonfrustrating to the frustrating situation was over four times the standard error. The mean regression amounted to 17.3 months of mental age.

   The results indicate that frustration not only affects actions involved in achieving inaccessible goals, such as attempts to find roundabout routes or aggression against physical or social barriers, but that it may also affect behavior not directly frustrated or involved in overcoming the frustration. They suggest that the level of intellectual functioning is dependent upon the immediately existing situation and that the total situation is important in hindering or promoting the child's creative achievement.

   Emotional expression was affected by frustration. With frustration came a proportionate decrease in happiness of mood and an increase in restlessness, hypertension, and aggressiveness.

   The amount of intellectual regression and the amount of increase in negative emotionality were positively related to the strength of the frustration.

7. Beier, Ernest G., "The Effect of Induced Anxiety on Some Aspects of Intellectual Functioning: A Study of the Relationship Between Anxiety and Rigidity." *American Psychologist*, 4 (July, 1949), pp. 273–74.

   A group of women graduate students were given a mildly unfavorable interpretation of the Rorschach results. On a series of tests requiring attention, reasoning, and flexibility, given immediately afterward, the experimental subjects did less well than a matched unthreatened group. The test performance of the anxiety-threatened group was best described as rigid and poorly organized.

8. Castaneda, Alfred, David S. Palermo, and Boyd R. McCandless, "Learning and Performance as a Function of Anxiety in Children and Task Difficulty." *Child Development,* 27 (September, 1956), pp. 327–32.

Using an adaptation of Taylor's Manifest Anxiety Test, thirty-seven fifth-grade children were tested to determine their degree of anxiety. They were then given a test in a complex learning situation. Comparisons were made to test the relationship between anxiety and performance whereby the following conclusions were drawn:
 1. A significant (statistically) interaction was found between anxiety and task difficulty.
 2. Highly anxious subjects showed inferior performance on difficult tasks but superiority on easier tasks.

9. French, John, "Organized and Unorganized Groups Under Fear and Frustration," "Studies in Topological and Vector Psychology," Studies in Child Welfare, XX. Iowa City, Iowa: University of Iowa (1944), pp. 229–308.

Eight organized groups and eight groups in which members did not know each other were presented with three insoluble problems and asked to solve one in forty-five minutes. At the end of the time, the experimenters gave each participant a questionnaire to fill out, told them the experiment was over, went out, and locked the door. Smoke was poured into the locked room and fire sirens were sounded.

The group activities were observed in the frustration and fear situations through a one-way screen and a recording was made of the discussion. The actions and comments were classified into four categories:
 1. "We" feelings and motivation
 2. Motivation and frustration
 3. Frustration and aggression
 4. Interdependence and aggression

The organized group's reactions fell most frequently in the first category, while the unorganized group's reactions displayed behavior that could be classified in the last three categories.

10. Gaier, Eugene L., "The Relationship Between Selected Personality Variables and the Thinking of Students in Discussion Classes." *School Review,* 60 (October, 1952), p. 404–11.

An investigation of the relations among the learning processes and achievement, and three selected personality characteristics (anxiety, rigidity, and negativism) was made of eleven students in a social science course at the University of Chicago. Data on the learning processes in the classroom were obtained through observation and individual interview. Data on achievement were gained through the comprehensive examination given by the University to determine the course grade and credit. Personality data were gained through the use of the Rorschach test. The students were studied for a period of four months.

The following findings were reported:

1. The anxious person spends about half his time thinking about himself rather than the topic at hand. The correlation between thoughts about self and anxiety level was .45. Most of these thoughts revolved around feelings of inadequacy both as a person and as a class member.

2. The anxious person spends considerable time thinking about specific things in the classroom, such as people's dress, a chair, the blackboard, and so forth.

3. Anxious people do as well on knowledge of specific information as nonanxious people but they do rather poorly on problems involving analysis, application, or synthesis.

4. The rigid person spends a great deal of time in class thinking about himself.

5. The rigid person continues to think about specific words and phrases long after the class has moved to another subject.

6. The rigid person is easily irritated or bored with the class.

7. Rigid students tended to be best in knowledge of specific information.

8. About a third of the time in class is spent by negative individuals in evaluating (negatively) other students and the teacher and depreciating the ideas being discussed.

9. Negative persons spend considerable time thinking of things completely irrelevant to the class discussion.

In summary, it was found that particular personality characteristics, which can be identified before a course begins, will determine the nature of the individual's class participation.

11. Kvaraceus, W. C., "Delinquency—A By-Product of the School." *School and Society,* 59 (May 13, 1944), pp. 350–1.

From a comparison of the records of 761 delinquents handled by the Passaic Children's Bureau over a five-year period with the records of a control group from the general school population, it was found that: forty times as many delinquent boys repeated three or more school terms than other boys; seventy-five times more delinquent girls repeated three or more school terms than other girls; other students received high marks thirty-two times more frequently than delinquents; most of the delinquents left school as soon as they became sixteen while few of the other children did; 60 per cent of the delinquents expressed a marked dislike for school or for some persons closely connected with the school or classroom; *there was a significant decrease in the delinquency rate during the months when school was not in session.* It was concluded that aggressive behavior (delinquent conduct) is a result of frustration, and is believed to be frequently caused or brought about by the school.

12. Mandler, George, and Seymour B. Sarason, "A Study of Anxiety and Learning." *Journal of Abnormal and Social Psychology,* 47 (1952), pp. 166–73.

    Forty-two students were divided into two groups on the basis of an anxiety questionnaire. The two groups were subjected to an experimental work situation which included the giving of an evaluation report of the success of each member. The evaluation was designed to give each person a feeling of success, failure, or neutrality. The results were:
    1. The low anxiety group performed better initially.
    2. A wider dispersal of achievement was found in the high anxiety group.
    3. The high anxiety group tended to improve its initial performance.
    4. Intervening evaluation report elicited improved performance for the low anxiety group but depressed the high anxiety group.
    5. Optimal conditions for the high anxiety group was that no further reference be made to the test situation. Optimal conditions for the low anxiety group was an intervening failure report.

13. Montague, Ernest K., "The Role of Anxiety in Serial Rote Learning." *Journal of Experimental Psychology,* 45 (February, 1953), pp. 91–96.

    Thirty anxious and thirty nonanxious subjects, as determined by the Minnesota Multiphasic Personality Inventory, were studied to determine whether anxiety interfered with the rate of learning.

    The subjects were instructed to learn three lists of nonsense syllables of varying difficulty.

    Anxious students did not perform as well as nonanxious subjects on the difficult tasks. Anxious subjects showed greater improvement as tasks became easier, and surpassed nonanxious subjects on the easiest tasks.

14. Ramond, Charles K., "Anxiety and Task as Determiners of Verbal Performance." *Journal of Experimental Psychology,* 46 (August, 1953), pp. 120–24.

    Thirty-three highly anxious subjects and forty nonanxious students, as measured by the Taylor Manifest Anxiety scale, were studied in an investigation of the relationship between drive level and performance in a simple trial-and-error learning situation. The subjects were undergraduate psychology students at the State University of Iowa.

Nonanxious students responded correctly significantly more often than did anxious students on presentations in which a weaker response was correct.

No significant difference was found between the performance of the anxious and nonanxious students on presentations in which the stronger response was correct.

Emotional Needs

15. Bettelheim, Bruno, and Emmy Sylvester, "Therapeutic Influence of the Group on the Individual." *American Journal of Orthopsychiatry*, 17 (1947), pp. 684–92.

    A study was made of the effect of a group upon emotionally disturbed children at the Orthogenic School, University of Chicago, Illinois. No organic cases or children with less than normal intelligence were admitted. The age range of group members was from seven to twelve years. Children usually participated in groups of six.

    Group situations were permitted to evolve casually and naturally from activities of the children, but they were modified and planned in accordance with the child's existing needs.

    The therapeutic influence of the groups came from the active influence of the group or its individual members, and from non-positive actions or attitudes. Help for disturbed children came when

    1. Group permissive gave support.
    2. Group permitted gain of status.
    3. Group assisted in the integration of hostile tendencies.
    4. Group assisted in the integration of contradictory tendencies.
    5. Group helped face the traumatic past by a secure present.
    6. Group gave strength through belonging.

    It was concluded that a group with good social climate and adequate assistance, whether permanent or not, constitutes a reservoir of strength from which the individual child may draw support for his new steps in mastery.

16. Bills, Robert, "Non-Directive Play Therapy with Retarded Readers." *Journal of Consulting Psychology,* 14 (April, 1950), pp. 140–49.

    The study tested the hypothesis that the difficulty which some retarded readers show is due mainly to inconsistencies within their value systems, and if nondirective play therapy can aid the individual in changing his attitude toward self or in re-evaluating his self-concept, then corresponding changes will occur in subject-matter ability after nondirective play therapy.

Third-graders with a discrepancy between their mental age and reading age were chosen for study. They were studied over three periods of thirty school days each. During the first thirty days no therapy was given and the growth of eighteen pupils was measured; during the second thirty days eight of the pupils were given six individual and three group therapy sessions while the remaining ten pupils served as a comparison group; during the third thirty days all children followed the normal school procedures.

It was found that the group receiving therapy made greater gains in the therapy period, significant at the .001 level of probability, than in the control period.

17. Burrell, Anna Porter, "Facilitating Learning Through Emphasis on Meeting Children's Basic Emotional Needs: An In-Service Training Program." *Journal of Educational Sociology,* 24 (March, 1951), pp. 381–93.

The study listed the hypothesis "that one source of difficulty in learning relates to the status of the child's emotional needs and that serious frustration of these needs may be one of the primary causes of failure to learn." Three teachers, one fourth-, one fifth-, and one sixth-grade, and their classes constituted the experimental group. Three teachers and classes of similar ability and background served as a comparison group. Each experimental teacher selected five pupils to study and to attempt to help. In addition, the teachers met frequently with a consultant to discuss the pupils and the general problem of meeting emotional needs. Tests—The Wishing Well, the Ohio Social Acceptance Scale, Otis Quick Scoring Ability Test, Pintner General Ability, Stanford Achievement Test, and the Wetzel-grid—were used at the beginning and end of the semester. "From the summarized data it would seem that the work with the selected children of the experimental group substantiated the hypothesis that guided this study; that an attack upon the problem of improving learning through emphasis on meeting the child's emotional needs by concentrating attention upon a few selected students who had learning difficulties, would produce changes in social acceptability and achievement. Furthermore, working with selected students in the experimental groups not only resulted in improvement in terms of social acceptance, learning, and personal adjustment of the few students but resulted in gains experienced in these areas by the members of the total experimental classes."

18. Fleming, Robert, "Psychosomatic Illness and Emotional Needs." *Educational Leadership,* IX (November, 1951), pp. 119–23.

Thirty-eight children with a history of psychosomatic manifestations such as stomach upsets, allergies, kidney difficulties, and frequent headaches were identified in an elementary school by the school health authorities. Twenty-six of the pupils were considered in an experimental group and twelve in a comparison group. Teachers of pupils in the experimental group engaged in an in-service program consisting of a series of conferences devoted to discussions of the emotional needs of children and their implications for working with children. Also, teachers of the experimental group analyzed a series of human relations films.

Teachers with the experimental group sought to work with pupils in a manner "which would free them, which would make them secure, which would help them like school, which would help them recognize success, which would help them work on things for which they saw purpose, which would give them opportunities to see more clearly what they were doing in school, and which would help them become better participants in their group."

Of the children, 96 per cent in the experimental group showed significant decrease in the intensity of the symptoms, whereas 50 per cent of the children in the comparison group showed significant improvement. In terms of frequency of symptoms, 66 per cent of the experimental group decreased from daily manifestations to occasional manifestations, whereas 41 per cent of the comparison group continued daily manifestations. Attendance of the experimental group improved 49 per cent over attendance during the same period the preceding year. The comparison group had a 40 per cent loss in attendance over the previous year.

Nine parents made up a sub-group in the experimental group to test the hypothesis that the teacher plus parent would result in more change. Individual conferences were held with the parents and they saw some of the human relations films. In terms of attendance, decrease in intensity and frequency of symptoms, the children whose parents and teachers worked together showed greater improvement.

19. Mann, Frank A., "The Frequency of Unmet Emotional Needs as Evidenced in Children's Behavior." *The Journal of Educational Sociology,* 24 (March, 1951), pp. 414–24.

A study was made of 1,358 children from six schools to see where they manifested behavior thought to indicate unmet emotional needs and to determine the relationship of this behavior to social status, acceptance, and intelligence. The population consisted of 743 boys and 615 girls from 52 classes ranging from kindergarten through the ninth grade. The results of teacher observation, The Wishing Well (a test of emotional needs), the Ohio Social Acceptance, a test designed to determine friendship patterns within a classroom, Warner's Index of Status-Characteristics, and intelligence quotients were used as data. Of the sampling, 20 per cent were found to be unusually aggressive, 7 per cent submissive, 8 per cent consistently withdrawing, and 2 per cent showed symptoms of psychosomatic illness. The most prevalent unmet needs were reported to be: for belonging, for achievement, for love and affection, and for understanding. Test results indicated that the need for understanding was unmet in the greatest percentage of aggressive boys and the need for achievement was unmet in the greatest percentage of aggressive girls.

Using the Index of Status Characteristics, the social class status of 506 children in two schools was determined. A greater percentage of children in the lower classes were characterized by teachers as aggressive. Symptoms of psychosomatic illness seemed to be concentrated in the three lower class groups.

Teachers did not see as many unmet needs in pupils from their own social status, in pupils with highest ranges of intelligence, in pupils not accepted by their sex. Test results disagreed with the teacher's judgment in many cases in these areas.

20. Park, Lawrence, "Prejudice and Unmet Emotional Needs." *Journal of Educational Sociology,* 24 (March, 1951), pp. 406–13.

The study explored the hypothesis that as children's emotional needs are better met, these children's attitudes toward minority groups change in a positive direction. Six teachers with six classes (fourth, fifth, and sixth) participated in a semester-long attempt to meet the emotional needs of selected pupils in their classes more adequately. Six other teachers and their classes were used to widen the sample. Tests (Wishing Well, Human Relations Inventory, and Ohio Social Acceptance Scale) and data from personal folders were used to determine position of student before and after the semester. No mention was made to the teachers involved of the hypothesis being tested—emphasis was on meeting emotional needs.

It was found that: (1) children whose needs were better met during the interim of the study made significant decrease in their attitude of prejudice, particularly toward the Negro; (2) children whose needs were apparently less well met increased their prejudice toward "Negro people," (3) children whose emotional needs didn't change also did not change in their attitudes toward this group. The relationship was not so strong in regard to Jewish and Catholic groups, where the attitude of prejudice was less in evidence.

21. Rogers, Carl R., "Mental Health Findings in Three Elementary Schools." *Educational Research Bulletin,* 21 (March, 1942), pp. 69–79.

In three elementary schools with a total of 1,542 children it was found that: one-third of the children were regarded as problems by teachers; 30 per cent showed evidences of being poorly adjusted though not to a serious degree; 12 per cent were seriously maladjusted and showed evidence of poor mental health.

Evaluation

22. Alexander, Audrey M., "Teacher Judgment of Pupil Intelligence and Achievement is Not Enough." *Elementary School Journal,* 53 (March, 1953), pp. 396–401.

Thirty-five teachers of grades three through eight, who had worked with their students at least six months, were asked to list from their classes:
1. the five most intelligent pupils
2. the five least intelligent pupils
3. the five highest achievers in relation to mental capacity
4. the five lowest achievers in relation to mental capacity

Teachers were correct in their judgments concerning mental ability 57 per cent of the time and in their judgments concerning relationship of achievement to mental ability 25 per cent of the time.

23. Whitner, Chester L., "Just How Much Do Teachers' Marks Vary?" *Education*, 52 (October, 1931), pp. 97–99.

Ten freshman English examination papers were submitted to ten instructors in English at the University of Wisconsin. Scores assigned one paper ranged from twenty to sixty-five. The rank assigned a single paper by the instructors varied as much as six ranks. The study provides strong evidence of variability in the marks assigned pupil work by teachers.

Group Interaction

24. Back, Kurt, "Interpersonal Relations in a Discussion Group," *Journal of Social Issues*, 4 (Spring, 1948), pp. 61–65.

The discussion patterns of two groups were studied with regard to distribution of participation, type of participation, and direction of participation. It was found that:
1. By dominating the discussion, the highest contributors could make their position permanent.
2. Faculty leaders exert a distinct influence on the participation pattern of members.
3. As faculty leaders contribute a higher percentage of work-centered and friendly remarks than the group, the group's percentage of work-centered and friendly remarks increased.
4. A greater amount of negatively-toned responses tends to anchor the relative positions in the group; greater emphasis on friendly interactions assures a smooth change in positions.

25. Deutsch, Morton, "Social Relations in the Classroom and Grading Procedures." *Journal of Educational Research*, 45 (October, 1951), pp. 145–52.

Deutsch compared the results obtained through cooperative and competitive methods of grading. Fifty matched students were placed in ten discussion groups. In the competitive situation, the subjects were told that each would be graded in comparison with other members of the group. Subjects in the cooperative group were told that group members would be given the same grade, that the individual rewards would be based on the total performance of the group. Three human relations problems were submitted to each group. Observers noted that the cooperative groups were friendlier, showed greater tolerance, made more encouraging comments to each other, and made fewer aggressive remarks.

No significant difference was found between cooperation and competition, in friendliness outside of class, in group activities outside of class, or in achievement.

26. Johnson, A. D., "An Attempt to Change Interpersonal Relationships." *Sociometry*, 2 (July, 1939), pp. 43–48.

    Two attempts were made to bring isolates into groups of fourteen-year-old boys. In one case, an adult group leader worked directly with the isolate and in the other the youth group leader, as shown by sociograms, assumed the responsibility of working the isolate into group acceptance. In the situation in which the adult leader attempted to work directly with the isolate, no change resulted. The youth group leader was able to help the isolate win some acceptance by the group.

27. Klugman, Samuel, "Cooperative vs. Individual Efficiency in Problem-Solving." *Journal of Educational Psychology*, 35 (February, 1944), pp. 91–100.

    One hundred and thirty-six children from the fourth-, fifth-, and sixth-grades, with IQ's between 90 and 109, solved arithmetic problems working alone and in pairs. When pupils worked together, they solved more problems correctly but took a longer time. Klugman concluded that the higher scores and longer time needed to solve the problems were due to the presentation, discussion, rejection, and acceptance of the larger number of possible answers which occurred when children were working together.

28. Lewin, Kurt, "The Dynamics of Group Action." *Educational Leadership*, 1 (January, 1944), pp. 195–200.

    An effort was made to change students from the consumption of white to the consumption of wholewheat bread. From each student was obtained a rating of his eagerness to reach the goal and his like or dislike of wholewheat bread as compared with white bread. The results showed that after requests to change, the eagerness to succeed was lowest in the individuals who disliked wholewheat bread most and that it increased with the degree of liking for wholewheat bread. After group decision, however, the eagerness to reach a group goal was largely independent of personal likes or dislikes. The experimental studies indicated that it was easier to change ideology or cultural habits by dealing with groups than with individuals.

29. Moreno, J. L., and Helen H. Jennings, "Sociometric Control Studies of Grouping and Regrouping." *Sociometry Monographs*, No. 7, Beacon House (1947), pp. 20–29.

Three groups of girls, each group consisting of sixteen persons, were studied for thirty-two weeks. The first group, the control group, was assigned to cottages without any sociometric testing or design. The second group, Group A, was assigned to cottages on the basis of sociometric procedure, but not on a maximum affinity basis. The third group, Group B, was assigned according to sociometric procedures, and maximum affinity was carefully adhered to. All groups were checked with sociometric measures every eight weeks.

It was found that the tested subjects find a better position in the group from the start. The sociometric assignment protects the newcomer against social blocking at an early stage. They are integrated with the group more quickly; the greater the original affinity between a newcomer and the prominent members of the group, the better that subject is accepted by the whole group; hit-or-miss assignment appears to facilitate social blocking and often establishes an isolated position; sociometric studies can cut down some of the adjustment otherwise needed.

30. Rosenthal, David, and Charles Cofer, "The Effect on Group Performance of An Indifferent and Neglectful Attitude Shown by One Group Member." *Journal of Experimental Psychology*, 38 (October, 1948), pp. 568–77.

Twelve control and twelve experimental groups were established from male members of a psychology course. All groups were given the information that they were participating in a dart-throwing experiment to compare the intellectual and motor processes of college students with those of different academic, occupational, and social status. All groups were encouraged to attain at maximum potential.

In the initial tests the control and experimental groups were equal in ability.

The difference in groups was that a "plant," who after the initial test displayed indifference, neglect, and negativism but not to a sufficient degree to cause isolation, was placed in each experimental group. Nine tests were given to each of the groups.

Although the "plant" achieved on an average with his group, his indifference and neglect provoked deterioration of motivation toward group goals as well as disintegration of commonality of group thought and feeling.

Groups of five showed greater increase in positive attitudes and achievement under favorable conditions than groups of four, and faster deterioration under unfavorable circumstances.

Group-Centered Procedures

31. Asch, Morton J., "Non-directive Teaching in Psychology." *Psychological Monographs*, 65 (1951), p. 4.

Traditional and nondirective methods of teaching were compared. Twenty-three students at Syracuse University, enrolled in a second semester course in introductory psychology, were selected as the experimental group. Teaching methods followed the nondirective theories advanced by Rogers, Combs, and Snyder. This group was told the pages in the textbook (and other textual data) which would contain essential information. They were asked to write a reaction report each week, as long or short as they pleased, pertaining to the subject or not. They were permitted to discuss anything in class and the instructor clarified, objectified, or summarized student remarks. The instructor did not further structure the course; pupils evaluated their own learnings. Grades were self-assigned in conference with the instructor.

The control group pool consisted of 101 students enrolled in three second semester psychology classes. These students were assigned the same materials that had been suggested to the experimental group. In addition, they were assigned a term paper, required to take two quizzes, a midterm and final examination. From the control group pool, twenty-three students were selected who most closely matched the experimental students in honor point averages and scores on the Ohio State Scholastic Aptitude Test.

The two matched groups were given examination on factual material, social attitudes, and emotional adjustment. Emotional adjustment scores favored the experimental group at the 1 per cent level. The experimental group scored higher on the social attitudes test but not significantly so. The control group was superior on information gained at the 1 per cent level on an objective test and the 5 per cent level on an essay test.

32. Faw, Volney, "A Psychotherapeutic Method of Teaching Psychology." *American Psychologist*, 4 (April, 1949), pp. 104–09.

From a comparison of the results in three sections of a psychology class (one a student-centered group handled in a nondirective therapeutic fashion, one an instructor-centered group handled in a directive fashion, and one taught by alternating the two methods) it was found that: the student-centered group had two and one-half times as many student comments as the instructor-centered class; the student-centered class tended to express personal feelings and experiences in connection with the topic being discussed, whereas the instructor-centered group seemed to discuss the issues in a purely intellectual way with few references to their own experiences; the student-centered group expressed preference for student-centered discussions by a ratio of 29 to 2 and the combined method favored student-centered discussion 22 to 11; in all three examinations given, the student-centered group scored higher than the other groups.

33. Levine, Jacob, and John Butler, "Lecture versus Group Decision in Changing Behavior." *Journal of Applied Psychology*, 36 (February, 1952), pp. 29–33.

The effects of a lecture and group discussion as method of changing behavior of twenty-nine supervisors were compared. Three groups were formed:
   1. a control group (nine members) which received no instruction
   2. a discussion group (ten members)
   3. a lecture group (eleven members)

The supervisors in the discussion group improved. The lecture group members did not change at all and persisted in over-rating the higher skilled and under-rating the underskilled workers.

34. Perkins, Hugh V., Jr., "Climate Influences Group Learning." *Journal of Educational Research*, 45 (October, 1951), pp. 115–19.

Six in-service teacher groups participating in an established program of child study were used as subjects in an investigation of the difference in learning in group centered and leader centered classrooms. Three of the classes were group centered and three were leader centered. Withall's technique for assessing classroom climate in terms of the pattern of teachers' categorized statements was used to describe the climate of each group in the study. Records were made of comments which revealed child development concepts, attitudes toward children, information to support statements, and increased insight.

Group-centered groups displayed greater objectivity and warmth in their attitudes toward children whereas the attitudes in leader-centered groups were proportionately more emotional, conventional, and cold. Group-centered classes were superior in concepts acquired, attitudes expressed supporting information supplied, and insight.

35. Rehage, Kenneth J., "A Comparison of Pupil-Teacher Planning and Teacher-Directed Procedures in Eighth Grade Social Studies Classes." *Journal of Educational Research*, 45 (October, 1951), pp. 111–15.

Two classes of eighth-grade social studies at the Laboratory School of the University of Chicago, matched on the basis of intelligence and social acceptance, were studied for thirty weeks to determine the relative effectiveness of teacher-pupil planning and teacher-directed procedures.

No significant difference was found in the amount of subject matter learned, but the pupil-teacher planning group showed greater insight into the processes of group planning.

36. Withall, John, "The Development of a Technique for the Measurement of Social-Emotional Climate in the Classroom." *Journal of Experimental Education*, 17 (March, 1949), pp. 347–61.

Using the conclusion from Lippitt's study that different leadership styles produce different social climates, Withall constructed a climate index which measured whether the teacher's approach was learner-centered, problem-centered, or teacher-centered. In application of the index it was found that most of the class situations studied were teacher-centered, and that pupil reaction to the events in the class were predominantly positive when class sessions were pupil-centered and predominantly negative when the sessions were teacher-centered.

37. Zelany, Leslie Day, "Experimental Appraisal of a Group Learning Plan." *Journal of Educational Research*, 34 (September, 1940), pp. 37–42.

A comparison of student growth in college sociology classes taught by the *group discussion* and the *recitation* methods was made by the author. In the five comparisons made, it was found that more sociological facts were learned, more attitudes were changed, more personalities moved in the direction of leadership, cooperation, and sociability through group discussion. Although the amount of difference between groups was not statistically significant in any case, the advantage in every case was with the group discussion procedure. Further, students like the group discussion method better.

Learning

38. Carpenter, Finley, "The Effect of Different Learning Methods on Concept Formation." *Science Education*, 40 (October, 1956), pp. 282–85.

Carpenter tested two groups of thirty-five each on their ability to associate nonsense syllables with various shapes and colors of blocks. One group was taught to make the associations and learn the concepts functionally; the other group learned by rote.

The experiment was continued until all in each group could name and classify each block.

A test was given one week later and it was found that 77 per cent of the functional group could name and identify the blocks and 29 per cent of the rote group could name and identify the blocks. The author concluded that:

    1. Functional learning of concepts is more efficient than rote learning.

2. Concepts that refer to classes of material objects are more thoroughly understood when the student has an opportunity to manipulate and study the objects than when only factual information is given in lectures.

39. Kelley, Earl C., *Education for What is Real.* New York: Harper and Brothers, 1947.

Dr. Adelbert Ames of the Hanover Institute has developed some experimental demonstrations of the principles which govern the development of perceiving. Material objects are presented to a subject in such a manner as to restrict his obtaining all the clues he would ordinarily secure. Different observers perceive and interpret the objects differently. Dr. Kelley interprets the demonstrations as follows:
"We do not get our perceptions from the things around us but the perceptions come from us. Things around us have no meaning except as we ascribe meaning to them."
"The name and position we give to the object do not lie in the objects themselves, but in what we ascribe to them out of our past experience."
"The only reality we can experience is what we make of the objects around us, and is always unique for each of us."
"Perception is a directive for action. The only way to know perception is faulty or valid is by action . . . Reality comes from what we make of our clues, received by our sense organs, when we act upon them."
"Selection of the factors in the environment is determined by a combination of past experience and purpose."

40. McClelland, David C., and John W. Atkinson, "The Projective Expression of Needs: Part I, The Effect of Different Intensities of the Hunger Drive on Perception." *Journal of Psychology,* 25 (January-April, 1948), pp. 205–22.

Atkinson, John W., and David C. McClelland, "The Projective Expression of Needs: Part II, The Effect of Different Intensities of the Hunger Drive on Thematic Apperception." *Journal of Experimental Psychology,* 38 (December, 1948), pp. 643–658.

McClelland, David C., John W. Atkinson, and Russell W. Clark, "The Projective Expression of Needs: Part III, The Effect of Ego-Involvement, Success, and Failure on Perception," *Journal of Psychology,* 27 (January-April, 1949), pp. 311–30.

McClelland, David C., *et al.,* "The Projective Expression of Needs: Part IV, The Effect of the Need for Achievement on Thematic Perception." *Journal of Experimental Psychology,* 39 (April, 1949), pp. 242–55.

Perception was tested by having the subjects guess the nature of a "faint" really nonexistent image projected on a screen and by having them make up stories based on somewhat ambiguous (thematic apperception) pictures. Hungrier subjects, deprived of food for sixteen hours, "saw" more food-related objects on the blank screen and used more food-deprivation themes in the stories based on the pictures.

In other comparable studies, students who had just experienced failure on tests showed by their perceptions and stories greater need for achievement than did control subjects.

41. Tyler, Ralph, "Permanence of Learning." *Journal of Higher Education*, 4 (April, 1933), pp. 203–05.

Eighty-two students, typical of those enrolled in the elementary zoology course at Ohio State University, were given a test at the beginning of the course, at the completion of the course, and at the end of fifteen additional months during which they had taken no zoology courses. The purpose was to determine the percentage of the gain made during the course that was lost in the ensuing fifteen months. Tyler found a 77 per cent loss in ability to name animal structure appearing in diagrams, a 26 per cent loss in identifying technical terms, and a 21 per cent loss in recalling information. On the positive side, he found no loss in skill in applying principles and a 25 per cent gain in interpreting new experiments.

Motivation

42. Buhrick, Harry P., "Incidental Learning Under Two Incentive Conditions." *Journal of Experimental Psychology*, 47 (1954), pp. 170–72.

Seventy-four students were assigned by random procedure to two experimental conditions. In one situation, the students were to be paid according to the quickness with which they learned fourteen geometric forms placed on a memory drum. In the other situation, the subjects were given the same task but offered no pay and told not to exert themselves.

The high incentive group learned the whole task quicker (significant at the 2 per cent level) but the low incentive group learned the figure order sooner (significant at the 2 per cent level).

43. Bills, Robert E., "The Effect of a Value on Learning." *Journal of Personality*, 21 (December, 1952), pp. 217–22.

An experiment was conducted to discover how agreement or disagreement of the student's and instructor's values affects the learning of the student.

Two groups of students, thirty-seven in one and ninety-three in the other, were chosen from two child psychology classes. These students were tested on the first day of class to determine their attitude toward psychology. From these two groups, fifty-one pairs of students, one with a positive attitude toward psychology and the other with a negative, were chosen and matched on the basis of general ability test scores.

At the end of the course, an objective examination, based on the factual material of the course, was given. A comparison of the final marks of the two groups supported the conclusion that agreement or disagreement between student's and instructor's values influences final class marks even when those marks are based on an objective examination.

44. Brown, William F., Norman Ables, and Ira Iscoe, "Motivational Differences Between High and Low Scholarship College Students." *Journal of Educational Psychology,* 45 (April, 1954), pp. 215–23.

Ninety-seven students from the Dean's list and forty-six students from the Scholastic Probation List, all University of Texas freshmen with comparable scores on the ACE, were sent letters requesting that they come to the Psychology Department at any time during a three-day period to cooperate in a one-hour study. After the three-day period had elapsed, those who had not appeared were sent another letter. Those who didn't appear after the second letter were phoned and appointments made. Of the Dean's list students, 97 per cent appeared, while only 50 per cent of the Probation List students appeared, even after phoning.

Three hundred and sixty-seven male students were asked to cooperate in an attitude study sponsored by Cornell University. The same general procedure was used that was followed as in the University of Texas study. School pride and cooperation were stressed in the original letter requesting help.

Cooperation was compared with honor point averages. Students who cooperated on the study had a significantly higher honor point average than did those who did not.

45. Hurlock, Elizabeth, "An Evaluation of Certain Incentives Used in School Work." *Journal of Educational Psychology,* 16 (March, 1925), pp. 145–59.

Four groups all did the same tasks in arithmetic. The first group was praised for the improvement they had made and encouraged to do better, another was reproved before other pupils for their many careless mistakes and the inferior quality of their work, while a third group was ignored in that nothing was said about their work although they heard the remarks made to the others. The fourth group, a control group, worked in another room under usual conditions. All three experimental groups did better than the control. The praised and reproved groups improved rapidly at first, but from then on, while the praised group continued to improve, the work of the reproved group declined. The work of the ignored group was not as good as that of the reproved group.

Self-Knowledge and Self-Direction

46. Buck, Nina M., and Ralph H. Ojemann, "The Relation Between Ability in Scientific Thinking and Behavior in Situations Involving Choice." *Journal of Experimental Education*, 11 (December, 1942), pp. 215–19.

Twenty-three high school freshmen were studied to determine the relationship between ability in scientific thinking and behavior in situations involving choice. A paper-and-pencil test of scientific thinking was given and scored. Later, two observers recorded and scored the behavior of the students in ten performance situations. Each was judged on the nature of his approach to the problem and his attempt to validate his choice scientifically.

The correlation between thinking scores and behavior scores was low, .31. The two subjects having the highest thinking scores had quite low scores on the behavior tests.

The outstanding difference between high and low score subjects on the behavior situations seemed to be a well-formed purpose which was the subject's own and which he was attempting to carry out.

47. Raimy, Victor C., "Self Reference in Counseling Interviews." *Journal of Consulting Psychology*, 12 (May-June, 1948), pp. 153–63.

An analysis was made of 111 recorded interviews of fourteen counseling clients for statements showing the person's attitude toward himself. In successful counseling cases there was a marked shift from an unfavorable to favorable self-concept, which was absent in unsuccessful cases. Rainey concluded that a person's self-concept was a core factor in his personality organization.

48. Rogers, Carl R., Bill L. Kell, and Helen McNeil, "The Role of Self Understanding in the Prediction of Behavior." *Journal of Consulting Psychology*, 12 (May-June, 1948), pp. 174–86.

A number of delinquent children were rated on a variety of factors including physical status, family record, social influences, education, and self-insight. Self-insight meant the degree to which the child understood his own situation and problems. An independent follow-up study rated the children's later readjustments, which were then correlated with the factors in their histories. A youngster's self-insight was found to be the best prediction of his later adjustment. His social experiences and family record were also related to the outcome, but education, economic, and physical factors were not.

49. Williams, Herbert D., "An Experiment in Self-Directed Education." *School and Society,* 31 (May 24, 1930), pp. 715–18.

Thirteen boys, selected from the worst cases of juvenile delinquents, age eight to sixteen years, found in a review of 2,600 cases, were brought to a central technical high school for one semester. They were placed in a room set aside for them. It was equipped with desks, blackboards, and a table with supplementary readers, story books, and texts for the various grades.

No formal instruction was given. The only rule enforced was that the boys keep busy and refrain from bothering others. Otherwise, they could do as they pleased. Whenever interests were discovered they were encouraged, and extra help was provided. Boys could relate their findings to the group, but no one was required to listen.

Forms A and B of the Stanford Achievement Test were administered at the beginning and end of the semester. A gain of six to fifteen months' progress in the various subjects was made in the four-month period, with the greatest gain shown in language and arithmetic and the smallest in history and literature.

Teacher-Pupil Relationships

50. Lewin, Kurt, "Experiments in Social Space." *Harvard Educational Review,* 9 (January, 1939), pp. 21–32.

An experiment was conducted by Lippitt and White at the Iowa Child Welfare Research Station to observe the effects of democratic and autocratic atmospheres on clubs that had been experimentally created. Observers noted the properties of groups.

Two groups of boys and girls, ten to eleven years of age, were selected for mask-making clubs. Both groups were equated on such qualities as leadership and interpersonal relations. Eleven meetings of the groups were held. The democratically operated group always met two days before the autocratically controlled group. The democratic group chose its activities freely. The autocratic group was ordered to do whatever the democratic group had done. All factors except the group atmosphere were kept constant.

In the democratic group all policies were a matter of group determination. Alternate procedures were suggested and the group could choose the course it wanted to follow. Group members were free to work with whomever they chose, and the leader attempted to be a group member, giving objective praise and criticism. In the authoritarian group the leader determined the policy, dictated the techniques to be used, told each member with whom he should work, criticized an individual's activity without giving reasons, and remained aloof from group participation. During the meeting of the clubs, observers noted the number of incidents of aggression and the actions of the leader per unit of time. In both groups the leader was still leading. Both leaders were less submissive than average members of the group, but the difference between the ordinary group member and the leader was much less pronounced in the democratic situation. The autocratic leader took twice as much action toward members of the group as did the democratic leader.

In the authoritarian group almost thirty times as much hostile domination occurred—such as demands for attention and hostile criticism in child-to-child relationships—as in the democratic group. The democratic group exhibited more cooperation, praise of the other person's work, constructive suggestions, and matter-of-fact behavior. "We" centered statements, rather than "I" centered, occurred twice as often in the democratic group as in the autocratic group.

51. Lippitt, Ronald, and Ralph K. White, "An Experimental Study of Leadership and Group Life." *Readings in Social Psychology* (Newcomb and Harley, eds.). New York: Henry Holt and Company, 1947, pp. 315–30.

An attempt was made to determine the reaction of four clubs of three variations in adult leadership—"democratic," "authoritarian," and "laissez-faire."

The adult-leader role was found to be a strong determiner of the pattern of social interaction and the emotional development of the group. Four clear-cut types of social atmosphere emerged.
 1. Aggressive reaction to the autocratic leader with aggression toward out-groups.
 2. Apathetic reaction to the autocratic leader with internal expressions of aggression.
 3. Reaction to democratic leader with attempts to overcome sources of frustration.

Previous group history and preceding social climates had an important effect in determining the group's perception of a leader's behavior and its reactions.

52. Michael, William B., Earle E. Herrold, and Eugene W. Cryan, "Survey of Student-Teacher Relationships." *Journal of Educational Research*, 44 (May, 1951), pp. 657–73.

A questionnaire which was designed by the authors to measure the attitudes of students toward the behavior and practices of teachers was given to 489 boys and 487 girls in eleventh and twelfth grades in five selected high schools in northern New Jersey and eastern Pennsylvania.

They found that:
1. The relative importance of six factors ranked with respect to their contribution to classroom enjoyment were:
   —teacher's method of teaching
   —teacher's personality
   —confidence in the teacher's knowledge of the subject matter
   —good marks obtained in the course
   —short assignments
   —no special emphasis on discipline
2. Most girls were willing to undergo long assignments and strict discipline for good grades, whereas most boys were unwilling to do so.
3. Both boys and girls were in favor of allowing volunteers to answer questions rather than have the teacher pick someone.
4. Both boys and girls preferred teachers who participated in extracurricular affairs to brilliant teachers who did not.
5. Students prefer answers to mathematics problems after solving the problems rather than before.
6. There was no systematic relationship found to exist between the scholastic averages of students and their attitudes with respect to the points in 1, 2, 3, 4, and 5 above.

53. Ojeman, Ralph, and Frances Wilkenson, "The Effect on Pupil Growth of an Increase in Teacher's Understanding of Pupil Behavior." *The Journal of Experimental Education*, 8 (December, 1939), pp. 143–47.

The data in this study are consistent in showing that when teachers learn to know their pupils as personalities in their home environments, the teachers tend to become more effective guides for learning. The pupils achieve more in academic areas and teachers become more effective in helping pupils improve their personalities.

54. Sparks, Jack N., "Teachers' Attitudes Toward the Behavior Patterns of Children." *Journal of Educational Psychology*, 43 (May, 1952), pp. 284–91.

Do teachers rate the same problems as most detrimental to the future of the child exhibiting them that they rate as most troublesome to the school situation?

Seven hundred and sixty-two Iowa teachers, chosen randomly from all sizes of schools in the state, and sixty-one graduate students provided data. Teachers were grouped on two criteria: (1) amount of training and (2) years of teaching experience.

1. The teachers did not rate the behavior problems in the same order in terms of seriousness to future adjustment of the child displaying them and troublesomeness in classroom situations.

2. Amount of education seems to make a difference in the attitudes of teachers toward the seriousness of certain behavior problems in relation to the future of the child.

3. Those traits of virtue with which our society is most concerned (honesty, social and sexual morality, and so forth) are more important to teachers than the personality traits which indicate the state of the child's personal adjustment.

Index

A

Ability:
 confidence in, 49
 decision-making, promoting, 221–42
 intellectual, individual differences in, 145–46
 ranges of, 54
Ables, Norman, 323
Absentees, 59
Acceptance, 33, 36, 47
 aids to, 58–59
 empathy and, 57
 by group, 111–15
  hindrances to, 112, 113–14
  maintaining, 115
  winning, 112–13, 114
 of less-developed child, 155
 as mutual faith, 113
 of others, self-improvement and, 57–58
 promoting, 82–83
 pupil:
  effect of community, 61–63
  of others, 72–79
  of teacher, 79–82
  teacher's role in, 63
 of pupils by teachers, 36, 53–60
 research in, 305–6
 of self, 36
  fear and, 66–68
  guilt feelings and, 68–70
  insecurity and, 70–71
  by pupils, 61–72, 166, 167
  by teachers, 49–52, 284
 total group, 62–63
Accomplishment, praising, 65
Achievement:
 differences in, 33, 37
 group, 102
 and personal worth, 66
 providing sense of, 133, 134
 recognizing, 63–66

Activities:
 community, participation in, 272–74
 group, records of, 127–29
 and individual differences, 141, 142
 newspaper reports of, 276–77
 observing, 166
 organizing for, 25–26, 37
 provision for variety in, 149–50
 records of, 230
 social, 91, 267
Administrators, school, 252, 255–56, **261**
Adolescents:
 development of, 155
 teachers and, 214
Age-groups:
 characteristics of, 110–11
 and purposes, 204
Agenda:
 as control, 125
 of faculty meetings, 252–53
 group, 120–21
 long-term, 121
 necessity for, 131
Aggression, 62
Aggressive children, 113–14, 157–**61**
 characteristics of, 157–58
 helping, 158–60
Alexander, Audrey M., 314
Alper, Thelma G., 306
Anxiety, research in, 306–10
Asch, Morton J., 318
Assemblies, 259
Assignments:
 definite, 12
 school policy on, 250–51
 stereotyped, 168
Atkinson, John W., 321
Attendance records, 12
Attitudes:
 attempts to direct, 73
 changes in, 19

330 INDEX

Attitudes (Cont.)
parental:
acquisition of, 80
effect of, 153
pupil, toward teachers, 80–82
of teacher, 60
Authoritarian society, 26
Authority:
planning, 132
shared, 94–96
teacher, 49, 60

B

Back, Kurt, 315
Background:
cultural, 143
home, differences in, 142–43
of pupils, 55
value, 211–12
Barker, Roger, 307
Behavior:
acceptable, 69
adjusted to situation, 286
class, present and past, 105
code of, 60, 124, 126, 294
defining in terms of objectives, 225–26
growth and, 227–29
misinterpreting, 55
objective consideration of, 52
observing, 233–34
patterns of, 26
records of, 233–34
understanding, 57
Beier, Ernest G., 307
Belonging, desire for, 108–9
Bettelheim, Bruno, 311
Bills, Robert, 311, 322
Brainstorming sessions, 189–90
Brown, William F., 323
Buck, Nina M., 324
Buhrick, Harry P., 322
Burrell, Anna Porter, 312
Buswell, Margaret M., 305
Butler, John, 319

C

Carpenter, Finley, 320
Castaneda, Alfred, 308
Chamber of Commerce, local, 266
Checklists:
class report, 129–30

Checklists (Cont.)
group development of, 134–36
human relations, 83–85
individual differences, 177–78
intellectual growth, 196–97
self-direction, 242–44
school and community leadership, 277–79
Christmas gifts, eliminating, 71
Churches, 265
Citizenship education, 36
Civic groups, 265
Clark, Russell W., 321
Class committees, 78
Class diary, 128
Classes:
conflicts between, 250
organized for activities, 25
quality teaching in, factors of, 33
testing of new teachers, 113
sharing authority in, 94–96
Class groups (see also Groups):
contributions to school, 256–62
leadership in, 99–102
morale of, development, 92–93
organization of, 96–97, 98–99
participation in community projects, 274–75
planning committee in, 97–99
pupil responsibility to, 102–3
role of individual in, 106–7
social groups within, 63
social relationships of, 77
structure of, formation of, 93–97
teacher in, 15–16
typical operation of, 123–24
unity in, 91–92
Class minutes, 127, 128
Class recorder, 128
Classrooms:
arrangement of, 133
attitudes toward, 77
chaos in, 125, 131
comfort in, 92
order in, 11, 125
physical appearance of, 111
Class size, 30–31
Cliques, 59
Cofer, Charles, 317
Committees:
class, 78
community advisory, 276

INDEX 331

Committees (*Cont.*)
  joint planning, 259
  planning, 97–99
  reports of, 127–28
  as sources of ideas, 299
  student-faculty, 253
  work, 122–23
  work plans of, 232
Common purposes, 59, 93, 96
Communication:
  with administration, 261
  with community, 276–77
  level of, in community, 30
  school, 260–61
  mass, 264
Community:
  activities of, participating in, 272–74
  attitudes of, 30–31
  cooperation with schools, 42
  educational aspects of, 264–66
  effect on pupil acceptance, 61–63
  emotional and intellectual climate of, 30
  exerting leadership in, 263–77, 298–99
  knowledge of, 110
  learning about, 263, 264–67
  level of communication in, 30
  mores of, influence on purposes, 205–6
  projects of, student participation in, 274–75
  relationships between adults and young people in, 30
  reports to, 275–76
  role of teacher in, 30–32
  schools in, 30–31
  working with, 42
  world, students and, 275
Community leaders, beliefs of, 266–67
Comparative-standard marking, 239
Concepts, changes in, 18–19
Conferences:
  faculty, 252–53
  group, 269, 270
  individual, 148
  teacher-parent, 236, 269–71
Confidence:
  achievement and, 134
  of teacher, 49, 52
Conflicts:
  purpose, 203
  value, 152, 214–15, 216
Conformity, 184, 185

Contributions, recognizing, 65, 102
Control:
  of classes, 11, 125
  democratic, 15–16
  group, 124–27
Cooperation, community-school, 42
Courtesy, acceptance and, 59–60
Creative potential, fostering, 33
Creative products, as indication of personality, 165–66
Creativity:
  allowing time for, 189
  fostering, necessity for, 183–84
  interpretation and, 186–88
  necessity for honesty, 186
  promoting, 40
    barriers to, 184–85
    conditions for, 186–91
  regulations and, 186
Cryan, Eugene W., 326
Cultural background, individual differences in, 143

D

Deadlines, as means of control, 125
Decisions, 96, 221–42
  classroom, 29
  group, 94, 95, 103, 104
  promoting ability to make, 221–42
    (*see also* Judgment-making)
  pupil, regarding purposes, 170–73
  records of, 105
  shared, 114–15
  suggestions and, 284
Demands, unreasonable, 153
Dembo, Tamara, 307
Democracy:
  essentials of, 27
  self-control in, 29
  self-direction in, 28–29
  value acquisition in, 28
  concepts of, 27
Democratic procedures, in classroom, 15–16
Deutsch, Morton, 315
Development:
  of democratic society, 27
  and encouragement, 15
  patterns of, 54
  rates of, 154–55
  of working skills, 16

Diagnostic tests, 233
Diaries, record, 230, 232
Directing, teaching and, 14, 24
Disagreements, handling, 104
Disappointments, accepting, 285
Discipline, 31
 defined, 207
 process of, 127
 school policy on, 250
Dress, 71

E

Economic position, individual differences in, 143
Economic problems, decreasing, 70
Education:
 citizenship, 36
 community-school cooperation and, 42
 as community-wide process, 263, 265–66
 formal, function of, 39
 teacher, in-service, 300
Egocentricity, overcoming, 285–86
Embarrassment, 58
Emotional climate, 24–25, 49
 of community, 30
 individual differences and, 150
 of learning situations, 47
Emotional disturbances, 36
Emotional handicaps, 145
Emotional needs:
 of gifted children, 163
 meeting, 36
 research in, 311–14
 unmet, 152
Emotions:
 effect on learning, 21–22
 promoting value of, 188–89
Empathy, 57
Encouragement:
 of joint planning, 116–17
 at times of failure, 65
 of underdeveloped child, 155
 of uninterested students, 156–57
Energy, lack of, 143
Environment:
 classroom, 24
 community (see Community)
Evaluation:
 of behavior, 126
 of class procedures, 105–6
 of completed projects, 130

Evaluation (Cont.)
 of group growth, 127–31, 293–94
 of growth progress, 236–37
 human relations, 291–93
 in individual differences, 294–96
 joint, 39
 of present procedures, 288–91
 of procedures, 130
 research in, 314–15
 of self, 170
 of values, 40, 215–16
Experiences:
 analyzing, 168–69
 and individual differences, 40, 146
 learning and, 18–20, 21
 sharing, 75
 student, analysis of, 25
Experimental studies, ideas and, 300–301
Experimental teaching, 301–2
Experimentation, 254, 255–56
Expression:
 creative (see Creativity)
 individual differences in, 148–49, 151

F

Faculty:
 attitude toward discipline, 249
 experimentation by, 255–56
 homework policy of, 250–51
 leadership of, 41, 249–62, 298–99
 problems of, 253–55
 scholars on, need for, 193–96
 taking action in, 252–55
 working through students, 256–62
 working with, 285–86
Failure:
 encouragement at times of, 65
 learning from, 100–102
 possible reasons for, 152–54
 teacher, 287
Faith:
 mutual, 112–13
 in pupils, 108
Family, pupil acceptance and, 61–63
Faw, Volney, 318
Fears, decreasing, 66
Feelings:
 promoting value of, 188–89
 recording, 190–91
Field trips, 35, 251
Files:
 class, 128–29
 library, 174

Financial status, insecurity and, 70–71
Fleming, Robert, 312
Flow chart, as class record, 129
Folders, sample, 230–31
Forlano, George, 306
Formal education, function of, 39
Friendliness:
  demonstrating, 112
  encouraging, 58, 59, 260
French, John, 308
Frustration:
  as cause of aggression, 158
  facing, 285
  group, 101–2
  as motivating force, 102
  teacher, 288

G

Gaier, Eugene L., 308
Generalizations, formation of, 175–76
Gifted children, 162–63
Goals:
  definition of, 223–26
  determining, 170–73
  failure in, 65
  formulation of, guiding, 201–20
  helping pupils to clarify, 169
  helping pupils establish, 39
  planning and, 11–12
  proposed, 236
  social, 27–28
  vocational, 202
Graduate study, 300
Group control, 124–27
  agenda and deadlines as, 125
  code of behavior for, 124–25
  morale as, 125
  punishment and, 125–27
Group growth:
  checklist, 134–36
  evaluating, 127–31
  records of, 127–29
Group maturity, development of, 103–4
Group morale, 93, 105–6, 125
Group motivation, 203
Group punishment, 125–26
Groups (see also Class groups)
  acceptance by, 111–15 (see also Acceptance, group)
  civic, influence of, 265
  classroom, teachers as members of, 15–16

Groups (Cont.)
  community, 272, 273
  competition between, 76–77
  individual feelings for, 61
  participation in, 28–29
  progress of, determining, 105–6
  unity in, beginning of, 91–92
  work, 97, 98
Group structure, formation of, 93–97
Group unity, 59
Group work:
  accommodating individual differences in, 149–50
  and aggressive children, 159–60
  control of, 124–27
  evaluation of, 293–94
  of gifted children, 162–63
  period of, 121–24
  pitfalls in, 131–34
  plan of, 120–21, 131–32
    beginning, 115
    preliminary, 110–11
  records of, 127, 128, 129
  research in, 315–17, 318–20
  selection of projects for, 119–20
  size of groups, 122–23
  for withdrawing child, 161–62
Growth:
  behavior and, 226–28
  deciding on most important area of, 288
  degrees of, 227–29
  evaluation of progress in, 236–37
  group, 127–31 (see also Group growth)
  individual differences in, 148
  slow rate of, 154–55
Guidance:
  in goal formation, 201–19 (see also Motivation; Purposes)
  in group work, 121, 122
  motivational, 207–9
Guilt feelings:
  decreasing, 68–70
  increasing, 70

H

Handicaps:
  emotional, 145
  physical, 144
Health, individual differences in, 143–44

Health examinations, 144
Hearing defects, providing for, 148
Herrold, Earle E., 326
Home background, differences in, 142–43
Home visits, 166, 271–72
Homework, 31, 250–51 (*see also* Assignments)
Honesty, creativity and, 186
Honor rolls, 63
Hostility, 52
How Children Develop, 110
Human relations (*see also* Acceptance)
  checklist in, 83–85
  evaluation of, 291–93
  improving, 49–60, 82–83
Hurlock, Elizabeth, 323

I

Ideas:
  new, seeking, 299–301
  responding to, 58
  sources of, 299–300
Imitation, avoiding, 284
Immaturity, 52
Improvement, belief in possibility of, 108
Inadequacy, feelings of, 49, 51, 52
Independence, desire for, 112
Individual differences:
  in achievement, 33
  checklist, 177–78
  in cultural levels, 143
  economic and social levels, 143
  emotional, 145
  evaluation in, 294–96
  experience and, 40, 146
  in growth and expression, 148–49, 151
  in health, 143–44
  in home background, 142–43
  importance of, 141–42
  intellectual, 145–46
  learning, 164–66
  in needs, providing for, 147–48
  providing for, 37
  purposeful activity and, 141, 142
  varying standards for, 66
  within class group, providing for, 149–50
Individuals:
  evidence of concern for, 147–51

Individuals (*Cont.*)
  instruction for, 164–77
  records of, 128
  role in groups, 106–7
  types of, 151–63
    aggressive, 113–14, 157–61
    gifted, 162–63
    "less-developed," 154–55
    underachieving, 152–54
    uninterested, 155–57
    withdrawing, 161–62
  values of, 218–19
  working alone, 123
Inferiority, feelings of, 143
Insecurity, 50
  caused by financial status, decreasing, 70–71
  feelings of, 143
In-service teacher education, 300
Integration, learning and, 17–18
Intellectual climate, 30, 33
  creating, 183–96 (*see also* Creativity; Scholarship)
  defined, 183
  evaluation of, 296–97
Intellectual growth, checklist, 196–97
Intelligence:
  individual differences in, 145–46
  operational, learning and, 22
Intelligence tests, 145, 146
Interests:
  common, 59
  distinguished from motivation, 208, 209
  planning and, 119
Interpretation:
  pupil, opportunity for, 187–88
  by teacher, avoiding, 186–87
Interviews:
  with parents, 241, 271–72
  pupil, 241, 271–72
Iscoe, Ira, 323

J

Jennings, Helen H., 317
Johnson, A. D., 316
Joint projects, 92, 257–59
Judgment, 29, 33, 39, 235
Judgment-making:
  collection of data for, 226–30
  criteria for, 223, 224
  definition of goals for, 223–26

Judgment-making (*Cont.*)
importance of, 221-22
including parents in, 237-41
pupil:
keeping records for, 230-33
promoting, 235-37
self-direction and, 222-23
Judgments, avoiding, 169, 235

K

Kell, Bill L., 324
Kelley, Earl C., 321
Klugman, Samuel, 316
Knowledge:
acceptance and, 72
applying to daily living, 195
of community, 110
organization of:
individual, 175-76
individual nature of, 40
and teaching, 14
varied, 193-94
reorganization of, 19-20
sharing, 176
Kuder Preference Checklist, 170
Kvaraceus, W. C., 309

L

Labels, group, 70
Leadership:
checklist, 277-79
in class groups, 99-102
community, 263-77
encouraging, 64
evaluating, 298-99
faculty, 41, 249-62
provided by teacher, 54, 107-9
pupil, 33
selecting, ability for, 96
sharing, 107-8
status, desire for, 146-47
teacher's concept of, 63-65, 102
Learning:
about individual pupils, 164-65
of complex skills, 19
defined, 17
effect of physical condition on, 22
effect of purposes on, 20-21
emotional climate and, 47
environment and, 18-20, 21
experience and, 18-20, 21

Learning (*Cont.*)
intelligence and, 22
living and, 17
multiplicity of, 20
research in, 16, 20, 320-22
pupil organization of, 175-76
uniqueness of, 20
Learning process, 16-26
emotional conditioning in, 21-22
perception and integration in, 17-18
teaching and, 22-26
theories of, 16-22
Lecturing, 23-24
"Less-developed" children, 154-55
Letter marks, 238
Levine, Jacob, 319
Lewin, Kurt, 307, 316, 325
Libraries, 173, 174
Lippitt, Ronald, 326
Logs, record, 231
Love, assuring aggressive child of, 158-59

M

McCandless, Boyd R., 308
McClelland, David C., 321
McLendon, Ida Ruth, 306
McNeil, Helen, 324
Malnutrition, 143
Mandler, George, 310
Mann, Frank A., 313
Marks and marking:
comparative-standing method, 238-39
elimination of, 239-41
and feeling of personal worth, 66
individual differences and, 151
letter, 238
limitations of, 238-39
percentage, 238
Materials:
cost of, effect on planning, 172-73
illustrative, 193
individual differences and, 149
sharing, 258-59
survey of, 173-75
Maturity, 52, 96
fostering, methods of, 103-4
group, development of, 103-4
increasing, 287
of teacher, increase in, 283-87
Mental disturbances, 36

Mental health:
  and guilt feelings, 68
  promoting, 36
Merit rating, 3
Michael, William B., 326
Minutes, class, 127, 128
Mistakes:
  allowing pupils to discover own, 104
  profiting by, 100–101
Montague, Ernest K., 310
Morale, group:
  as control, 125
  development of, 93
  maintaining, 105–6
Moreno, J. L., 317
Motivation:
  classroom, levels of, 204
  discipline and guidance, 207
  forced, 201–2
  group, 203
  influences on, 204–6
  research in, 322–24
  strengthening, 202, 203, 207–9
  values and, 208–9
Movies, role of, 264

N

Name-calling, 70
Names, calling pupils by, 55, 58, 60, 114, 164
Needs:
  individual differences in, 147–48
  recognizing, 285
  satisfaction of, 286
Newspapers:
  educational aspects of, 264
  reporting to community in, 276–77
Nicknames, 60

O

Obedience, blind, 28
Objectivity, 52
Ojemann, Ralph H., 324, 327
Open-house program, 277
Operational intelligence, learning and, 22
Opinions, changes in, 19
Order, classroom, 11, 125
Organization:
  for activities, 25–26, 37
  class, 96–99
  of individual programs, 37
Overprotection, 154

P

Palermo, David S., 308
Paper-and-pencil tests, 170, 225, 230
Parents:
  attitudes of, effect on child, 153
  classroom visits, 267–68
  conferences with teachers, 236
  cultural levels of, 143
  influence on purposes of children, 204
  interviews with, 241
  planning with, 31
  pupil-written letters to, 233, 241
  reactions to pupil success, 290
  relationships with children, 113
  reports to, 12, 66, 237–41
  role in setting judgment criteria, 224
  school improvement by, 268–69
  visited by teacher, 166
  visits to school, 267
  working with, 267–72
Park, Lawrence, 314
Participation:
  effect of family position on, 62
  learning, 29
  in planning, 107, 115–19
Percentage marking, 238
Perception, learning and, 17–18, 184
Periodicals, professional, 299
Perkins, Hugh V., 319
Personality:
  as center of value, 27
  of teachers, uniqueness of, 288
Personnel folders, reviewing, 110, 111
Persuasion, 213
Physical condition, learning affected by, 22
Physical defects, 144
Physical violence, protecting from, 67
Planning:
  group:
    beginning of, 115–19
    importance of, 131–32
    methods of encouraging, 117–18
    selection of projects, 119–20
  improvement and, 289
  importance of, 11–12, 131–32
  individual participation in, 106
  individual work, 173–75
  joint, 39
  preliminary to group work, 110–11

Planning (Cont.)
to provide for individual differences, 37
records of, 232
steps in, 118
work, 120–21, 131–32
Planning committee, 97–99
functions of, 97–98
organization of, 98–99
Poverty, effects of, 143
Praise, 65, 104
Preliminary planning, in group work, 110–11
Problem census, 119–20
Problems, pupil, 58
Problem-solving:
criteria for, 118–19
group, 79
helping pupils in, 67
scientific method of, 29
teaching steps in, 104
technique of, improving, 284
Professional organizations, 256
Progress:
determination of:
in group work, 105–6
helping pupil in, 65
discussing with pupils, 134
evaluation of, 107
as evidence of successful teaching, 289
group, reports of, 122
growth, evaluation of, 236–37
importance of following, 132
judging by quality of teaching, 96
pupil, 12
Projects:
community, student participation in, 274–75
completed, evaluation of, 130
cooperative, 78, 102
forced, 132–33
joint, 92
school improvement, 256–62
selection of, 119–20
Psycho-drama, 73–74
Punishment, 125–26
for aggressiveness, avoiding, 160
group, 125–26
individual, 126
use of, 126–27
Pupil placement, 43

Pupils:
acceptance by:
of others, 72–79
of teacher, 79–82
aggressive, 113–14, 157–61
contributions to school, 256–62
decisions of, regarding purposes, 170–73
determining progress of, 12
fears of, decreasing, 66–68
getting acquainted with, 111
gifted, 162–63
interests of, teaching and, 14–15
knowledge of, 110–11
learning to know, 164–66
"less-developed," 154–55
new, welcoming, 58–59
organization of learning by, 175–76
protecting, 67
records kept by, 151, 230–33
records of, 55 (see also Records)
relations with school administration, 261–62
responsibility to group, 102–3
role in group, 106–7
self-acceptance of, 61–72
self-understanding, promotion of, 166–70
teacher acceptance of, 53–60
treating as adults, 60
underachieving, 152–54
uninterested, 155–57
weaknesses in, 53–54
withdrawing, 161–62
work plans of, 173–75
Purposes, 201–9
age-group and, 204
of children, 108
class, pupil formulation of, 25
common, 59, 93, 96
community influences on, 205–6
conflicting, 203
effect of learning on, 20–21
establishing, 23, 24
influenced by entertainment media, 206
influence of teacher on, 206
as judgment criteria, 224–25
motivation and, 202
parental influence on, 204
planning, 170–73
of pupils', when different from teachers', 54–55

338 INDEX

Purposes (Cont.)
 revealing, 206
 utilizing, 207–9
 values of, 206–7
 working on, 169–70

Q

Quality teachers:
 becoming, process of, 283–302
 examples of, 34–42
Quality teaching:
 approaches to obtaining, 42–43
 definition of, 33–34
 prerequisites of, 33
Questions, student, 58, 169

R

Radio:
 community reports by, 277
 educational aspects of, 264
Raimy, Victor C., 324
Ramond, Charles K., 310
Ranking, pupil, 63–64
Reading, records of, 128
Reality, accepting, 284–85
Rebelliousness, feelings of, 49, 51
Recognition:
 of achievement, 63–66
 of contributions, 65
Record-keeping, role of pupil in, 133, 230
Records:
 attendance, 12
 of behavior, 233–34
 of class decisions, 105
 cumulative, examining, 164–65
 of group activities, 127–29
 importance of, 12
 of ideas and questions, 232
 individual, 55, 128
 kept by pupils, 151, 230–33
 planning, 232
 reading, 128
 of teacher, 233–35
Regression, 66
Regulations, routine, 186
Rehage, Kenneth J., 319
Rejection, 163
Reports, 12, 66
 checklist for, 129–30
 class, 129–30
 comparative-standing, 238–39

Reports (Cont.)
 committee, 127–28
 to community, 275–77
 descriptive, 240–41
 of group progress, 122
 to parents, 237–41
 Portland study of, 239
 pupil-written letters to parents, 233
 typical, 237–39
Research, 305–28
 leadership, 34, 247
 learning, 16, 20, 320–22
 pupil, 174–75
 scholarship and, 195–96
 as source of ideas, 299–300
Resentment, feelings of, 51
Resource people:
 community, 268–69
 at staff meetings, 300
Resources:
 lack of, 172–73
 survey of, 174–75
 teaching, sharing, 254
Responsibility:
 developing sense of, 102–3
 in group work, 103
 shared, 94–96
 of individual to group, 61, 102–3
Ridicule, avoiding, 58
Rogers, Carl R., 314, 324
Role of teacher, 14–32
 in community, 30–32
 in decreasing fears, 66–68
 in decreasing insecurity, 70–71
 in developing judgment ability, 221–22
 in handling guilt feelings, 68–70
 helping, not controlling, 57
 in helping pupil accept himself, 63
 human relations, 49
 leadership, 107–9
 learning process and, 16–26
 and nature of society, 26–32
 and nature of teaching, 14–16
Role-playing, 73–74
Rosenthal, David, 317

S

Salary scales, 3
Sample folders, 230–31
Sarason, Seymour B., 310

Sarcasm, avoiding, 58
Schedules, class, 121
Scholarship:
 contact with, necessity for, 191–93
 contributions of, 193–96
 interpretation of, 192
Schools:
 becoming acquainted with, 249–52
 control of, 31
 cooperation with community, 42
 policies of, 250–52
 reputation of, 31
 support of, 31–32
School staffs, selection of, 43
Scientific method, 29
Scrapbooks, 175
Seating arrangements, unorthodox, 251–52
Security:
 providing, 109
 sense of, 169
Self-acceptance:
 pupil, 106–7
 by teacher, 49–52
Self-confidence:
 effect of fear on, 66
 working for, 156, 161
Self-control:
 in democracy, 29
 of teacher, 286
Self-direction:
 checklist, 242–44
 defined, 221
 in democracy, 28–29
 developing, 15–16
 evaluation of, 297–98
 judgment-making and, 222–23
 promoting, 39, 202, 209, 235
 research in, 324–25
 of teacher, 284
Self-discipline, 31
Self-evaluation, 170
Self-respect, 66
Self-understanding, promotion of, 166–70
Shortcomings, recognizing, 285
Simpson, Ray, 204
Skills:
 complex, learning, 19
 explaining and illustrating, 24
 lack of, 153
 social, development of, 283–84

Social position:
 effects of, 143, 153
 individual differences in, 143
Social pressure, research in, 306–10
Social relationships:
 in class groups, 77
 satisfying, 286
Social skill, development of, 283–84
Social activities, 91
Social goals, 27–28
Social groups, within classes, 63
Society:
 authoritarian, 26
 change in, 183–84
 democratic, 26–30
 nature of, 26–32
Socio-drama, 168
Sociograms, 77–78
Sparks, Jack N., 327
Speech disorders, 144
Staff meeting, 300
Standardized tests, 169
Standards:
 faculty, 41
 judgment, 224
 teacher, 49
 unreasonable, 153–54
 varying, for different individuals, 66
Stereotypes, 40, 50
Straw vote, in selection of project, 119–20
Student government, 260–61
Study procedures, individual differences in, 146
Suggestions:
 accepting, 284
 planning committee and, 97–98
Superiority, feelings of, 49, 50, 51
 in group work, 103
 pupil, 62
Sylvester, Emmy, 311
Symbols, value, 220

T

Tape recordings, class records, 129
Teachers:
 in authoritarian society, 26
 becoming acquainted with schools, 249–52
 deciding on major contribution, 287–88
 examples of, 3–10

Teachers (*Cont.*)
  feelings toward pupils, 53–60
  as guides for pupils, 16
  leadership of, 107–9
  maturity of, increase in, 283–87
  as members of classroom groups, 15–16
  minimum acceptable level of, 10–13
  pupil acceptance of, 79–82
  quality:
    examples of, 34–42
    process of becoming, 283–302
    records of, 233–35
    role of, factors affecting, 14–32
  self-acceptance by, 49–52, 284
  self-direction by, 284
Teaching:
  better, search for, 3–13
  defined, 23
  as directing and telling, 14
  effect of community on, 29–32
  experimental, 301–2
  experimentation in, 254, 255–56
  learning process and, 22–26
  nature of, 14–16
  as organization of knowledge, 14
  present, evaluation of, 288–91
  as process of experience analysis, 168–69
  pupil interests and, 14–15
  quality in:
    definition of, 33–34
    obtaining, approaches to, 42–43
    prerequisites of, 33
  unsatisfactory, defined, 10
  of values, 210–11
Teaching methods:
  community and, 31
  experimenting with, 301–2
  and teaching situations, 32
Television, impact of, 264
Telling, teaching and, 14, 23–24
Tests, 12
  diagnostic, 233
  intelligence, 145–46
  paper-and-pencil, 170, 225, 230
  standardized, 169
  vision and hearing, 144
Textbooks:
  individual differences and, 149
  planning and, 12
Thinking, 22

Trust, promoting, 109
Tyler, Ralph, 322

U

Underachieving children, 152–54
Understanding:
  of feelings of others, 74–75
  of self, 33
Uninterested children, 155–57
Unity, group, 91–92
Unreasonable demands, 153–54
Unsatisfactory teaching, defined, 10

V

Vagharsh, Bedoian H., 305
Values:
  acceptance of, 212, 213
  acquired, 28
  clarification of, 209–20
  conflicts in, 152, 214–15, 216
  current, determining, 211
  democratic, 26–27, 28
  exploring and developing, 33
  group control, 124–25
  individual, 218–19
  life, development of, 286–87
  motivation and, 208–9
  multiplicity of, rejecting, 50–51
  of others, teaching, 215–17
  pupils' evaluation of, 40
  reviewing, 219–20
  of teacher, 210–11, 212, 213
  teaching, 210–11
Value symbols, 220
Vision defects, 144, 148
Vocational goals, 202

W

Weaknesses:
  accepting, 51–52
  helping pupils overcome, 53–54
White, Ralph K., 326
Whitner, Chester L., 315
Wilkenson, Frances, 327
Williams, Herbert D., 325
Wishing Well, 170
Withall, John, 320
Withdrawal, 62, 161
Withdrawing children, 161–62
Work committees, 122–23
Work-groups, 97, 98, 121–22

INDEX 341

Work periods, 121–24
Work plans:
  committee, 232
  group, 120–21
  pupil, 173–75, 232
Workshops:
  classes as, 121
  teacher, 300

World community, student contributions to, 275
Worry, 153
Wright, Erick, 307

Z

Zelany, Leslie Day, 320